For Carl

Sarah is a student
to be proud of!

To Carl—

I'm not really sure why Professor Grossman wrote that. I just asked him to sign it to you. Anyway. I wanted to give you this as a token of my appreciation for everything that you have done for me. You and the rest of the team were so extremely supportive of me last year with my mom. Even my freshman year, when I was "crazy bad", you never gave up on me. I truly respect you for all you have done for me and this team. Thanks for everything,
—Sarah

The Art of Alibi

English Law Courts and the Novel

JONATHAN H. GROSSMAN

The Johns Hopkins University Press

BALTIMORE AND LONDON

© 2002 THE JOHNS HOPKINS UNIVERSITY PRESS
All rights reserved. Published 2002
Printed in the United States of America on acid-free paper
2 4 6 8 9 7 5 3 1

The Johns Hopkins University Press
2715 North Charles Street
Baltimore, Maryland 21218-4363
www.press.jhu.edu

Library of Congress Cataloging-in-Publication Data

Grossman, Jonathan H.
The art of alibi: English law courts and the novel / Jonathan H. Grossman.
p.   cm.
Includes bibliographical references and index.
ISBN 0-8018-6755-X (hardback : alk. paper)
1. Legal stories, English—History and criticism. 2. English fiction—History and criticism.
3. Courts in literature. 4. Law and literature. 5. Law in literature. 6. Literary form. I. Title.
PR830.L43 G76 2002
823.009'355   2001002200

A catalog record for this book is available from the British Library.

TO MY PARENTS

Marc and Penny Grossman

with special thanks

to Eli

for waiting for me

to finish

❦ CONTENTS ❦

ILLUSTRATIONS

ACKNOWLEDGMENTS

ALIBIS, even when true, draw their strength from the support of others, and so has this book, concerned in part with the history of alibis. The case it makes for placing the English novel at the scene of the law courts could never have been made without the incisive comments that Nina Auerbach penned in purple and green ink on the staid black-and-white manuscript pages or without the long-distance advice and suggestions provided by John Sutherland. Both scholars, in surprisingly similar ways, energized and inspired my attempts to understand nineteenth-century fiction.

It is with pleasure that I also acknowledge that the arguments here stem from an ongoing exchange of drafts and thoughts with Rayna Kalas, Jane Penner, John Plotz, Kristen Poole, and Julian Yates. I could not have asked for better first colleagues and comrades. I am grateful as well to three other expert readers: John Richetti, who inspirited this book as a history of the British novel at its inception; Hilary Schor, who insightfully critiqued the manuscript in its entirety as it neared completion; and Stuart Curran, who all along the way provided no-nonsense guidance, professional and intellectual.

My thinking while I was writing this book was regularly enriched by conversations with my parents, to whom the book is dedicated out of long-standing respect and love. My sister and brother, Gillian Grossman and Nicholas Grossman, and my close friends Adam Parker and Etsu Taniguchi influenced my concerns here more deeply than they may know. Years of writing and researching brought me into contact with a number of people who supplied all kinds of judicious counsel, helpful information, and productive critiques of the manuscript, and I thank Daniel Bivona, Patrick Brantlinger, David Brownlee, Martin Brückner, Carl Dawson, David DeLaura, Barbara Gates, Ezra Greenspan, Steve Helmling, Matthew Kinservik, Ron Lear, Irena Nicoll, Maggie Parker, Don Reiman, Charlie Robinson, Talia Schaffer, Jan-Melissa Schramm, Peter Stallybrass, Christina Taneyhill, Irene Tucker, Darryl Wadsworth, Jane Weiss, Thomas Wortham, Molly Wyman, Liza Yukins, and the members of the Nineteenth-Century groups at both the University of Delaware and the Johns Hopkins University. As if this list of generous contributors weren't already long enough, I am much indebted to some people whose names I do not even know—anonymous readers at journals (a version of chapter 4 was published in *Nineteenth- Century Literature* 52 [1997]). My research assistant for a time was Jaime Hastings, to whom credit belongs for showing me the painting by Hutchison discussed at the end of the book. Maura Burnett was my editor at Hopkins, and she expertly shepherded the book into production, where, in its final reworking, it received careful and thoughtful copyediting by Elizabeth Gratch.

There were many times in the writing of this book when I seriously agreed with my partner Jana Portnow's joke that the book might be better titled "Alibi/Schmalibi." Yet her own careful readings and sharp editing of the manuscript also helped me to think otherwise. Day in and day out, she lent her limited spare time to this work, and she usually proved to be a better reader of it than I was. As she knew I would, I must acknowledge, though it might be self-indulgently sentimental to do so, the daily companionship of our hound dog, Chloe, whose heedless selfishness and horrifyingly innocent predatoriness helped remind me that a precoccupation with justice and narrative is only important to some of us.

FIG. 1. Abraham Solomon, *Waiting for the Verdict*, engraved by W. H. Simmons (1866). © The British Museum

Introduction

WALKING DOWN the Strand in 1871, one would come upon a massive, unprecedented construction project at the heart of London: the building of the Royal Courts of Justice. The Victorians were erecting a palace to the judicial process, one they had begun planning in the 1830s. Throughout the nineteenth century similar projects were under way across the nation. Previously positioned as spectators of the gallows, ordinary people now imaginatively understood themselves in relation to the physical space of these new civil and criminal courts and the trial narratives they produced. This book is about how readers and authors became immersed in this trial-oriented culture as never before and about how their novels were shaped by the complementary and competing storytelling structure of the law courts.

We can begin to understand the important relationship between narrative form and the law courts that was established by the Victorian period by looking closely at Abraham Solomon's celebrated 1857 painting *Waiting for the Verdict* (see fig. 1). In Solomon's picture the prisoner on trial is not shown, and we are confronted instead with two striking parallel planes. In the foreground we see the anxious family of the accused, and in the background the courtroom. The two scenes are at once linked and separated. Both explicitly make claims upon the viewer's judgment. In part this is because, as Martin Meisel observes, "in the absence of the Accused, we have no way of deciding the issue [of guilt or innocence]."[1] Also, however, the picture ethically balances the two scenes so that neither triumphs over the other. If the stylized pathos of the family demands the viewer's sympathy, the bath of almost religious light emanating from the courtroom stymies any simple translation of the picture into familiar melodramatic terms in which the law figures as an institutional villain disrupting the family. Instead, the absent protagonist's plot exists in both planes as if in two interdependent narrative fields. No wonder a sense of story weighs so heavily on this picture. It is twice-told within its frame.

Because the family occupies the foreground and more than two-thirds of the painting, our perspective centers on their story. Details that indicate the family's long attendance on the court—such as the picnic basket on the left or the remnants of feathers and flowers in the foreground which reveal the sleeping child has earlier dismantled his plumed hat—further enmesh us in their unfolding situation. We have a cultural, not an insider or professional, view of this law court; like the family, we are "waiting for the verdict." The central female character (whose wedding band suggests she is the accused's wife) at a glance even seems to be looking outward toward us, breaking the frame and appealing directly to us as part of her circle. Actually, she is looking blankly inward, as the position of her arms in a posture of abstracted self-despair confirms. As spectators, we are invisible. In a sense we read the private story of the family, novelistically portrayed primarily as speaking and acting characters, against the court's different, public rendering of that same story, which, if we look closely, we can see being penned in the far background by a legal functionary. This moment of narrative doubling shapes our larger understanding of the content and form of the accused's family story—of the social world these characters inhabit and of their story's connection to, and difference from, the kind of story being told in the law court.

My concern in this book is with the similar shaping of novels through their evocations of the law courts. So, although Solomon's painting may certainly be connected to the theater or other visual arts, I want to suggest that we can productively understand *Waiting for the Verdict* as a visual realization of the relation between two of its era's most prominent narrative paradigms—the novel and the law courts. For me the painting captures how a realistic novel-like story (presented in the foreground) may be figured against the law court projected as a defining background. It suggests the competition and connection that novels' stories may mount to those of the law courts, juxtaposing two central, inter-locking sites of nineteenth-century narrative production. And this picture may even be understood as not rendering a real scene so much as representing the minds of its contemporary viewers, who may think of justice and truth as pro-duced by the epistemology of the novel counterbalanced by that of the law court. In such intersections, I see Solomon—whom the *Art-Journal* applauded for having moved on from the ranks of those painters who mindlessly made lit-erary scenes in "books . . . the foundation of . . . their works"[2]—presenting to us one possible view of the Victorian novel itself.

Solomon's painting and the subsequent mass-produced, engraved version of it, shown here, were hugely popular. Shortly after the picture's exhibition *Punch* condescendingly derided the painting's public acclaim, and later that same year "art-rebellion . . . rag[ed] in Liverpool" when *Waiting for the Ver-dict* was not chosen for a prize.[3] Solomon himself capitalized on his picture's popularity, producing *Not Guilty* (1861), a painting that resolves the first pic-ture's narrative tension by banally showing the accused happily reunited with his family. *Waiting for the Verdict* had clearly tapped into a broadly felt and established Victorian sense of narrative and justice. Nor is it hard to find pop-ular Victorian novels to which one might connect the picture. Its dual narrative logic, expressed somewhat differently, recalls the obvious imaginative structur-ing of novels in relation to the processes of the courts in such key near-con-temporary works as Charles Dickens's *Bleak House* (1853) and Wilkie Collins's *The Woman in White* (1860). (This similarity was made explicit in the 1980s when Penguin, with some strategic cropping, used Solomon's painting as a cover for its edition of *Bleak House*.)

But what interests me is not so much the rich field that late Victorian fiction provides for examining the forensic form of the novel but, rather, how and why the nineteenth-century English novel became so deeply tied to the storytelling structure of the law courts in the first place. What happened to create this affili-ation? How did the tie between the novel and the law courts that may be seen figured in *Waiting for the Verdict* arise?

This book reconstructs the historic shift in the novel's form that linked it so powerfully to the law courts. Currently, if we look into either literary criticism or novels, it is easy enough to find analogies between the novel and the law courts as storytelling forums: readers or authors are like judges; a narrator performs as a witness or a lawyer; characters testify; and so on. When, in *Adam Bede* (1859), George Eliot famously compared her novel's form to a mirror, she wound up in precisely this type of legal analogy, observing of her own writing: "The mirror is doubtless defective; the outlines will sometimes be disturbed; the reflection faint or confused; but I feel as much bound to tell you, as precisely as I can, what that reflection is, as if I were in the witness-box narrating my experience on oath."[4] For her, as for many other novelists, the law courts, understood as a containing structure for retelling stories, provided a constitutive way of imagining her novel's form. Literary critics have not missed this point either. Ian Watt, for instance, continues even today to be much quoted in the law and literature field for observing in passing that "the novel's mode of imitating reality may . . . be equally well summarised in terms of the procedures of another group of specialists in epistemology, the jury in a court of law."[5] Yet, if we stay within the frame of Solomon's painting and reconstruct how the novel's relation to the law courts it depicts arose, we discover not merely an illuminating analogy for the form of the novel or even a parallel discourse but a cultural and historical entwining of the novel with the narratologically structured space of the court. Instead of fashioning or uncovering more metaphorical maps likening novel to court, this book pieces together some of the animating historical forces and key developments lying behind this mapping.

One central claim I make is that, after a surprisingly gradual shift in the eighteenth century from a system of justice centered on the scaffold to one focused on the trial scene, the period from the 1790s to the 1840s was uniquely dominated by the development of a narrative paradigm oriented to the law courts as a storytelling forum. There were exciting and powerful changes occurring to the novel—and especially to crime fiction—which preceded the 1840s and 1850s invention of the detective mystery and the concomitant rise of the modern policed state.

This study begins by broadly tracing eighteenth- and early nineteenth-century legal and literary history. I argue that the novel, in becoming the ascendant literary genre of the nineteenth century, played an active role in a process through which a reinvented criminal trial supplanted the spectacle of the gallows as the culmination of justice. I then turn to show how in particular two Romantic era authors—William Godwin and his daughter, Mary Wollstonecraft Shelley—

shed the novel's eighteenth-century alliance with gallows literature and molded a fresh form and role for the novel, one predicated on the cultural consumption of trial narratives and a new juridical ideology of justice. This trial-oriented narrative paradigm in turn shaped key early Victorian novels. In the 1830s and 1840s both Charles Dickens and Elizabeth Gaskell imagined their first novels forensically, likening them to—and distinguishing them from—the storytelling forum of the court. At the same time, Edward Bulwer created an entirely new subgenre, the Newgate novel, which more intensely than ever before tied the novel to the trope of the legal trial. On the one hand, the result of such work was that Victorian novels commonly incorporated self-reflecting and self-defining analogies to the law courts. On the other hand, the establishment of the novel's juridical patterning conjured up its repudiation as well, and therein, I argue, lies a central reason why detective fiction was invented in the 1840s and 1850s.

So, although detective fiction and its relation to disciplinary systems has been well fathomed by critics as diverse as D. A. Miller and Ian Ousby, this book is the first to argue that in the era between gallows literature and the detective mystery, between Tyburn's scaffold and 221-B Baker Street, the law courts crucially shaped the formal structures and political aims of the novel. In so doing, it aims broadly to present a new history of crime fiction and refigure our understanding of the link between storytelling and justice. Until now the advent of the mystery genre in the 1840s and 1850s, along with the rise of the police, has partly obscured our view of a trial-oriented paradigm that developed in earlier nineteenth-century novels. During this time the courthouse was not only beginning to be newly defined and built as a central urban building; it was for the first time powerfully shaping the way that novels conceptualized their own storytelling structure. Crime stories would never be the same.

The reconstructive process that illuminates this crucial aspect of the English novel reenvisions how prevailing figurative scenes of justice have shaped narrative paradigms across different eras. Sculpted scenes of justice—a scaffold, a law court, a detective at a crime scene—provide intertextual frameworks for telling tales of transgression. In this book the novel thus meets the law upon grounds that both partly recall John Bender's linking of eighteenth-century prison design with the early novel and stretch our current approaches.[6] In particular, I hope to steer in a new direction a discussion that began in earnest with Alexander Welsh's *Strong Representations: Narrative and Circumstantial Evi-*

dence in England (1992). In that study Welsh showed how weaving together corroborating circumstantial detail became increasingly essential to telling both literary and legal stories. Since its publication work in law and literature has largely been following Welsh's model: the novel as a form of discourse is compared to the form of legal discourse. Thus, judges' opinions, trial transcripts, and such are brought together with any parallel legal language or rhetorical constructions in novels. Building on this approach, *The Art of Alibi* addresses how the genre also defined itself against and through the cultural and material presence of the law court—a symbolic and real *place* where stories are reconstructed. Thus, I began this introduction with the building of the Royal Courts of Justice and the narratival spatial relationship imagined in Abraham Solomon's painting *Waiting for the Verdict*. This book sets out to reconstruct the history of the novel's own juridical architecture.

From Scaffold to Law Court, from Criminal Broadsheet and Biography to Newspaper and Novel

D URING THE ERA stretching from the English novel's eighteenth-century beginnings up to its establishment as the nation's ascendant literary form in the Victorian period, the gallows, which was both a public, physical site around which the climax of justice was focused and a central symbolic figure in the culture, was gradually supplanted by the criminal trial as both the actual public climax of state justice and its imaginatively defining scene. As a part of this shift in the form of justice, the literary genre of criminal biography, closely allied with the scaffold scene, was reconceptualized as a genre allied with the law courts and tied to the expanded publication of trial reporting in the newspapers.

This change in narrative form began as punishment in England became increasingly private and hidden over the course of the eighteenth and nineteenth centuries, with the gallows finally, rather belatedly, disappearing behind prison walls in 1868. As punishment moved out of sight, the long-standing public process of the courtroom trial, itself freshly amplified as a mode of re-telling narratives, came to occupy a newly central place both in the process of state justice and in a marketplace that turned the materials of state justice into print products. The newspapers (publishing trials as they happened) and the

novel (tapping this culture and marketplace of trial narratives) together replaced the older genre of criminal broadsheets and biography.

I

For most historians the history of how punishment changed from the eighteenth to the nineteenth century is still told primarily in terms of a decrease of
physical violence by the state against bodies. According to Leon Radzinowicz,
the history of punishment recounted the progressive enlightenment of British
society. Since Michel Foucault's *Discipline and Punish* (1975) this history
has been retold, somewhat more accurately, as the deployment of discipline
by other—micro and mental—means. Yet two subsequent works, one by
J. M. Beattie, concerned with secondary punishments, and one concerned with
capital punishment, by V. A. C. Gatrell, together suggest that the history of
punishment in this period might also be better understood as a decline in punishment as spectacle. Together these works—Beattie's *Crime and the Courts in
England* (1986) and Gatrell's *The Hanging Tree* (1994)—suggest that public
punishment, more than physical punishment, was disappearing in England
from the eighteenth century to the mid-nineteenth century. As John Stuart Mill
observes in 1836, "the spectacle, and even the very idea, of pain, is kept more
and more out of the sight of those classes who enjoy in their fulness the benefits
of civilization."[1]

As Mill's observation suggests, a subtle reconceptualization of our traditional history of punishment has long been in order. Beattie formulates a
summary of the history of punishment accordingly: "In the first half of the
eighteenth century few questioned the rightness of the massive physical terror
deployed by the State to punish convicted criminals and to discourage others.
By the early nineteenth century, [however,] . . . all physical punishments—
hanging, public flogging, the pillory—were being widely questioned" (139).
This summary would, at first glance, hardly raise the eyebrows of students of
either Radzinowicz or Foucault, but notice that Beattie focuses on what people
"questioned," that is, on an attitudinal shift, not an actual shift. He is right to
do so. The level of state violence is an elusive statistic to gauge. The violence or
suffering inflicted by new punishments, such as solitary confinement, cannot
be defined. Moreover, the newly central "nonphysical" punishments of trans-

portation and imprisonment were often de facto death sentences and generally themselves involved brutal and repeated corporal discipline, such as starving, whipping, or sleep deprivation. Michael Ignatieff's study of the rise of the penitentiary from 1750 to 1850 makes it only too clear that, in the tighter web of the bureaucratic disciplinary regimen devised in the nineteenth century, the ordinary criminal was not necessarily better off than his eighteenth-century predecessor.[2] Thus, we find in Beattie that society's general "rejection of physical violence as an acceptable means of punishment" corresponds to "the decline of physical violence [being used] as a penal weapon" (614), but we must be careful not to confuse this explicit change in penal weapons—official punishments—with a decrease in "violence" by the state in the eighteenth and nineteenth centuries.

Instead, Beattie focuses on the social effects: "The penal consequences of this larger change in attitude and outlook marked a crucial stage in the fundamental transformation of punishment," and "punishment ceased to be mounted with an eye to those who watched, and was concentrated (at least in intention) single-mindedly on the prisoner in order to reform and rehabilitate him." In short, as is historically well-known, the point of punishment was no longer to serve up an example to the populace. Beattie thus continues: "This transformation is perhaps seen at its clearest in the way the pillory fell into disfavor, the punishment that might stand as a paradigm of the old penal order" (614). Yet his smooth transition hides his striking insight: though not itself a violent "physical" penalty, the pillory is nonetheless a paradigm for the era of bloody punishments. While the pillory frequently matched other punishments as a scene of grotesque and even fatal violence, officially it displayed a person's guilt as his or her punishment. As part of a continuum of sentences that included hanging and whipping, the pillory represented the barest form these penalties took by keeping only the public display of punishment as their common denominator while sparing the body. When the pillory was finally completely abolished in 1837, its removal signified that public punishment was disappearing.

First, a major decline occurred in the public display of punishment in the eighteenth century. As Beattie shows, transportation to the colonies and imprisonment were, taken together, the dominant new methods of punishment that arose in the eighteenth century. Previously, sentences typically resulted in a public whipping or were mitigated by the plea benefit of clergy, which allowed first-time offenders in capital cases to be released after a letter—such as *T* for *thief*—was branded onto their thumb. Beattie concludes in the usual terms: "by the end of the eighteenth century one penal regime was rapidly giving way to another. The older forms of punishment were public and violent. They attacked the body." Yet he adds a caveat: "The more private forms of punishment inside prisons were not necessarily less cruel, nor indeed less violent, for . . . the disciplines of many penitentiaries could only be maintained by vicious and frequently administered corporal punishments." For Beattie studying the disciplining of the body in penal history, the goal of punishment had become no longer "primarily to create a frightening deterrent but to reduce crime by bringing about a change in the prisoner himself. The essence of the new cause was to attack not the prisoner's body, but his mind and soul" (617). It is clear from Beattie's work, however, that these new, prevailing, official, secondary punishments of transportation and imprisonment removed punishment from the public streets of England. If, as Beattie emphasizes, punishment was becoming individualized, state discipline was also being concealed. Paying attention to this rise of "private forms" of secondary punishment, we might, at least momentarily, reject the idea that the decline of the spectacle of punishment resulted from a different method of treating offenders and suggest, instead, that the new individual and reformative ways of treating offenders were a result of dismantling the theatrical stage of punishment. Private disciplinary lessons had to follow when public corrections were no longer tolerated by the increasingly powerful middle class. Punishment itself was put out of sight.

Hence, the eventual completion of the radical, eighteenth-century transformation of punishment was not the eradication of capital punishment but, rather, its concealment in 1868 behind prison walls. It is true that earlier in the 1830s an actual and enormous decrease in executions occurred. At that time the laws known as the Bloody Code, which mandated capital sentences for scores of petty property offenses, were dismantled. With this reform the spiraling number of death sentences came to an abrupt and necessary end, having increased out of all proportion. As Gatrell shows, by the nineteenth century the justice system had become altogether too effective in sentencing people to death. Despite the tradition that juries, firmly guided by judges, routinely brought in patently false verdicts to mitigate punishment, the system not only still needed to dispense reams of royal pardons but also faced a perpetual public bloodbath. Gatrell calculates that the rate of hangings that took place in London in the first half of the eighteenth century increased almost fivefold over the second half of the century and into the early nineteenth century (7). As he says, in the 1830s "the bloody code might fairly be said to have collapsed under pressure of the criminal law's mounting prosecutory effectiveness" (21).

This collapse, effectively brought on by the efficient machinery of middle-class bureaucracy, was a major part of the fall of the older, public penal regime. The spectacle of the scaffold lost its place at the center of the penal process. Offenders were not to serve primarily as human examples whose brutal death would presumably curtail future crime. Rather, the certainty of individual punishment was considered the most effective deterrent. Instead of being selected almost lottery-like from a list for capital punishment, convicted people would each receive a punishment proportional to the offense committed, as Cesare Beccaria had recommended in *An Essay on Crimes and Punishments* (English translation 1767) and Jeremy Bentham had carefully reasoned out in *An Introduction to the Principles of Morals and Legislation* (1780). Public hangings persisted—along with an older penal ideology—but long before the last public hanging in 1868 the punishment of confinement in prison was at the center of a new, modern penal process. In the nineteenth century one new controversial cruelty would be another turn of this screw: the complete closeting of solitary confinement. Punishment was no longer primarily a grim show performed for the people. In part the point of providing such examples had been obviated by the hegemony of middle-class values. When the new middle-class norms became widely accepted and set the terms of debate, violent public displays of power were counterproductive. All that the public display of punishment created was a traffic jam or, at worst, a potential riot scene.

In fact, the beginning of the end of the public gallows scene might be dated to 1783, when complaints about traffic and the unruly crowd forced London executions to be moved to outside Newgate prison, ending the grim parade to Tyburn. Samuel Johnson protested that the "old method" was being vitiated: "No, Sir, (said he, eagerly,) it is *not* an improvement: they object that the old method drew together a number of spectators. Sir, executions are intended to draw spectators. If they do not draw spectators they don't answer their purpose."[3] Even at Newgate, however, these spectators continued to be intolerable in the eyes of the middle class, and by the 1860s it was a tired old refrain that the "pupils of the gallows" were learning nothing: "It is the spectacle, and the spectacle purely, they love."[4]

As Gatrell explains, the "abolition [of public execution] may be said to have been achieved *chiefly* by reference to that adverse image of the scaffold crowd which had taken shape over the previous century" (610). Thus, in Gatrell's study—even more clearly than in Beattie's work on secondary punishments—the attitudinal shifts at issue directly revolve around ending the public spectacle:

> There was a significant shift in polite society towards the end of the eighteenth century, and certainly into the nineteenth. Taboos began to encase the scaffold, thus altering its relationship with civility irretrievably. . . . The old curiosity became disreputable. People were advised to keep personal and emotional distances between themselves and all unseemly spectacles. Distaste for any association with hanging was projected on to the crowd with enhanced energy: the scapegoated crowd became the target of contempt, not the hanging itself. (240)

This new disdain was no minor matter. Nor was it a displaced response to the hanging itself, as Gatrell would have it. Rather, as the aristocrats had done, the middle classes were asserting a sensibility in which their ruling-class identity was grounded in a shared contempt for the common crowd, what Edmund Burke had notoriously called the "swinish multitude." Collections of common people were newly disparaged as "the masses" (a way of seeing tellingly checked, as Raymond Williams cautions, if the "mob" is composed of the viewer's friends, coworkers, relatives, and others known to be diverse individuals).[5]

Contempt for the scaffold crowd in particular was crucial to the mainstream middle classes. It reproduced the old aristocratic view of the plebes while repudiating a central motif of the old aristocratic structure and behavior. Not only was the elimination of the spectacle of the scaffold a triumph of middle-class bureaucracy over aristocratic pomp, but also, for middle-class individuals, the feeling of disdain for the scaffold scene could help to locate and define identity in opposition to an older ideology of justice. The monarchial spectacle of the scaffold, with its stock audience of aristocrats and poor, had no place for the middle class, and the ruling middle class eventually responded by deciding they had no place in their justice system for the spectacle itself (which is not to say they never attended it). Ultimately, doing away with the scaffold stage and other public scenes of punishment would be an intrinsic part of the uneven and mostly unconscious process of asserting both a new "middling" individuality and a new configuration of power dominated by bureaucratic professionals.

Not surprisingly, then, in 1849, in a letter to the *Times*, a middle-class writer denounces not the grim hanging he has seen the day before but the brutalized and brutal crowd the spectacle of the hanging had created. The audience is the appalling show to this writer: "A sight so inconceivably awful as the wickedness and levity of the immense crowd collected at that execution this morning could be imagined by no man, and could be presented in no heathen land under the sun." His protest is not to be confused with "the abstract question of capital punishment." He wants only that "the Government might be induced to give its support to a measure making the infliction of capital punishment a private solemnity within the prison walls." An editorial that same day tries to defend public executions, but the letter writer—who happens to be Charles Dickens, himself a master of depicting mob scenes—is the voice of the respectable middle class, whose members have come to dislike witnessing executions.[6] Nineteen years later the scaffold was finally hidden, completing a process of hiding punishment begun over a century earlier.

As Gatrell succinctly puts it, the dominant middle-class perception was that, "far from making statements about right order, public executions were making statements only about *dis*order" (16). Moreover, the abolition of public hangings "defended polite Victorians' representation of their own civility" (610), and so, at the end of his study of capital punishment Gatrell concludes "that Victorians' civility only veneered the state's violence over; that in hiding penal violence they consulted their own feelings and not those of the punished; and that within the secret prison power was to be—and is—wielded more efficiently than ever it had been at Tyburn" (610–11). Thus, again, in the history of capital punishment in the nineteenth century, as in the history of the secondary punishments in the eighteenth century, the transformation of punishment was ultimately a story less about the eradication of physical penalties than about the hiding of punishment.

The disappearance of the scaffold in the nineteenth century verified that an enormous shift had taken place. It was the last step in a process through which punishment became an off-stage horror. For the majority of people punishment had become a subject of indirect knowledge. Already its terrors were perpetually having to be brought to light, "exposed." Meanwhile, the old public spectacles became specters. That is, they persisted primarily in representational forms, a gothic presence of the past making for an uneasy and largely specious dividing line between enlightened modern life and barbaric past life. For, when the gallows themselves were finally shrouded, it was not the end of capital punishment but the death of an era in which a dominant and shaping figure for the public had been the scaffold. To end up on the gallows, to be fated to ride up Holborn hill, to be destined to "swing," these had been the commonplaces in constructing the life of the rogue or the rebel, and, as such, the scaffold had interpenetrated the entire British population's conception of self, even when envisioned only as a marginal and upside-down self-possibility. At a time when judges deliberately punished primarily in order to provide an example, the criminal law as a whole was a far-reaching ideological system, as E. P. Thompson and Douglas Hay especially have revealed in unveiling it as a battleground for class struggle.[7]

Of course, the justice system was no less an ideological apparatus in nineteenth-century England. The scaffold and public punishment had simply been by and large supplanted. The legal reformer and Utilitarian philosopher Jeremy Bentham helped point the way of change; his detailed plans for reorganizing the entire justice system, though rarely directly implemented, influenced and epitomized two major directions of its transformation. On the one hand, Bentham confirmed and extended the revolution in punishment occurring in his time. He famously saw a new epistemology and architecture for discipline in the panopticon penitentiary, which maximized the prisoners' physical visibility in order to engender mental self-surveillance in them and thus individual reformation. On the other hand, Bentham also worked tirelessly toward completing his *pannomion,* a rationalized legal code grounded on the greatest happiness principle. In so doing, he helped drive the nineteenth-century's construction of a new, reformed foundation for the law courts, one implicitly reinforcing their public import and design, rather than, as with the prison, transfiguring it.[8]

Bentham's contemporaries in the midst of implementing reforms in the early decades of the nineteenth century saw the justice system in similarly expansive terms and knew that a revolution was taking place in their culture's conception of justice. As Randall McGowen summarizes: "Between 1808, when Samuel Romilly inaugurated his campaign for the mitigation of the criminal law, and 1836, when a bill was passed granting defense counsel the right to address juries in felony cases, a debate took place which challenged eighteenth-century notions of justice and propounded a new conception of the judicial process. In this debate, both sides appealed to justice as a form of instruction, teaching lessons to a wider public."[9] There were many different lessons to be taught, in which the new modes of punishment would play their part, but behind such telling concerns as the mitigation of death sentences and a felon's right to a defense counsel lay a larger, tacit transformation. Without spectacles of punishment the public's focus necessarily shifted to the trial. The display of punishment, which had schooled people for centuries, was gradually replaced by the public spectacle of the courtroom as the central display of justice. "The image of justice," as McGowen aptly calls it, changed, but more strictly in terms of "image" than McGowen suggests. For in the end the gallows scene lost its place to the trial scene for the "wider public" that is a watching public. In the nineteenth-century justice system the new, symbolic climactic scene of crowding would be in the courtroom, while new cathedralesque courthouses—such as the Manchester Assize Courts and the Royal Courts of Justice—would eventually make palpably present a new compelling juridical ideology whose upwelling itself may roughly be said to have begun in 1773–80, when the first stand-alone courthouse in England was constructed.[10] This transition was the changing image of justice.

Punishment became the postscript to the trial. Foucault notes that once "punishment had gradually ceased to be a spectacle," that is, once punishment had "become the most hidden part of the penal process," then it was "the conviction itself that mark[ed] the offender with the unequivocally negative sign: the publicity ha[d] shifted to the trial, and to the sentence."[11] Yet Foucault's work ignores the new import of the law courts because, like most historians, Foucault keeps his eyes on punishment. He follows the trail of punishment and bodies into the disciplinary web of society's normalizing institutions, and, in order to focus attention on what he sees as discipline's diffusion and redefinition, he ends up dismissing the court: "The minor court that seems to sit permanently in the buildings of discipline . . . must not mislead us: it does not bring, except for a few formal remnants, the mechanisms of criminal justice to the web of everyday existence; or at least that is not its essential role; the disciplines created . . . a new functioning of punishment."[12]

In response, it is tempting to stand Foucault's dismissal of the court on its head. The modern legal court should, after all, more clearly be seen as carrying on for the new ruling middle class, at a new level and in new ways, the conflicting and complex functions that the royal court had once performed for the nobility. The law courts would even seem to be a paradigm for the new technologies of power which Foucault describes.[13] It is helpful, however, to recall here that Foucault covers a pan-European history: as he himself recognizes, legal history is uniquely different in England. In England, unlike in the rest of Europe, where inquisitorial, secret prosecutions dominated, the court trial has an ancient and continuous history of being public and juried. The infamous secrecy of the Star Chamber is only the English exception that proves the rule. England had long had public trials along with public punishment. As public punishment declined in England over the course of the eighteenth and early nineteenth century, the spectacle of the criminal trial was an entrenched, almost inevitable, replacement.

Still, we must keep in mind that in the eighteenth-century heyday of public punishment the criminal trial, including the jury's verdict, was primarily a sentencing procedure. Particular trials might garner widespread attention, but the criminal trial as a spectacle functioned as the prelude to the public infliction of penalties. Thus, when Hay rightly, if with some exaggeration, suggests that "in the court room the judges' every action was governed by the importance of spectacle,"[14] one must remember, as Beattie notes, that "the image of the gallows . . . pervaded and dominated the courtroom" (12). The donning of a black cap to render death sentences or of white gloves at the end of an execution-free session were performances that belonged ultimately to the theater of the scaffold. In the eighteenth century, as Hay suggests, "the secular mysteries of the courts had burned deep into the popular consciousness, and perhaps the labouring poor knew more of the terrors of the law than those of religion,"[15] but, as Gatrell reminds us: "Humble people did not scratch images of judges in wigs or of courts in their pomp when they conjured up their images of justice or its opposite. The scaffold was the vehicle for the plebeian commentary" (195–96). This association was changing as public punishment declined.

I I

To varying extents, trials have been spectacles ever since the medieval days of trial (and punishment) by ordeal, oath, or battle. The English jury trial, established in the thirteenth century, is a public spectacle almost by definition; to be tried by jury is to be tried "by God *and the country*."[16] Nonetheless, it was not until the beginning of the nineteenth century that the ordinary criminal trial was widely understood in place of the scaffold and public punishment as the culmination of justice. As public punishment declined, the role of the law courts became more culturally central, and proof of this lies partly in the ways that the criminal trial as a spectacle was itself re-formed.

Even before the sweeping, official legal reforms of the 1830s, the criminal trial was being shaped into its modern form. As the legal historian John H. Langbein, who has done the most to uncover and trace these changes, reports: "Some of the most fundamental attributes of modern Anglo-American criminal procedure for cases of serious crime emerged in England during the eighteenth century: the law of evidence, the adversary system, the privilege against self-incrimination, and the main ground rules for the relationship of judge and jury."[17] Even the history of the formula "innocent until proven guilty" provides one conspicuous confirmation of the rise of the modern criminal trial. According to Beattie, "the notion in its modern form arose as an active principle only toward [the nineteenth century] as one aspect of a complex change in the character of criminal trials. The idea that men ought actively to be regarded as innocent before being tried was being expressed in the 1780s, and by 1820 it could be confidently asserted. . . . But it was only then that the characteristics of the modern jury trial were beginning to emerge, and only in the nineteenth century that they took firm shape: it was then that juries came to be selected specifically for each case, that the prosecution and defense were normally managed by lawyers, that the judge invariably summed up and instructed the jury to retire and deliberate over the evidence in a frame of mind that required that they be persuaded of the prisoner's guilt beyond a reasonable doubt before convicting him" (341). In short, it was only in the early nineteenth century that criminal jury trials emerged in the modern form with which we are familiar. They had been altered dramatically. Three of the main shifts in the way that criminal trials proceeded involved their pace, their lawyerization (with a concurrent change in the nature of cases), and their increased numbers. Together these changes go a long way toward charting how the criminal trial became a spectacle in its own right.

Perhaps the most obvious indication that criminal trials in the nineteenth century were no longer simply preludes to punishment (or exculpation) was that they began to take more time. As Langbein observes: "Nothing distances the trial procedure of the Ryder years [the mid-eighteenth century] from its modern counterpart so much as its dispatch. The sheer volume of cases is stunning. [The judge] Ryder saw more felony jury trials in a day or two than a modern English or American judge would expect to see in a year."[18] Beattie calculates that the time from arraignment to verdict at the Surrey assizes in the mid-eighteenth century was ordinarily thirty minutes (378). Although Gatrell reminds us that "even in the 1820s and 1830s, with an increased presence of lawyers in the court . . . trials remained uncommonly hasty" (536), criminal trials were slowing down by the nineteenth century. While there had been a rare few lengthy trials earlier, such as the special three-day prosecution of John Lilburne, leader of the Levelers, in 1649, the early twentieth-century judge Sir Frank MacKinnon was thinking along the right temporal trajectory when he mistakenly suggested that "the trial of [Thomas] Hardy for high treason in 1794 was the first that ever lasted more than one day," noting that "the Court seriously considered whether it had any power to adjourn."[19] Before the nineteenth century the infamous mandate that juries would be locked up "without meat, drink, fire, or candle" until they reached a verdict could not have been too terrifying, at least in felony trials. In general, eighteenth-century juries did not even retire from the courtroom to render their verdicts. In 1714 Alexander Pope mocked that "the hungry Judges soon the Sentence sign, / And Wretches hang that Jury-men may Dine" (*The Rape of the Lock*, 3.21–22). There were, however, a number of reasons for the rapidity of trials, the most salient being that though the outcome was not predetermined, they were not ordinarily expansive inquiries into guilt or innocence (often the accused spoke primarily so that—in this era of the Bloody Code—his or her sentence could be mitigated). "The coming of the lawyers," as Langbein calls it, would change this situation drastically.

As the employment of counsel in criminal trials became the norm by the late

eighteenth and early nineteenth century, trials began to take on a wholly different complexion—and a slower pace. The basis of the older form of trial was that
truth would best be revealed if the prisoner were confronted with both accusation and evidence without professional help or previous preparation in a verbal face-off between two opposing lay parties. The judge was supposed to take
an active role in helping the accused, rather than just referee the proceedings,
though in general he took on an inquisitorial role, asking questions, as did the
experienced and legally knowledgeable juries of this time.[20] In spite of the presence of a jury, the whole method had an obvious parallel and continuity with
the protocols of the justice of the peace. The arrival of the lawyers in the criminal courts transformed this process by turning it into presentations of conflicting narratives, or "cases."

The new presence of the lawyers, in other words, did not just mean professionals would now speak for each party: the whole nature of the inquiry was
shifted. Instead of enabling a civilized confrontation or merely determining
sentences, trials became the orchestrated, public assembling of opposing stories. A particularly telling marker of this change was that prisoners gained access to the depositions (taken when they were committed for trial) which contained the evidence against them. The defense could then prepare its account
accordingly. In 1839, when parliament enacted this right—which would clearly
have been a wrong within the former logic of establishing justice—procedural
rules were still being belatedly refitted to accommodate the changed practice in
court.

Three years earlier, in 1836, the new process had received its definitive legislative confirmation in the Prisoners' Counsel Act, which ensured the right
of the accused to be fully represented.[21] Lawyers for the defense could then
officially address the jury and make a closing argument as well as cross-exam-
ine witnesses as they had been. In general, the same politicians who had dismantled the Bloody Code confirmed that a new type of criminal trial had arrived. Adjudicated speak-outs had been firmly abandoned. Advocates were an
accepted part of the trial. The British tradition of the jury trial embraced *professional* "pleading." Not only did standard rules of evidence develop with the
introduction of the lawyers; they also became increasingly important in the
newly lawyered court, where cross-examination itself was taken to new lengths
by the experts. In Britain's courtrooms Foucault's general description of the

changing legal situation applies: "The question is no longer simply: 'Has the act been established and is it punishable?' But also: 'What *is* this act, what *is* this act of violence or this murder? To what level of reality does it belong? Is it a phantasy, a psychotic reaction, a delusional episode, a perverse action?' It is no longer simply: 'Who committed it?' But: 'How can we assign the causal process that produced it? Where did it originate in the author himself?'"[22] When the criminal trial became a battle of lawyers, it also became a newly complex storytelling forum.

In fact, the criminal trial became a novel spectacle, in both senses of the word *novel*. From the perspective of the watching and newspaper-reading public, avid consumers of crime stories, the mere increase in trial time gave space for courtroom drama and individualized narratives to develop. The crime continued to provide that necessary modicum of transgressive action, a plot for a narrative, but now there was also an agglomeration of details and a plumbing of character by the trial itself. The courts might still view themselves primarily as mechanisms for resolving disputes nonviolently, but the public would come to view the trial, like the novel, as responsible for producing the full story. The enthusiastic public consumption of Thurtell and Hunt's 1824 murder trial particularly registers this change. The *London Magazine,* for instance, provided a twenty-one-page account of the trial explicitly intended to cut newspaper-like repetition and "make the readers breathless while they read."[23] Meanwhile, the trial itself, taking two full days instead of two hours, was obviously caught between the old requirement that the accused make his or her own defense and the new fully lawyered form of trial which was emerging. Thurtell's traditional-style dramatic oration simply did not compare to the detailed case mounted by the prosecution, while an exhausted Hunt had a court clerk read his defense— a statement actually written by his lawyer. Even in this trial, but especially in cases in which the defense counsels could do more toward cross-examination and presenting their own witnesses, the lawyers introduced a competition for narrative control which further made trials novelistic by turning a forum previously orchestrated solely by the judge into one organized around the sort of multiply authoritative voices which M. M. Bakhtin sees as characterizing the novel as a genre.

It is partly this Bakhtinian polyglossia that provokes John Bender to claim straightforwardly that "the 'lawyerization' of the criminal trial could be called a form of 'novelization.'"[24] For Bender this novelization is tied to the rise of modern bureaucratic forms of authority, and he argues that the introduction of lawyers matters because with them the impersonal authority of rules of evidence came to replace the personal authority of the judge. Caught within a structure of rules, discourse in the court is invisibly controlled, and in this way the court begins to operate like omniscient realist fiction. Bender theorizes: "The reformulation of authority in terms of ostensibly autonomous rules finds its counterpart in the [novel's] convention of transparency"; Gustave Flaubert's literary dictum that a controlling authorial power must be "everywhere felt, but never seen" suggestively applies as well to the modern court's organization of narration.[25] Bender thus nicely links the rise of realistic fiction to the rise of rules of evidence in criminal trials.

Nonetheless, without discarding this argument, we might begin again. For, if the lawyerization of the criminal trial is a novelization in the sense of introducing polyglossia, the first thing to notice is that once the lawyers started doing the talking, the defendant was swiftly and almost completely silenced.

Because defendants in England could not testify under oath on their own behalf, if they did not manage their own defense they effectively handed over their voices to their barristers. In 1822 the French commentator Charles Cottu observed that the prisoner's "hat stuck on a pole might without inconvenience be his substitute at the trial. . . . Neither the sound of his voice . . . nor the convincing silence of guilt, laid bare and forced to yield, call forth the passions of the by-standers."[26] The old right not to incriminate oneself actually began to matter to an extent that it never had. In the nineteenth century the silence of the accused became a problem to be debated, as a slew of articles in popular journals attests.[27]

Alongside this new silence lies what Alexander Welsh has seen as the rise of new forms of representation which "openly distrust direct testimony."[28] As Welsh shows, in the later eighteenth and early nineteenth century an epistemological shift occurred in which firsthand testimony became increasingly subordinated to its corroboration by circumstances, and accretions of factual detail became necessary to make a convincing representation. Narratives—whether recounted in the courtroom, in the novel, in scientific inquiry, or elsewhere—more than ever came to depend on presentations of circumstantial evidence. In court the barrister had to weave material facts and testimony into a story to bear out the "whole truth"—no longer legible in the words of the accused or accuser. Thus, novel-like, the real, or at least realistic, story emerges piecemeal in court from the consensus of its seemingly contradictory or divergent parts and voices. All voices are held to the physical facts; no single voice is authoritatively trustworthy or paramount. In this form of narration telling one's own story in one's own words is a less credible procedure than having one's story reconstructed by an orchestrating third party, namely, the barrister as narrator.

As a result, after the introduction of defense counsel in criminal cases, imagining justice for even an ordinary citizen on the model of the courts would entail more clearly than ever before imagining such a narrator at work. When, in the eighteenth century, in the long shadow of the scaffold, Adam Smith contemplated how individuals measure justice, he postulated it was imagined by thinking up an "impartial spectator" in the mind's eye in order to pass sentence on the self as agent.[29] As a gross oversimplification, one recounts one's narrative and imagines judge and jury for it. In the nineteenth century the accused and the victim would need advocates—the phantom of a barrister—who would take up one's words and who would produce and orchestrate one's story for an audience. This imagined persona that was still one's self would stand apart from the self as agent and yet be able to mime one's voice, organizing the reconstruction of a dramatically effective narrative; the story told in this way would be judged and juried.[30]

So, whereas the silence of the defendant or the plaintiff ensured that barristers in court would take on a role predicated on representing another's voice in their own narration, the lay person imagining justice, or the reproduction of truth, with reference to the courts was forced to construct a narrator whose discourse not only orchestrated facts and testimony but also integrated into itself the outer and inner voices of characters, including his or her own. In part what this change required was what Margaret Anne Doody describes as a "narrating language . . . big enough to accommodate all points of view, which are ultimately to serve the author's own."[31] The coming of the lawyers thus formed a small part of, and contributed to, the contemporaneous shift that Doody is describing in the novelistic narrator's capacity to represent perspective and consciousness.

The imagined spectacle of the newly lawyered criminal courts was, in short, one catalyst in the developing art of narrating other people's minds. The court-room that had represented and would always represent a drama became more deeply entangled with a quite different art—the novelistic narration of the "psychology of possible human minds . . . imaginary psychology."[32] In the realm of the novel an arsenal of different narratorial techniques for unpacking characters' consciousness and narrating their speech was gradually becoming more central to the conventions of the form. Arguably, the most important among them was the ability to imagine a narrator who, rarely rendering explicit judgments, might slide in and out of the characters' consciousness to let the real story piece itself together. This was the free indirect style, in which an imagined narrator, maintaining the third-person reference, nonetheless rendered the mental and spoken language of those in the story. In novels this narrator blurred the clearly demarcated voice of Fielding's authoritative and judgmental narrator with the depth, individuality, and primacy of the characters' voices in Richardson. In much the same way the arrival of the lawyers in the criminal courts blurred the division between the first-person, subjective speech of parties to a case and the ostensibly objective and authoritative declamations of its judge.

This is not to imply that barristers were discoursing in the free indirect style and society, watching them, adopted it. Nor were the new procedures of the courts reconstructing the form of the novel. As part of a far-reaching epistemological change, the method and conception of how criminals were tried underwent a transformation, and this transformation (as well as the larger epistemological change of which it was a part) percolated in the imaginatively flexible art of the novel, in which such changes found powerful exploration and origination, expression and response. Hence, deeply entwined in the development of the free indirect style that Doody and others usually trace to the domestic fiction of Fanny Burney and Jane Austen is also William Godwin's *Caleb Williams* (1794), a novel that wrestles its narrator through tribunal after tribunal. Identifying such a connection may help us to transcend the plain fact that the confluence of the procedures of the law courts and literary form has a long history, leading back even to the origins of literacy itself.[33] Instead, we may begin to recognize more specifically how, with the introduction of counsel in criminal trials, the trial, which had previously been a brief dramatic scene preceding the tableau of the scaffold, transformed into a complex, storytelling procedure that we may productively see as intersecting with the novel's evolving, increasingly influential form.

In general, it might be argued that the system of justice in British society went through a revolution, though nothing particularly new had been invented in the tradition-bound legal world. Within the legal milieu the ordinary criminal trial had in large part simply been reshaped after the fashion of civil trials, in which silent defendants and plaintiffs, controlling lawyers, and lengthy trials had long been the norm. (Even in the eighteenth century a suit in the court of Chancery could take a Dickensian thirty years.) In a rough sense the 1696 decision to allow for defense counsel in state treason trials had slowly extended into ordinary criminal trials, and, in broadening so, the initial public impact of the treason show trials as a form of justice also kept slowly and surely expanding, becoming applicable to ordinary criminal trials and ordinary people. With the boundaries of behavior marked out for all by the figure of the outlaw, the new mode of producing criminals became a powerful part of imagining identity, albeit perceived from a kaleidoscope of diverse perspectives. In so doing, the criminal trial's changing legal form intermixed with the everyday art of making life stories, an art both recorded and created by literary forms.

It is no coincidence, then, that, alongside the eighteenth-century emergence of the realistic, but fictional, narrative form later called the novel, the word *alibi* also entered into ordinary English discourse. Technically the legal plea of "elsewhere," culturally speaking, an alibi indicated the mounting of a realistic story narrated in a law court. (This initial, specific sense of alibi as a story told in court contrasts with its use since the beginning of the twentieth century, when it began also to refer to a story that keeps one *out* of court or to any form of excuse tale.) Alibi's entrance into common parlance did not indicate the arrival of a forensic genre of realistic fiction: an alibi could, after all, be true. Rather, it was a sign of something broader: an emerging widespread awareness that stories were narrated in law courts. Alibi added a narrative dimension to the ancient truism that the courts were theatrical spectacles; it flagged the courts as places where stories were told, as in a novel, not as places where they were enacted, as in drama.[34] The rise of the alibi marked a crucial public recognition that the (novelistic) art of narrating intersected with the court.

As changes in punishment and trial procedure combined to link novels to trials more and more firmly, both media also suggestively shared a concurrent rise in sheer numerical presence. As public punishments declined in importance, a tide of criminal trials swept over and through society along with the novel. As Martin Wiener reckons, "the first half of the nineteenth century saw a very large increase in the number of arrests, trials, and convictions. The numbers prosecuted in assizes and quarter sessions rose from 4,605 in 1805 to 31,309 by 1842; thereafter, more and more of the load began to be shifted to magistrates acting summarily."[35] There was, as Gatrell tells us, not just "an explosion in the number of barristers and attorneys" from 1770 to 1820 (430)—Christopher Allen counts 379 practicing barristers in 1785, 1,835 in 1840[36]—there was also a staggering "prosecution boom" in the first half of the nineteenth century (19). No calculus can compute the relevance of such statistics to the nineteenth-century novel (just as the actual multiplication of trial scenes in novels in this period should not necessarily persuade anyone of their import to developments in novelistic form), but it is perhaps worth observing that it was in this context, and at the apogee of trials in the 1840s, that the novel solidified as the dominant literary genre.

While this surge in trials resulted in part from internal legal changes, such as the government's increasing willingness to reimburse the private citizens upon whom the burden of prosecuting ordinarily fell, the repercussions were social. Whatever the causes (including simply an increasing population), criminal proceedings, lengthened and novelized, were being produced for public consumption in abundance. As always, people attended. The "indefatigable" novelist (and early friend of William Godwin) Amelia Opie led the way; she hardly missed a single assize session in her life and was regularly accorded the privilege of sitting with the judge in court.[37] Moreover, in the course of the nineteenth century the provincial assize processions (in which the judges on circuit showily paraded into town twice a year), the rendition of an assize sermon, and the other social events connected with the assizes no longer overshadowed the actual subject matter of the session. Everywhere, including London, each session would more and more clearly be divided into its individual trials. The jury would no longer wait to render verdicts on up to a dozen trials at one time, and sentences would no longer be pronounced en masse at the end of the session.

From the perspective of the public each trial would become its own story, and many trials would garner a much larger audience than just the people packed into the public gallery: those who did not attend could read all about it.

III

In the mid-eighteenth century there was an old, established print industry of criminal broadsheets and biographies centered around the gallows. Over the next century it was joined and surpassed by a similar print industry that produced newspapers and novels centered around the trial. Roughly speaking, newspapers supplanted criminal broadsheets, and the novel replaced criminal biography. Taken together, the change was part of a larger trend that established the separate cultural categories of fiction, in the shape of the novel, and fact, in the shape of the news.[38] That, however, is another story. Our concern is with the general, broad shifts in the publishing business which surrounded the materials of state justice.

Crime literature had long included accounts of trials. Whether one looks back to the sensational Elizabethan crime chapbooks or the gallows broadsheets and criminal biographies of the eighteenth and nineteenth centuries, the publication of "tryals" is always commonplace. But before the second half of the eighteenth century the printed literature of crime was centered on the execution scene. This dependence is perhaps most obvious in the broadsheets, which relied on the execution crowds for a marketplace. Still, it is the style and content of the crime literature of this era which bind it to the execution scene. Like the execution that is its end, this literature is about the human body. Within formulaic plots broadsheets and biographies alike prize bodily description or movement. Preset, often euphemistic, phrases frequently might leave the "unhappy victim" merely "weltering in her gore," but it is clearly important to recount in narrative slow-motion and detail the violence of a crime and when possible to illustrate it, especially any chopped-off body parts. Transgression must be recounted in its root *physical* sense of stepping across boundaries— whether in violence or, as indicated by the popularity of Jack Sheppard's escapes, in the outer limits achieved by a moving body. Both broadsheet and biography focus on the narrative of body events the trial provides, not on the details of personality which might incidentally surface in a trial. The trial is but a brief stop in a transgressive body's progress toward the scaffold.

The criminal broadsheet or gallows literature, epitomizing the "low end" of the genre, from the publication of the smaller quarter-sheet up even to pamphlets, should be distinguished from the criminal biography. Broadsheets—cheap, short, hawked on the street, and generally tied to immediate events—have a more pronounced reportorial function. For them currency, the latest news, was a selling point, even if the story were recycled. Likewise, even if the story was a "cock," that is, "cooked" up, competition between the broadsheets hinged, in part, on manufacturing claims to all-encompassing factual detail and authenticity. In this way they are attempts at "full and true accounts" in a journalistic sense. But because this literature revolved around the ritualized, almost unindividualized, lesson of the execution, the broadsheets also were ritualized and unindividualized. As Gatrell reads them, the broadsheets are predictably "repetitive and their moralizing intrusive and formulaic" (175). In a sense, they are rituals in print. Each is a variation on a basic format, and the conventional titles—a typical one beginning with "A True narrative of the confession and execution of several malefactors at Tyburn"—are long in part because they advertise which components of the overall rigid schema are included in that particular text.

Formulaic repetition lowered production costs, but this alone cannot explain the underlying agreement between readers and writers in which formulaic repetition was not simply irrelevant but expected. Execution sheets could go to market with a crude woodcut print of the gallows scene which was was not only recycled but also did not even represent the right number of the hanged. It was an "emblem," as Gatrell calls it, not an illustration. "What drew the purchasers," reasons Gatrell, "was . . . the fact that execution sheets were totemic artefacts. They were symbolic substitutes for the experiences signified or the experiences watched. They were mementoes of events whose psychic significance was somehow worth reifying" (175). They were like the grim playbills of a scaffold theater, which always put on the same shows. The contradictory nature of the broadsheet's two functions as both souvenir and report are nicely captured in the fact that, as soon as the prisoner on the scaffold dropped, the cry went up of patterers selling the victim's "last dying speech and execution." As Henry Mayhew was informed by a running patterer: "We gets it printed several days afore it comes off, and goes and stands with it right under the drop; and many's the penny I've turned away when I've been asked for an account of the whole business *before* it happened. So you see, for herly and correct hinformation, we can beat the *Sun*—aye, or the moon either, for the matter of that."[39] It was not that the writers and printers were blatantly duping foolish buyers. Rather, readers and publishers had established an exchange with values, expectations, and conventions which belonged to a different (and not simpler) time, one in which the scaffold and public punishment provided a shaping tableau.

As Mayhew's report concerning the broadsheets and the people who sold them reveals, the genre maintained its conventions and highly stylized form until after the mid-nineteenth century. By then, however, they were operating in a field dominated by newspapers—the *"Sun."* Whereas broadsheets had once been the primary printed source of crime stories, in the nineteenth century they became, as Mayhew observes, a form both produced with reference to and seen as "a condensation from the accounts in the newspapers,"[40] and then they disappeared altogether.

Foucault paints this passing away of gallows literature and its replacement by the newspaper and the novel as the suppression of a subversive literature. As an archaeologist of power, he sets up his argument by suggesting that "we should compare this literature with the 'disturbances around the scaffold,'" that is, with the scaffold scene as a confrontation between the people and state power. It is true, as he suggests, that "in the wake of a ceremony that inadequately channelled the power relations it sought to ritualize, a whole mass of discourses appeared pursuing the same confrontation."[41] As Gatrell carefully reconstructs, however, only the bawdy "gutter" songs—the "flash" ballads—actually engaged in a discourse of resistance, confrontation, and bravado (109–96). The resistance to the law "from below" is not to be found in this branch of the print industry. In England, at least, the gallows broadsheets constitute essentially moralistic tracts for lawful behavior, albeit sometimes rendered in a street English offensive to polite middle-class sensibilities.

Despite moments of pity or apology for the offender, broadsheets remind their readers that poor people were also the unhappy victims of crime who could hope to put the law to their own uses and defenses. At least in part, the broadsheets were celebrating a justice that consumers, both poor and middle-class, affirmed. At the same time, broadsheets were undoubtedly indoctrinating docility. Their very repetitiveness inculcated only one "right" response to the punishment of vastly different people and crimes. When Hannah More interpolates a criminal broadsheet titled "The last Words, Confession, and Dying Speech of William Wilson, who was executed at Chelmsford, for Murder" into one of her religious tracts intended to chasten the poor, this simulacrum of a broadsheet is a concentrated version of the tract itself.[42] Although broadsheets may have spawned fascination with the figure and adventurous life of the criminal, they ultimately attempted to brainwash their readers into unprotesting acceptance of the offender's condemnation.

The end of the broadsheets did not come because, as Foucault claims, they "glorified the criminal" and therefore had to be suppressed.[43] Nor can their demise simply be explained, as Gatrell suggests, by the fact that "polite people retreated as much from the contamination of the image as of the event" of the hanging (195). Broadsheets, like the rest of this type of crime literature, were doomed because they depended on an ideology and industry formed around the climactic scene of fatal, public punishment.[44] They persisted, as did public hangings, but long before the end of both they were essentially replaced by newspapers, whose reportage was newly focused on the trial scene.

Logic would seem to dictate that the press would reshape its crime stories around the trial *after* the disappearance of the scaffold in 1868. By that point it is certainly safe to say, as Richard Altick does, that "the climax of the story was now to be reached when the jury returned its verdict and the judge delivered his sentence. The execution, described after the exclusion of the press simply by a curt official statement affixed to the prison gate, was anticlimactic."[45] Yet, remarkably, no real change in reporting occurred at this point. The lucrative niche market of execution broadsheets closed down with the disappearance of the public execution, but the shift to the court which Altick describes had been forming for over a century in a complicated and gradual manner: as punishment had increasingly meant that prisoners were whisked off into near-oblivion, a newly shaped law trial began to command the public's attention, and event-specific broadsheets and pamphlets were largely replaced by the more continuous reportage of newspapers.

The dramatic reduction in public executions in the 1830s helped shift the focus of crime reporting to the trial scene, but the decade from 1814 to 1824 also marked a significant turning point for newspapers. According to Altick, "not only did the newspapers, beginning with Thurtell [and Hunt's trial in 1824], report in detail, often verbatim, the narrative of the crime as it was gradually developed from the witness box . . . the same copious materials were gathered together and printed in hastily produced books for crime addicts to read at their leisure."[46] An 1824 article in the *Edinburgh Review* on the state of this sort of reporting suggests a historic rationale for the new situation: "All the newspapers abound with reports of trials, and all their readers freely talk over both the merits and the points, the form and the substance, the preparatory process, and the ultimate decision. This spirit of observation, inquiry, and improvement, became vigilant and active soon after the peace had deprived foreign affairs of their too interesting character."[47] Walter Scott comes to a similar conclusion in a letter that year: There is "no public news—except the more last words of Mr. Thurtell, whose tale seems to interest the public as long as that of Waterloo, showing that a bloody murther will do the business of the newspapers when a bloody battle is not to be heard."[48] It is no surprise, then, that Altick, who quotes Scott, designates the end of the war in 1815 as another turning point: "Until after Waterloo . . . it was the broadsides and the more detailed pamphlets which almost alone catered to the popular taste for murder in print."[49] It stands to reason that at the end of the war newspapers would turn from foreign news to domestic legal battles. And, as historians commonly note, incidents of crime were probably actually on the rise due to the return of large numbers of impoverished soldiers.

Perhaps more important, however, the end of the war coincided with major technological advances in printing, such as new paper-making machines and the installation of the first steam-driven press. While these inventions spurred even the broadsheets to record-high distributions, they definitively established newspapers as the dominant print medium. Thus, perhaps the most significant factor is one of the simplest: unlike the scene at the scaffold, trials produced ready-made and daily text for the voracious, growing industry of newspapers that fed a public with an addictive reading habit. Whether one considers the sensational trial of *Ashton v. Thornton* in 1817 (in which the accused saved himself by exercising the long unused, but never abolished, right to challenge the plaintiff to a trial by battle) or the strange, scandalous examination of Queen

Caroline in 1820 (in which the House of Lords essentially tried her for licen-
tiousness), it is clear that after 1815 the sort of inundation and consumption
which turned trials into a type of national, serialized media story was well organized. While Altick reports that "in 1751–52 . . . the case of Mary ('Molly')
Blandy, the 'Female Parricide' who was executed at Oxford after a sensational
trial, dominated the whole country's newspapers," he correctly calls this phe-
nomenon "an exception."[50]

Mary Blandy's eighteenth-century trial does, however, underscore developments in the history of British law trial reporting as it began to emerge from the
shadow of seventeenth-century prohibition. As James Sutherland recounts in
his history of the newspapers of the Restoration period, at first "journalists
were not only forbidden to report parliamentary debates, but also severely dis-
couraged from reporting important trials in the law courts." In stark contrast to
the nineteenth-century newspapers' regular transcription of court proceedings
and detailed coverage of important trials, newspapers in their earlier format
may have occasionally "succeeded in publishing some information about court
proceedings, [but] in an important trial anything approaching a shorthand account would have led to immediate trouble," according to Sutherland. Hence,
as he observes, "the word 'reporter' was used for the shorthand writer em-
ployed to take down trials and other proceedings, but it was not until the middle of the nineteenth century that it was used for newspaper reporters, who
were earlier referred to as news-gatherers." The order of the day in the seven-
teenth century prescribed that reports of trial proceedings appear only after
the trial and then only by special permission and direction of the authorities.[51]

Over the next century even these court-sanctioned accounts of ordinary
criminal trial sessions would undergo a metamorphosis. The historians Langbein and Beattie both find that their official sources, the Old Bailey Session
Papers and Surrey pamphlets, respectively, describe trials in greater and greater
detail from 1710 on.[52] Yet the big break for the reporting of trials in the newspapers came at the end of the century, when the law courts were opened to
reporting, along with parliament (the highest court). As a historian of Victorian
newspapers recounts: "In the courts, privilege was extended to correct reports
of a trial—and had been so since the 1790s. The great political trials in 1820 of
Henry Hunt and associates for conspiracy after Peterloo, and of Thistlewood
and the Cato Street conspirators, were published without interference, by rad-

ical printers in what appear to be verbatim editions."[53] To put a finer historical point on it, in 1799, in the case of *Rex v. Wright,* which came before the Court of King's Bench, the new right of the press to report ongoing and even pretrial public court proceedings was clearly articulated. Whereas judges had previously been reprimanding anyone who dared to take notes in their court, the judges were agreed in 1799 that *"it is of vast importance to the public that the proceedings of Courts of Justice should be universally known."*[54]

The newspapers of the nineteenth century certainly did not shirk this mandate. Trial reporting in the nineteenth century became so extensive that it was commonly condemned as an endangerment to fair trials, even though the press was not legally allowed to comment or expand upon trials before or while they were being held.[55] In 1824, for instance, the *Edinburgh Review* vehemently protested challenges to the newspapers' right to publish any public legal proceeding (that is, to challenges made on the basis, for instance, that only one side is being heard, such ex parte statements being deemed prejudicial to juries): "Grave personages are said to have declared that such publications of the truth are *high misdemeanors!* The faithful report of a public examination has been pronounced *highly criminal,*—as being in substance a libel tending to defame the individual charged, and to pervert the due course of law and justice."[56] But, if there was tension between newspaper and courtroom, the construction of front-row press box seats in the new courts of the 1830s patently confirmed what had been true since at least 1803 (when the presence of the press in the back row of the public gallery had been accepted): newspapers were a component of a newly established order of justice. (By contrast, in 1846 it was declared that the press would no longer be allowed into the Old Bailey on the days of executions.)[57] The *Solicitors' Journal* summed up a state of affairs well entrenched by 1858: "As a general rule, it is undoubtedly desirable that correct and impartial reports of proceedings in open courts of justice should be given in the press. As has been well said, the printing of such reports is only an extension of the area of the Court."[58]

In the nineteenth century newspapers brought the action of the law courts into ordinary lives. For the first time in British history a large number of people could be expected regularly to read a lengthy report of court proceedings. As Edward Bulwer Lytton observed in 1847: "There exists a Press which bares at once to the universal eye every example of guilt that comes before a legal tribunal"; to find this new "literature of Newgate and Tyburn, you have only to open the newspaper on your table."[59] Throughout the nineteenth century the *Times* had sections titled after particular courts, such as "Court of King's Bench." These columns were not discrete articles, telling of one case or one story; they recounted court proceedings. Even seemingly stand-alone articles were frequently transcripts of court proceedings. For example, later in the century the *Illustrated London News* used its regular column titled "Law and Police" to report the court proceedings of the Tichborne claimant for a number of weeks in 1871, but this sensational and lengthy trial at one point also briefly merited its own column with its own title, "The Tichborne Baronetcy Case."

One way or another, in the expanded space of the nineteenth-century newspaper, transcriptions of court cases were published, and entire sections recounting proceedings in a court the previous day were standard. Readers had regular printed doses of cases, and the execution scene (if there were one) necessarily faded into a single day's brief report. Whereas the broadsheet had once presented the scaffold as a socializing force, the newspapers began to inculcate a new forensic subjectivity. While foreign news helped establish a reader as English (in opposition to other nationalities) and coverage of the monarchy and parliament implied a reader who was a political subject, crime and trial reports constructed the newspaper reader as an answerable member of a law-bound state. The outdoor public spectacle of the scaffold with its broadsheets was tacitly replaced by a different sort of "mass ceremony," as Benedict Anderson calls the national ritual of newspaper reading. In the ideology of justice formed around the scaffold, the presence of the body was central, but now both the medium (newspapers) and subject (trial) emphasized language and narrative as the locus of discipline. This drill was, as Anderson puts it, "performed in silent privacy, in the lair of the skull."[60] As the Victorian Edward FitzGerald remarked to a friend: "I don't ever wish to see and hear these things tried; but, when they are in print, I like to sit in Court then, and see the Judges, Counsel, Prisoners, Crowd: hear the Lawyers' Objections, the Murmur in the Court, etc."[61]

Of course FitzGerald could find this "court in print" in books as well as newspapers. Some volumes were marketed essentially as extensions of the papers. Gatrell proposes James Harmer's *The Murder of Mr. Steele,* published in 1807 (two years before FitzGerald was born), as the book that for the first time dared "to appeal against a dubious trial and sentence by speaking directly to a general readership about the 'fairness' of legal process rather than deferentially to the authorities of state" (436). We may add to this *The Red Barn, A Tale, Founded on Fact* (1831) as perhaps the earliest novel to append a newspaper trial account to its true-crime fiction. In general, books for the public, such as *The Red Barn,* tended to see themselves as moving trial reporting out of the realm of ephemera and into the realm of supposedly timeless entertainment and moral instruction—into, that is, a crime literature market that would be dominated first by criminal biography and then by the novel.

Criminal biographies have long been recognized and debated as a "source" for the emerging novel.[62] Compared to their near-relation, the criminal broadsheet, these brief biographies were more expensive, longer, and less tied to current events. Moreover, unlike the broadsheets, which often made patchworks of their content and included a ballad or some rhymed verse, criminal biographies usually provided a more linear prose narrative, sometimes illustrated with high-quality engravings. The prosperous market that concerns us here worked by collecting or commissioning criminal biographies, which were sold as a set of volumes in which each volume was itself an anthology—most famously, various collections of this sort took the title of the *Newgate Calendar.*[63] These were frequently read by novelists, who then recycled crimes or characters from them, as the explanatory endnotes printed in countless novels today attest. Novelists may also have received a lesson in literary realism from the fact-filled accounts; as Maximillian Novak discerns, "*Robinson Crusoe,* England's first sustained work of realistic fiction . . . appeared, significantly enough, in the same year [1719] as the folio edition of the State Trials," which was specifically addressed to nonprofessional readers.[64] It has not been difficult, or mistaken, to see criminal biography as an ingredient of the novel. From our distant perspective some of Defoe's novels announce themselves quite blatantly as criminal biographies, and Henry Fielding's *Jonathan Wild* and *Tom Jones* are often seen as providing a bridge between the older and the newer forms.

Yet studies of criminal biographies also tend to emphasize just how different these texts are from the novel. Both Lincoln Faller and John Richetti discuss how criminal biographies, with their rehearsal of stereotypes, fall more into the category of repeated and ritualized myth than novel.[65] In the end, as

Faller argues, "the most valuable way to relate criminal biography to the novel ... is not in terms of its inherent forms or concerns, but rather in terms of the 'occasion' it made for the reading and writing of extended narratives about (to use Lukács's term) 'problematic' lives."[66] These texts, as Faller suggests, were not the precursors out of which later novelistic texts developed but a locus around which a market of writers and readers was established which then subsequently turned to the novel. From a literary viewpoint there was a jump from criminal biography to the novel.

What difference did this leap entail? Most obviously, the narratives of criminal biographies almost always end on the gallows. They have two basic formulas for getting there. A criminal biography generally turns out to be either a teleological picaresque story that relates the graphic movement of a transgressive body up until its final "lamentable" dead stop or a homily that rewrites the criminal's life as a series of archetypal stepping stones of sin progressing to a heinous moral collapse that is, usually, followed by a scripted recitation of repentance before the inevitable, abrupt departure for the beyond. Either way, the genre is rigidly shaped against the backdrop of the gallows. What strikes the reader, as Richetti says, is "the invariability of the criminal's biography; the progress toward death and judgement, and the execution itself [as] clear examples of ritualistic necessity."[67] In contrast, a different convention governs later crime novels such that even for legally culpable protagonists just the opposite seems to be true: the gallows scene becomes not an impossible but a less likely, and where it occurs, qualitatively different conclusion.

We are comparing starkly different narrative forms: fabrication in the crime novel is, by convention, fictional elaboration and expansion; in criminal biography fabrication is the refitting of plot to formulaic repetition, to legend, and of character to mythic types. Unlike criminal biography, the novel spins out language, so that any moment or character might be endlessly explored because that moment or character is as expandable as the language being used to create it. Moreover, the genre of the novel takes its own metamorphosis as an underlying assumption of its form: the novel's endless permutations—which cause some critics to throw up their hands at the mere thought of lumping novels together—expresses one of its fundamental principles. Not surprisingly, definitions of the novel are notoriously dangerous. The term itself—much more so than its well-plotted nineteenth-century incarnations—is a "loose and baggy monster." If, however, *novel* can be understood to describe not an entity, or even a process to which language is subjected, but a literary form that is intelligible only in the context of a specific set of cultural relationships, which it both reflects and produces, then, historically, *novel* names a departure from the genre of the criminal biography.

What have been less clear to literary historians are the underpinnings of that departure. As this chapter has tried to show, understanding the shift from criminal biography to novel requires first pairing that shift with a change in the paradigm of justice (epitomized by the switch from scaffold to court) and then seeing how, in a marketplace of print, the novel and newspaper were connected to the court while further recognizing that the novel, in tandem with the trial-oriented newspapers, had its own cultural functions and political aims distinct from those of the courts. That unique juridical self-fashioning is the literary history with which the rest of this book is concerned.

CHAPTER TWO

Caleb Williams and the Novel's Forensic Form

AFTER ATTENDING A PLAY IN 1830, Henry Crabb Robinson jotted down in his diary with some hyperbole that the "adoption of *legal* incidents as the source of romantic and dramatic interest . . . began with Godwin."[1] As Robinson, a barrister and a highly literate reader, perceived, the publication of his friend William Godwin's *Things as They Are; or the Adventures of Caleb Williams* in 1794 somehow marked an epoch in the history of law and literature. Godwin's novel ushered in, I will suggest, a twofold change: first, *Caleb Williams* helped shift the novel as a form away from the genre of criminal biography and, second, in so doing it produced a newly juridical conception of character and narrative form.

Godwin's novel brims with trial scenes; every one of this novel's three volumes depicts at least three tribunals of various types, with many more threatened or invoked. Caleb, once he knows the aristocratic Falkland has murdered the boorish squire Tyrell, seems almost always to be either accusing Falkland or defending himself against Falkland's preemptive, trumped-up charge of theft. The resulting repetition of trial scenes alone suggests a literary-legal turn that is unexplained by our current, ready-made crime novel genealogies, which tag this novel variously as a psychological thriller, a novel of pursuit, or even an early example of detective fiction.[2] Not that literary historians have ignored *Caleb Williams*'s trial scenes; these scenes have naturally formed an important part of a discussion concerned with the novel's reflexive narrative form—Godwin's story is filled with depictions of characters authoring stories.[3] We have, however, largely seen the novel's tribunals and self-consciousness about authorship and authority in terms of its broad, radical, political aims, tying the story to Godwin's famous political treatise, the *Enquiry Concerning Political Justice* (1793).[4] But the story also works in terms (no less political) of a more specific exposure of the contemporary system of criminal justice.

Specifically, *Caleb Williams* presents a historic struggle between criminal biography and the novel. In an effort to expose the deleterious shaping of character and society by the eighteenth-century justice system's narrative paradigms, Godwin intentionally shed the novel's gallows literature past. By turning instead, however, to tribunal scenes to shape his novel's story and form, Godwin—in spite of his more radical aims—thereby refitted a crucial aspect of the novel's mode of constructing narrators and characters for a nineteenth-century society that, like himself, had become enthralled by trial stories.

I

Most critics assume logically enough that *Caleb Williams* draws on various criminal biographies as sources. Godwin's own explanatory footnotes are almost all references to collections of criminal lives which fall into the genre of the *Newgate Calendar*. As these once-familiar texts have been left behind and the fame of the criminals' lives they depict has dimmed, scholars have fleshed out Godwin's notes and explored other references to criminal biography he makes in the novel.[5] The resulting assemblage of bits and pieces of context has, however, obscured Godwin's larger, original, coherent handling of criminal biography as a genre.

We can particularly begin to see that Godwin has gone beyond merely alluding to criminal biographies toward the end of *Caleb Williams*'s second volume. There Caleb, in jail awaiting trial on false charges of stealing Falkland's property, reenacts two celebrated prison escapes by the famous eighteenth-century criminal Jack Sheppard. The story does not just allude to Sheppard. Caleb's narrative in this section of the novel conforms at length to a recognizable criminal biography, as if Caleb were re-presenting a Jack Sheppard tale.

Caleb's escapes thus paradoxically become a kind of odd prison: he is trapped within the most predictable and shopworn of contemporary criminal life stories. Godwin's point is relatively clear: in this story Caleb's, and even Jack Sheppard's, ingenious escapes do not represent a real liberation from the state's system of justice. These physical breakouts are the lock-down of a larger cultural narrative. Caleb may tell us of his escapes from jail, but all of England might as well be Caleb's prison as long as he fails to deliver himself from the confinement of reenacting and retelling the same stale stories.

At the beginning of the next and final volume, the genre of criminal biography begins to emerge explicitly as Caleb's imprisoning narrative. As the volume opens, Caleb has escaped from prison and is hiding out with Mr. Raymond's honorable gang of thieves. Two of the gang return with a printed hue and cry that announces Caleb is a wanted criminal. They carefully compare Caleb to their printed text: "Having read for a considerable time, they looked at me, and then at the paper, and then at me again."[6] It is a match. This "description of a felon with the offer of a hundred guineas for his apprehension" recounts the crimes Caleb is supposed to have committed and describes Caleb minutely, confronting him with a textual double of himself (223). As always in this novel, the narrative situation is complex. Since Caleb, our narrator, is writing out his adventures, the handbill's double is implicitly paired not only with the "real" Caleb but also with the character "Caleb" that Caleb reconstructs in his own narrative. At another level the handbill's criminal character also represents Godwin's doubling of his textual creation—the novel's fictional character Caleb. Nor can the printed hue and cry be left out of the imaginary mirroring. This published hue and cry turns out to be the germ of a criminal biography that, it soon becomes clear, is the nonidentical double of both the narrative Caleb is writing and of Godwin's *Caleb Williams*. Godwin has brought Caleb typeface to typeface with his rogue double in an overdetermined textual cosmos. The two do not soon part. Caleb's encounter with the printed hue and cry reveals a manifest, mobile, letterpress shadow that continues to stalk him and the story itself.

Most immediately, the handbill's publication means that the conflict that has until this point been carefully kept within a select group suddenly erupts into a much larger, public arena. Caleb leaves Mr. Raymond's hideout to discover people everywhere are talking over his "history." In a public house someone complains that "he makes talk for the whole county" and that "one never hears of any thing else" (235). Earlier in the story Falkland may work through intermediaries and deploy the anonymous mechanisms of the law, but the conflict requires, and focuses on, the physical presence of the protagonists. In the third volume, when the conflict extends into print publication, Caleb is safe only as long as he is not identified as the nefarious character of the circulating story.

Or at least so Caleb believes. For when he disguises himself to keep others from connecting him with his hue and cry, he is promptly mistaken for another criminal described by a completely different handbill. In this bizarre adventure Caleb's initial disguise as an Irish beggar transfers him into the midst of another person's story—and into an almost identical predicament with a second hue and cry. This other "description . . . appeared to [two thief takers] to tally to the minutest tittle" (241), just like the first. From Caleb's perspective it would appear that acting as another character risks exchanging his own predicament for another's. Yet disguising his character is nonetheless one of the only paths of escape open to Caleb as he blindly flees his doubles sprung from the printing presses of a world of gallows literature.

Meanwhile, Godwin is clarifying the stakes of this strange, newly textual pursuit. First, he has Caleb's original hue and cry rename him: in it *Caleb*, meaning dog, becomes *Kit* (a byname of Christopher), suggesting cat. If this misnaming hints at the ease with which Caleb is made personally irrelevant—and one contemporary meaning of *kit* is "a group of people"—when the two thief takers next drag Caleb before a magistrate on the authority of the second, unrelated hue and cry, the scene confirms the generic nature of Caleb's fate. It matters little that he does not fit the second handbill's description; others will tailor him to fit the preconceived gallows story. The magistrate, who classifies Caleb as an "old offender" and quashes his protests that they have the wrong man, puts it succinctly: "If a man were too short, he said, there was no remedy like a little stretching" (244, 242).

The magistrate's grim joke catches at the dark comedy in Caleb's failure to see the larger framework of the justice system determining his personal predicament. And Caleb continually repeats such scenes. Throughout the novel ironic incidents and details mark a distance between Caleb, who comments intelligently on his own and others' individual behavior, and another, authorial presence, which sympathetically but persistently has Caleb betray that he (and the others) are unwittingly turning in prescribed circles. If readers were not adequately alerted by Godwin's warning in the preface that "the following narrative is intended to answer a purpose more general and important than immediately appears upon the face of it" (1), literary commentators have pounced on it. Although, as Marilyn Butler and Mark Philp write, Caleb is "full of acute insight into himself and his relationships with others, he is also, necessarily, the product of the flawed world he describes; learning to mistrust the narrator thus becomes the reader's first task." Godwin wants us to understand "the limits of the narrator's self-understanding."[7]

This lucid perception of Caleb must be our starting point. From there it is only a small, first step to see—as in the scene in which Caleb momentarily falls into another's hue and cry—that Godwin uses Caleb's limited self-awareness to expose his engulfment in a larger, political and historical system of justice, while Caleb, though occasionally glimpsing this larger reality, continues to see his problems and his fate as individual and local. The more difficult, second point—and my initial argument—is that in the concluding volume, in which Caleb and his narrative struggle against competing published stories, Godwin reveals that Caleb and his narrative are also engulfed, and stuck, in a contemporary narrative system that is itself part of the engine of justice. In the end Caleb's general inability to recognize the pervasive workings of the criminal justice system emerges, in part, as a failure to recognize the silent, controlling influence of literary genre.

That genre more and more explicitly emerges as criminal biography over the course of the final volume. Driven into hiding by the publication of the hue and cry, a disguised Caleb himself joins in producing criminal biographies: "By a fatality for which I did not exactly know how to account, my thoughts frequently led me to the histories of celebrated robbers; and I retailed from time to time incidents and anecdotes of Cartouche, Gusman d'Alfarache and other memorable worthies, whose carreer [*sic*] was terminated upon the gallows" (259). This "fatality" is hardly unaccountable. We see, as Caleb does not, that with a near criminal biography of himself just published, he has morbid, but good, reason to fixate on criminal biographies in which the hero's "carreer was terminated upon the gallows." Godwin's motivation is different. The decision to follow Caleb's two encounters with published crime accounts by having

Caleb himself "retail" criminal histories suggests that as an author Godwin is concerned with differentiating Caleb's narrative from the gallows literature upon which it so obviously draws. A battle of books escalates within *Caleb Williams.*

This battle's full complexity emerges in the aftermath of Caleb's brief tenure writing criminal biographies. Falkland's operative, Gines, tracks Caleb down, tracing him in part because he is writing gallows literature; Caleb recounts: "[Gines] was confirmed in [his speculations and suspicions] . . . by the subject of my lucubrations, men who died by the hands of the executioner" (264). Caleb flees, but Gines has discovered not just Caleb but also a better means of catching him. Expanding on "a true and faithful copy of the hue and cry" (268–69), Gines produces a "halfpenny legend" of Caleb (273), breathing new life into Caleb's textual double initially created by the hue and cry. Thus, shortly after Caleb is forced to give up authoring criminal biographies, he stumbles across a street hawker vending one: "The most wonderful and surprising history, and miraculous adventures of Caleb Williams" (268).

In an obvious way the street hawker's "adventures of Caleb Williams" is a ghost of Godwin's novel, *The Adventures of Caleb Williams.* The novel thereby links itself to its own genealogy, both to earlier realistic novels of crime and adventure and, more pointedly, to the criminal biographies with which these novels were entwined. At the same time, the street hawker's title distinctly fails to echo the crucial, authorial part of the novel's title, "Things as They Are," which reflects Godwin's perspective and his intentions in producing Caleb writing his own story: the novel is not the criminal biography. Even more important is the impact of Gines's criminal broadsheet on the ongoing plot. With his "Adventures of Caleb Williams" Gines produces a published story that attempts to imprison the character Caleb within the conventions of gallows literature. In doing so, Gines explicitly uses the genre of criminal biography much as Falkland has used the conventions of chivalric and romance stories to authorize the truth of his own story.[8] Later, in Wales, Gines's ploy will prove very effective. When a woman who has befriended Caleb discovers this published "Wonderful and Surprising History of Caleb Williams" (301), she will immediately and unequivocally condemn him. Caleb is confined by his society's literary clichés.

Caleb meanwhile believes, often along with us, that his world can be set to rights by the successful dissemination of an accurate rendition of his story. Such a belief is wholly mistaken—and to know this we need only remember the invisible, shaping perspective of Godwin, who has just completed an exposure of society's structures and their stifling and stultifying effects on individuals in his monumental *Political Justice*. In *Caleb Williams* the world presents a larger problem than just a struggle between individuals' narratives. These narratives are themselves determined and limited by genres, by institutionalized ways of seeing and speaking, and we are all implicated in both their platitudes and possibilities. Caleb's obsession with telling only his tale, with what he sees as his own personal story, is actually a blinder that keeps him—like Falkland—turning in circles. Caleb's problem is not that he needs to tell his story but that in telling that story he has recognized neither the larger story of how narratives work in and upon the world nor how the specific historical narrative form of criminal biography is structuring his actions, his viewpoint, his character, his narrative.

Godwin is cueing his readers to see Caleb's failure to suspend his self-obsession and recognize the larger generic framework shaping him along with others; perhaps nowhere is this clearer than in the moment when Caleb discovers his criminal broadsheet. In that scene Godwin has Caleb unwittingly expose his inability to connect his personal fate with the fates of others and thus with his larger context. Caleb learns from the broadsheet that Mrs. Marney, the kind landlady who sheltered and protected him, has been "sent to Newgate upon a charge of misprision of felony." His "instant feeling" is, in typically self-dramatizing fashion, "a willingness to undergo the utmost malice of my enemies" in order to save "this excellent woman from alarm and peril" (269). But he immediately shifts into a self-excusing, plaintive voice (recalling the earlier, unconvincing self-justification he gives for breaking into Falkland's private trunk during a house fire). He announces: "My sympathy for Mrs. Marney however was at this moment a transient one. A more imperious and irresistible consideration demanded to be heard":

With what sensations did I ruminate upon this paper? Every word of it carried despair to my heart. . . . A numerous class of individuals, through every department, almost every house of the metropolis, would be induced to look with a suspicious eye upon every stranger, especially every solitary stranger, that fell under their observation. . . . It was no longer Bow-Street, it was a million of men, in arms against me. Neither had I the refuge, which few men have been so miserable as to want, of one single individual with whom to repose my alarms, and who might shelter me from the gaze of indiscriminate curiosity. (269–70)

If Caleb's despair is understandable, Godwin here also has Caleb betray the fatal solipsism that produces it. Having dismissed sympathy for the unselfish Mrs. Marney, whose feelings he understands are such that, "if she should be the means of any mischief to [him], she should be miserable for ever" and whose imprisonment he has now caused, Caleb ironically bewails his own "solitary" fate (265). This unwanted wanted man even unintentionally points out that his "alarms" get their solid footing from his myopic self-involvement. The mobilization of "every department, almost every house of the metropolis" meanwhile underscores the broad, social nature of his plight (as well as representing the larger horror of how such broadsheets work to transform society into a massive, oversuspicious surveillance force). Caleb's response to his criminal broadsheet thus reveals an individual insightfully recounting his irreducible, private experience of how justice is served up in his world, but it also betrays how as part of that experience he has been blinded to his life story's connection to others' life stories, to their common shaping by political structures ("Newgate") and their unification by genre (the criminal biography he is reading and in which Mrs. Marney is now a character).

Crucially, then, it is not, as Kenneth Graham thoughtfully suggests, Caleb who is "seeing his life reduced to a literary convention" by the broadsheet but, rather, the reader, cued by Godwin, who watches this happen.[9] In the scene in which Caleb discovers this criminal broadsheet Godwin plays upon his reader's perspective, weighing his novel against the narrative Caleb is writing: for a moment there in Caleb's and the reader's foreground is the genre of criminal biography, a genre that has been lurking in the background and quietly overshadowing Caleb's attempt to tell a purely personal history (and win justice for himself alone).

As Caleb discovers a criminal broadsheet of himself, the reader discovers that Caleb is unable to gauge his own position (or writing) in the literary context of criminal biography in which he is enfolded. He fails to see that his own path has much earlier fallen into the scripted, false escapes of a Jack Sheppard, that later he writes about the lives of criminals because he finds himself in an analogous position (not because of some unaccountable "fatality"), and that now the criminal broadsheet he holds in his hand, which he himself notes is slightly more detailed than ordinary for "this species of publication" (269), has as much to do with the narrative structures and institutions of society as with himself. No wonder Caleb blithely proceeds to take another page from the *Newgate Calendar,* setting up a respectable life as a watchmaker-schoolteacher-etymologist in Wales just like the famous scholar-criminal Eugene Aram. His life falls relentlessly into the conventional, which exists even for those categorized as criminal; or, better said, his own life story sinks into the genre that is framing it.

Not surprisingly his criminal broadsheet quickly catches up with him in Wales. Laura Denison, whom Caleb describes as his "comforter . . . friend . . . mother" but from whom he has nonetheless concealed his troubled past, discovers the circulating, published criminal biography (298). She immediately banishes him. Driven, as it were, from his own life by a spurious published story of it, Caleb tries to regain control by writing the story of his life himself, beginning "the writing of these memoirs" (303). Although Caleb intends his written text to reverse (again) the roles of hunter and hunted in Falkland's and his fatal embrace, Caleb is actually spurred by Gines's publication of the criminal biography defaming his character, more than by any act of Falkland's. The ink slinging of the third volume comes full circle. The initial narrative that Caleb produces and which we read turns out to be formed as a contradiction to a published criminal biography: "I began these memoirs with the idea of vindicating my character" (326).

We have, it turns out, been reading not only Caleb's adventures but also the story of how he came to write them, and it is important to note that this writing pervades his entire story. Thus, long before the explicit pursuit by publication takes place in the third volume, Caleb tries with writer-conscious logic to explain away his betrayal of a Miss Peggy and a jail keep who have trusted him with some tools:

> In these proceedings it is easy to trace the vice and duplicity that must be expected to grow out of injustice. I know not whether my readers will

pardon the sinister advantage I extracted from the mysterious conces-
sions of my keeper. But I must acknowledge my weakness in that respect;
I am writing my adventures and not my apology. (194)

"Readers" may "pardon" away. Caleb sentences himself here, in both senses of
the word. His uneasy self-justification means he will continue to perform and
to recount, as he does throughout his initial narrative, his part in the inseparable pair of keeper and prisoner, pursuer and pursued, "persecutor and . . .
persecuted" (306). Moreover, readers know full well that Caleb is hardly just
writing his "adventures," as he claims. Elsewhere he has insisted precisely that
he is writing his defense, his vindication—an "apology" that ostensibly should
require him to confront, instead of skirt, the "sinister" moments like this one in
which he unintentionally reveals himself as unwitting accomplice to his own
protested fate. But Caleb has no sense of genre. Whether "memoirs" or "adventures," his narrative fatefully discounts the force of genre, even when it invokes it.

From the moment Caleb begins his story, the contemporary genre of criminal biography and the contemporary system of justice—in a conjunction that
only explicitly presents itself in the third volume—form the invisible walls of a
conceptual prison for him. This is why Caleb has little to say about the long
years that have elapsed since he began writing. He skims across this time, first
to report his current weariness with writing his narrative and his unchanged
situation, then to recount a meeting with Mr. Collins (Falkland's steward and
one of Caleb's many mentors) in which, among other things, Caleb shows his
weariness by uncharacteristically acquiescing to Collins's plea not to burden
him with his story, and finally to put down his pen. There is no liberation
derived from his reactive narrative act. We have drifted beyond the story's end,
and Caleb still has no resolution to his struggle. Nor can he get outside it; he
is next stymied in an attempt to sail away to a foreign country, provoking him
to resume writing in a frenzy in which he decides to try (again) to push the
moment to its crisis. It is no accident that we have been carried beyond the unified, initial narrative, yet Caleb is still in the same predicament. Caleb does not
understand that his initial narrative belongs to the current order of oppositions
that structure the contemporary system of justice. His narrative functions like
his prison breakouts; only now Caleb is explicitly moving on a symbolic plane.

Writing beyond the opposition formed within the novel by Caleb's "Adventures of Caleb Williams" and Gines's "Adventures of Caleb Williams," Godwin reveals that the conflict of these narratives is stalemated within a single genre.

Only at the novel's end, in the final trial scene, when Falkland at last breaks down and provides that specious cure-all, a confession confirming the truth of Caleb's "artless" story (324), does Godwin signal a way out for his readers. The "hateful scene" that Caleb inflicts upon a pathetic, wrecked, and aged Falkland provides no salutary resolution for Caleb but does lead him to the significant realization that the way Falkland has treated him (both for good and bad) has been motivated by a larger code of honor and chivalry which he has imbibed from romance narratives (320). Caleb's previous simplistic conception of Falkland as his personal enemy and unremitting tyrant melts, and he at last escapes the initial symbiotic struggle of individual wills. At the same time, Caleb discovers that "an overweening regard to [self] . . . has been the source of [his] errors!" (325), a belated self-analysis that not only censures the earlier narrative and narrator but also goes a long way toward making sense of them. Yet even this diagnosis has the ironic drawback of being a last hurrah of egocentricity, as if to say, "I do declare, I talk about myself too much." Worse, as Gary Handwerk argues, this "acceptance of guilt . . . seems to absolve [Caleb] from further self-examination and from applying to himself the historicizing analysis he has applied to Falkland."[10] Caleb may see that the code of chivalry, along with its narrative expression in romances, has shaped Falkland's behavior, but at the end of the story his own equivalent problem is left to the reader.

Caleb's final failure is Godwin's final bait to the reader. It enables us to see clearly that throughout the novel, as in much satiric or ironic writing, the specific viewpoint the main character lacks has been precisely what the author intended to conjure in the reader, the protagonist's failure to develop tacitly galvanizing the reader's development. As Caleb's use of superlatives inevitably becomes merely melodramatic with repetition, and as the syntax of his adventures becomes increasingly wooden, words and acts begin to expose Caleb and his narrative rather than the people and events he is ostensibly describing. Godwin constructs a tension between the novel's twin faces of intense individual psychology and of open-ended contact with a historical present by constructing a psychologically insightful narrator who fails to see the larger, shaping forces of his historical context. In doing so, Godwin presses the novel into service as a genre that liberates its readers by exposing the generic limits that structure reality.

Godwin thus has not really taken up the various *Newgate Calendars* and *State Trials* as sources to draw on for his novel. How could he, when he was himself engaged in a battle of publications indivisible from the larger legal battles then raging around seditious radicalism? Shortly after beginning *Caleb Williams,* for instance, Godwin protested that upon leaving the show trial of Thomas Paine he "saw hand-bills, in the most vulgar and illiberal style distributed, entitled, The Confession of Thomas Paine."[11] Here was the same, hackneyed story. Hence as Maximillian Novak argues of *Caleb Williams:* "Godwin's use of the Newgate Calendar was highly imaginative and creative. He saw in this series of lives not only a fascinating group of narratives but a catalogue of wrongs on both sides of the law: wrongs shocking enough to condemn the entire machinery of justice. . . . Godwin saw in the lives of criminals a vivid proof that true justice played no part in these bloody and violent careers. To read the Newgate Calendar was to experience vivid evidence of the breakdown of humane relationships in contemporary society."[12] And, as we have seen, to rewrite criminal biography from this perspective is to write *Caleb Williams.*

So, while Caleb's initial narrative futilely contradicts a single criminal biography, Godwin's novel challenges, to better effect, criminal biography as a genre. It marks a turning point in the history of the novel. As Novak discerns, "it was not the creation of a wholly new psychological fiction from [criminal biography] that made Godwin original; Defoe had done much the same in *Roxana* and in parts of *Moll Flanders* and *Colonel Jack.*"[13] It was, we might now say, that, whereas previous eighteenth-century novels were transforming criminal biography into a different narrative form, Godwin took up the genre of criminal biography in order to repudiate it. In a much quieter fashion Godwin's *Caleb Williams* was to the conjunction of criminal biography and the English novel something like Cervantes's *Don Quixote* (1605) had been to the conjunction of romance and novel. Here, too, irony undercut one narrative system while engendering another. After *Caleb Williams* the novel of crime subtly changed from referring itself to criminal biography to distancing itself from it.

I I

It is no accident that an author whose purposes were politically radical reoriented the English novel away from criminal biography. Moving beyond the eighteenth century's complex system of justice, in which the gallows held pride of place, was inseparable from moving beyond the lingering system of narratives associated with that form of justice. Yet, in searching for a more anarchistic community, Godwin also unwittingly helped to solidify a system of state justice which was gradually being established in tandem with the novel itself. This form of justice was newly rebuilt, like *Caleb Williams,* around the storytelling forum of trials. Thus, although within his novel Godwin ostensibly intended an exposé of the social impact of his contemporary adversarial trial system, in practice Godwin turned out to be as trapped by genre as he had shown Caleb to be: this novel, as a novel, ultimately helped tie the form and its conception of subjectivity more firmly than ever before to the law courts.

Instead of linking his novel to the crises over English Jacobins or the radical philosophy of *Political Justice,* we might begin by examining the moment in which Godwin wrote *Caleb Williams*—a time when the law courts invaded his own life. Here is Godwin in January 1793, the month he began *Caleb Williams,* writing in the preface to *Political Justice:*

The period in which [*Political Justice*] makes its appearance is singular. The people of England have assiduously been excited to declare their loyalty. . . . Every man . . . is to be prosecuted, who shall appeal to the people by the publication of any unconstitutional paper or pamphlet. . . . It is now to be tried whether, in addition to these alarming encroachments upon our liberty, a book is to fall under the arm of the civil power. . . . It is to be tried whether an attempt shall be made to suppress the activity of mind, and put an end to the disquisitions of science. Respecting the event in a personal view the author has formed his resolution. Whatever conduct his countrymen may pursue, they will not be able to shake his tranquillity.[14]

Tranquillity is, however, clearly under siege. As he sets out to write *Caleb Williams,* Godwin finds himself haunted by the knowledge that he may be tried for treason as the author of *Political Justice*. Understandably, he protests here that the real trial ("It is now to be tried. . . . It is to be tried") will be whether or not *Political Justice* provokes prosecution. After all, what is he to do if taken to court—object to the whole process by citing relevant passages from *Political Justice?*[15] Yet, in upstaging the possibility of his legal trial by invoking a larger ethical trial, Godwin reveals his own interpenetration by the very legal system he would transcend. There is something flawed about introducing a book that calls into question fundamental contemporary understandings of justice by pleading, as Godwin does here and in letters to the newspapers during this period, "at the bar of my country."[16] Yet the passage, with its internalized courtroom perspective, makes a likely preamble to the trial-filled *Caleb Williams*.

Neither while he was writing *Caleb Williams* nor later did the government prosecute Godwin for *Political Justice*. Godwin's daughter, Mary Shelley, reported that she frequently had heard her father say that "Political Justice escaped prosecution from the reason that it appeared in a form too expensive for general acquisition. Pitt observed, when the question was debated in the Privy Council, that 'a three guinea book could never do much harm among those who had not three shillings to spare.'"[17] That kind of narrow escape could not have been very comforting for Godwin. He would have realized the novel he was writing provided no such excuse; *Caleb Williams* was explicitly designed to reach those "persons whom books of philosophy and science are never likely to reach" (1). To make matters worse, his own personal legal fears were enmeshed in a larger, ongoing legal conflict. Trial after trial of English Jacobins would command his attention while he wrote the novel *Things as They Are* (fig. 2 shows Godwin in court the year of the novel's publication).

Having suffered through the in absentia trial of Thomas Paine in December 1792, Godwin began *Caleb Williams* in January 1793 preoccupied with the new case of Daniel Crichton. The trial and conviction of this tallow chandler for speaking a few treasonous phrases (he damned the king) led Godwin to write protesting letters to the newspaper—and these letters, advising jurymen or addressed to the attorney general, perhaps reveal more about the temper of Godwin's mind than about Crichton's predicament. Godwin wishes, for instance: "Would to Heaven it were practicable for this cause to be tried over again, and that the laws of my country would permit me, who am no lawyer, to

FIG. 2. William Godwin, *right,* contemplating a 1794 treason trial in progress, with Thomas Holcroft, by Sir Thomas Lawrence. By permission of Kenneth Garlick

plead it."[18] He was enmeshed in a legal world—one that he usually saw (and appealed to) not in terms of a particular law court but as if the court equated to his fellow citizens' consciences. The court was, to him, "us." The subsequent trial of his friend Joseph Gerrald in early 1794 is even more revealing of Godwin's juristic mind-set. Although this trial undoubtedly influenced *Caleb Wil-*

liams's ending (as Gary Kelly, Peter Marshall, Nicholas Williams, and others have shown), one might also argue that by this time *Caleb Williams,* nearly completed, was casting its own spell over Godwin's view of Gerrald's trial. In a long letter written to Gerrald before his trial, Godwin mind-walks himself into Gerrald's place, projecting his address to the jurymen, who themselves are "made of penetrable stuff: probe all the recesses of their souls."[19] Godwin, in this letter, is a writer who easily glides in his imagination into others' minds in the interest of imagining a forensic defense—a move that he has been practicing for over a year in the pages of *Caleb Williams* and which reflects how deeply the actual various ongoing legal trials affected him.

With these treason trials—as well as the French Revolution—in mind, Godwin withdrew his first preface to *Caleb Williams.* "Terror was the order of the day; and it was feared that even the humble novelist might be shown to be constructively a traitor" (2), he says of this time in the second part of the preface eventually published. Ostensibly, he is explaining why he withdrew the preface's first part (in which he provides something of a key to his novel's larger "purpose") from the first edition. But he is also providing a second key to the novel. The preface as a whole—written, withdrawn, and published with an added explanation—tells a story about an author both fearing and facing the possibility of a criminal trial. With this key, then, we might begin to explore how through his particular depictions of trial scenes and through the formal innovations to which these depictions gave rise, Godwin's novel laid bare a modern interdependency between life story and trial narrative.

For literary critics the focal point of all the novel's tribunals has consistently been the crowning trial scene, with its dramatic reversal (so different from Godwin's original ending, in which Caleb goes mad). A few chapters earlier, however, a little noticed but perhaps just as important "incredible reverse" occurs (279): Caleb's long-awaited, official state assize trial is nullified. It is a remarkable moment: this trial that does not take place has prompted Caleb's imprisonment, his desperate escapes, his flight to London, his disguises there, and his recapture, all amounting to some fifteen chapters that make up the core of Caleb's story and roughly a third of the novel's length. "Was it for this that I had broken through so many locks, and bolts, and the adamantine walls of my prison; that I had passed so many anxious days, and sleepless, spectre-haunted nights; that I had racked my invention for expedients of evasion and concealment . . . ? Great God!" The reader may be equally dumbfounded. Caleb can only conclude of this reversal that his "unexpected deliverance" is somehow also a "catastrophe" (279). It is a nonevent that is perhaps best described as the dramatic anticlimax of the novel's trial scenes, much as the final trial forms an anticlimax to Caleb's struggle to have his story confirmed over Falkland's. And it begs the question: why, in this novel wracked with tribunals, does Godwin forgo the most obvious and predetermined one of them all?

The answer, I think, is that this trial is before the bar, and Godwin has set out with his novel not to show the government in action but to show its pervasiveness—how, as he writes in his preface, "the spirit and character of the government intrudes itself into every rank of society" (1). For Godwin the point, then, was almost specifically *not* to reproduce a full-blown government court case of the sort he was regularly attending. The closest we come to a court trial is the magistrates' trials, and these, like the one Falkland's friend Forester holds for Caleb or that Falkland convenes for himself after Tyrell's murder, are pointedly construed as the characters' aping of the court in an attempt to give their homemade "transaction all the momentary notoriety and decisiveness of a trial" (100). In contrast, of the extended encounter with the law courts involving the Hawkinses—the father and son first persecuted for trespass by Tyrell and then wrongly executed for his murder—we hear nothing but a few brief reports before a final, terse announcement that they "were tried, condemned and afterwards executed" (104). Like Tyrell's and Falkland's lawyers, Swineard and Munsle, the physical court and legal machinery lie out of sight. Instead, Godwin depicts quasi-legal tribunals that are his characters' productions, as if (again) to say, I have gone to court, and it is us. In this sense his novel is built around the absence of Caleb's official law trial. Legal trials have not taken over Caleb's life; life has become trial-like.

Almost every encounter in this novel erupts into a trial, complete with accusation and defense. Dialogue consists less of conversation than forensic confrontation, with each side typically pronouncing upon conduct, declaring positions, or testifying to what has supposedly happened. When, for instance, Caleb meets an old man he hopes will free him from his captors, their passing encounter naturally becomes a "contest" over the merits of his "case" (249). Even before Caleb finds himself perpetually making his case, the tribunals are innumerable because they are ubiquitous. They arise everywhere in a society in which, as E. P. Thompson has described it, "the rules and categories of law penetrate every level of society, effect vertical as well as horizontal definitions of men's rights and status, and contribute to men's self-definition or sense of identity. As such law has not only been imposed *upon* men from above: it has also been a medium within which other social conflicts have been fought out."[20]

In *Caleb Williams* the legal trial in particular fatally models and structures interactions. Individuals pit themselves against one another in a contest over competing cases designed solely to force one side to capitulate, rather than, Godwin intimates, allowing calm rationality that aims at reconciling each individual's private judgment to prevail.[21] With instructive exceptions, such as Mr. Raymond's reasoned plea to his band of thieves, the tribunals in the novel illustrate its epigraph—"Man only is the common foe of man." Caleb is himself our preeminent example, blindly bent on achieving justice understood only as victory because, like most of the other characters, criminal or not, he has accepted the premises of the criminal justice system that encompasses him. As Caleb realizes in the tale's final tribunal, he is "the author of this hateful scene" (320). The protagonists in this novel make trials.

And here that means they are caught up in justice as a competition of narratives. As Forester pointedly counsels Caleb in order to prepare him for his first tribunal: "Make the best story you can for yourself; true, if truth, as I hope, will serve your purpose; but, if not, the most plausible and ingenious you can invent. That is what self-defence requires from every man where, as it always happens to a man upon his trial, he has the whole world against him, and has his own battle to fight against the world" (162–63). Forester's advice describes modern justice: not trial by jury but trial by narrative. Unfortunately for Caleb, Forester quaintly assumes that if Caleb's story is true it need not be "plausible and ingenious," an assumption immediately proved inaccurate by Caleb's first trial, which demonstrates that "the power of ingenuity" can indeed "subvert the distinctions of right and wrong" (173). Rhetoric, or to be more specific forensics, matters. Godwin gives little quarter in this novel to that dying eighteenth-century legal notion that "it requires no manner of skill to make a plain and honest Defence."[22] As Godwin discovers, however, Caleb, like "every man," is then left only to obey, and internalize, a commandment of literary imagination: "Make the best story."

Make the best story. Not just here but throughout the novel telling the story fuses with being on trial. Early in volume two, for instance, Caleb decides to observe Falkland as he judges a crime similar to that of which Caleb suspects him. In the novel's original manuscript Godwin gives Caleb's inspiration for this act: "I [Caleb] recollected that the great master of the human passions has represented the guilt of the regicide in his tragedy of Hamlet as finally laid open by the exhibition of a scene in his presence resembling that of the crime he had perpetrated. I immediately hastened to the room where they were assembled. I vowed that, like the Prince of Denmark, I would 'tent' the principal spectator upon the present occasion 'to the quick.'"[23] The bookish Caleb makes poor use of his reading. He should, as Godwin insinuates, at least pause before reliving *Hamlet*'s blood-and-body-strewn "tragedy." Yet Caleb is smitten by the excited realization that the trial—which he has turned into an instrument of revelation—can work the same trick as Shakespeare's famous play within a play. And like the play before the guilty king, the trial of this honorable, poor peasant for the sudden killing of "a human brute persisting in a course of hostility" provides Caleb with a revelatory reflection of the story of Falkland's murder of Tyrell from within the story (129). Within this book "In Three Volumes" the story that comes out at this trial explicitly, if distortedly, mirrors "those [incidents] which belonged to the adventures of the preceding volume" (128). The play within the play becomes a volume within a volume, a *mise-en-abîme* in which Caleb and Falkland even pointedly exchange "a silent look by which [they] told volumes to each other" (126). The kink here is that not a book but a trial mirrors the larger story. The two realms of trial and narrative are thereby thoroughly muddled—and this muddle becomes even more evident in the novel's later trial scenes, when Caleb directly retells his narrative. It is not just that a trial scene is reflecting, or reconstructing, the story; the story itself is revealed as the nonidentical partner to a trial.

This can be quite apparent, as when Caleb holds court in his own narrative and judges Falkland's crime at this peasant's trial. Caleb has been attempting for some time to convince himself of Falkland's guilt. At the close of the chapter before the trial his suspicions reach a climax: "In spite of persuasion and in spite of evidence, Surely this man is a murderer!" (125). Caleb eagerly resolves "to discover the state of [Falkland's] plea before the tribunal of unerring justice" (126), and at the trial at which Falkland presides Caleb sets himself up to judge the judge. Falkland flees. His flight provokes Caleb to pronounce him "guilty." With as yet "no evidence that was admissible in a court of justice," Caleb does pose to himself the question of how he has arrived at his verdict: "If it be such as would not be admitted at a criminal tribunal, am I sure it is such as I ought to admit?" (129, 130). But the question is rhetorical; he has already made up his mind. The true arena of judgment here is his narrative, with its own evidentiary rules, not a criminal tribunal.

Not only is this narrative's most common scene of action the trial, but Caleb's way of telling the story is an extrapolation from a trial scene. It is not just that Caleb metaphorically frames his narrative as if it were an appeal to a higher court, pleading in the first paragraph for "a justice which my contemporaries refuse" and then declaring at the end that "these papers shall preserve the truth: they shall one day be published, and then the world shall do justice" (3, 315). Caleb explicitly presents himself to us as our narrator as though he were testifying in court: "I do not pretend to warrant the authenticity of any part of these memoirs except so much as fell under my own knowledge, and that part shall be stated with the same simplicity and accuracy that I would observe towards a court which was to decide in the last resort upon every thing dear to me" (106). On the face of it, this avowal is ridiculous. Caleb perpetually extends his first-person narrative into places that could not possibly fall "under [his] knowledge," and he recounts even that which he hears in psychological and tendentious ways that glaringly belie "simplicity and accuracy." Just having Caleb play character witness for himself may be enough to make some readers wonder what exactly here is real and what true. Yet readers are not therefore, absurdly, to disbelieve his entire story. Rather, the question that arises is why, despite Caleb's failure to respect the limiting boundaries of his first-person narrative, his homespun, courtlike vow to tell the truth still makes some sense.

One obvious reason Caleb's claim does not jeopardize his role as our narrator is that we accept that he is not making systematic but, rather, opportunistic and contingent use of analogies to a trial scene: Caleb plays the role of judge one moment and compares his narrative to testimony another. Readers accept at the outset that his written narrative manifestly gives him a site and authority that starkly contrast with the context of an actual trial to which it nonetheless refers. Caleb tells his story not as it would "realistically" be told in court nor as he might render it were he testifying.

Instead, Godwin's novel "realistically" renders the realm of Caleb's trial-oriented mind. As our first-person narrator, Caleb presents a mind that has been constructed by the social situations that Caleb, as a character, has experienced: Caleb may tell us about his trials, but we are also hearing about the type of person which a society suffused with trials produces. We find a mind that does not want, Falkland-style, to settle things with a duel nor, picaro-like, to snake through adventures nor even, as in later detective fashion, to set about the investigative task of exposing the true criminal. Caleb's ductile mind plunges right into an acrobatic courtlike struggle to "make the best story," an injunction he has adopted as his own: "I will tell a tale—" (314). This novel is thus a psychological portrait of how life stories are conceived and told in a society in which a dominant scene and form of justice is the storytelling forum of the trial.

Like the shaping of Caleb's story by criminal biography, Caleb's narrative records the difficulty of an individual struggling against penetrating forms of judicial authority. But this time the justice system has subsumed the very act of telling one's story, and not just the kind of story one tells. Godwin thus sets us down in the midst of a loop: the trial scenes bid Caleb to tell his story, and Caleb justifies telling it by invoking a trial. The legal machinations do not call on Caleb, a character, to tell his story; they produce Caleb as a character producing himself—narrating, self-justifying.

Godwin's novel, as a form, partakes of this overcharged circuitry of trial and story, and new literary techniques come into existence in order to narrate this newly jurisprudential character. In purely technical terms we can begin by observing that Caleb not only functions here as an authorial character but also that, in doing so, his "first person" no longer presupposes that an authoritative, omniscient, third-person narrator is missing. Godwin explains:

> I began my narrative, as is the more usual way, in the third person. But I speedily became dissatisfied. I then assumed the first person, making the hero of my tale his own historian. . . . It was infinitely the best adapted, at least, to my vein of delineation, where the thing in which my imagination revelled the most freely, was the analysis of the private and internal operations of the mind, employing my metaphysical dissecting knife in tracing and laying bare the involutions of motive, and recording the gradually accumulating impulses, which led the personages I had to describe primarily to adopt [their] particular way of proceeding. (339)

Leaving aside the grisly surgical metaphor, which John Bender discusses in detail elsewhere,[24] Godwin gives us an essentially authorial explanation here (in an 1832 preface) for his narrative method. At first he seems to explain that he switched from third-person to first-person because this shift allows him entrance into Caleb's mind. Yet, as the lengthening sentence, with its increasingly convoluted syntax, suggests, a more complex and odd disclosure surfaces: Godwin imagines the story from Caleb's point of view because there, in imagining Caleb's mind, he finds the freedom to revel in *other* characters' thoughts. For Godwin the adoption of first-person narration licenses the rendering not only of Caleb's mind but also of Caleb's crossings into other minds. Godwin thus tacitly ascribes his own power as a novelist to imagine and narrate characters' thoughts to the mind of the character he depicts narrating. The result is that for the first time in the history of the English novel a character-narrator methodically renders a first-person story using third-person authorial techniques; as Godwin puts it with specious simplicity: "The hero of my tale [is] his own historian."

One might think that readers would see such a story as fantastic and perceive Caleb as akin to George Eliot's telepathic, clairvoyant character in *The Lifted Veil* (1859). After all, Caleb is not merely taking it upon himself to report the motivations, thoughts, and psychology of others (so that when, say, he is talking to the sympathetic Mr. Collins, he can mind-read the "secret struggle of his mind" [311]); as a narrator, he silently and telepathically wanders in and out of others' minds even in adventures in which his absence is explicit.

For example, when Caleb narrates how Mrs. Marney discovered Gines was following her, we can hear him shift from his seemingly objective narration into a stream of questions arising in Mrs. Marney's consciousness:

> She once again caught a glance of her pursuer. This circumstance, together with the singularity of his appearance, awakened her conjectures. *Could he be following her?* It was the middle of the day, and she could have no fears for herself. But could this circumstance have any reference to me? She recollected the precautions and secrecy I practised. . . . She thought that, if she should be the means of any mischief to me, she should be miserable for ever. (265; emph. added)

With the italicized question Caleb, as if quoting, launches us into Mrs. Marney's thoughts. As our narrator, Caleb modulates into what Roy Pascal calls a "dual voice,"[25] in which Mrs. Marney's thinking is present as well as Caleb's narrating perspective. Rendering Mrs. Marney asking herself, "Could he be following *me?*" Caleb maintains a third-person *her* in place of the *me.* The narrator's grammar dictates, even as it relays, the thinker's words. This narrative technique is a brand of the free indirect style, one method of making minds transparent, as Dorrit Cohn in particular has explained.[26] In this passage it can be compared to the more straightforward mode of tagged, indirect discourse that includes the introductory expressions "she recollected that" and "she thought that," which have a counterpart in the phrase "awakened her conjectures." The difference provided by the free indirect style, whose development both in *Caleb Williams* and in general is central to the novel as a form, is that, as our narrator, Caleb goes beyond reporting to us what is on other people's minds: he mimics their minds.[27]

Yet, if there is never a doubt that Caleb is not psychic, the explanation for his everyday divinations lies partly in his story's saga of trials, which has newly helped to complicate the novelistic portrayal of humans as storytelling beings. Godwin's endowment of Caleb as a character-narrator with omniscient narratorial powers makes sense as Caleb's own trial-oriented attempt to "make the best story." His first-person narratorial omniscience represents a viewpoint that arises when (though not necessarily only when) one reconstructs one's story as an imagined defense and becomes, as Harald Kittel has aptly described Caleb, "a narrator-character who consciously strives to offer a coherent point of view by integrating accounts from different sources into his own narrative."[28] So, Caleb may announce he is telling his story from the standpoint of providing defensive testimony, yet that turns out to mean not that he acts like a witness but that he puts on a solo performance in which he plays all the parts.

Consider the strange structure of volume one. Caleb announces at the end of the first chapter: "To avoid confusion in my narrative, I shall drop the person of Collins, and assume to be myself the historian of our patron" (9–10). Ten chapters follow, and then he announces: "I shall endeavour to state the remainder of this narrative in the words of Mr. Collins" (97). He then proceeds to do so in the final chapter. Rendering other people's inner thoughts is just Caleb's most open trespass in his attempt to draw together other people's accounts to tell his story. He commonly handles other people's speech in much the same way. It is no accident of typography that, with the explicit exception of the single chapter in Mr. Collins's words, quotation marks—themselves under tremendous pressure as free indirect discourse in print develops—hardly appear in this novel, though other characters' speech is regularly reported. This character-narrator is a novelistic ventriloquist.

Harald Kittel cites a particularly clear and suggestive example of free indirect speech, taken from the trial scene discussed earlier in which Caleb watches Falkland judging a peasant:

> When the accused was called upon for his defence, he readily owned the misunderstanding that had existed, and that the deceased was the worst enemy he had in the world. *Indeed he was his only enemy, and he could not tell the reason that had made him so. He had employed every possible effort to overcome his animosity, but in vain.* (127; emph. added)

Caleb moves here from narrating the event and reporting the peasant's speech to narrating his speech; in Caleb's voice we can hear the defendant saying, "He was my only enemy, and I don't know why; I tried everything to overcome his hatred with no success." Yet, instead of incorporating the voice of a "peasant" (126), Caleb's free indirect speech adapts the speech so it sounds more like Falkland speaking of Tyrell, that is, in just the way that lends credence to his story at this point. This is typical of Caleb, whether he is relaying thoughts or speech. He may not completely ignore speech patterns and dialect when he reports or narrates the words of different characters, but, in marked contrast to a free indirect style in which idiomatic shifts are a signal of the characters' voices and an integral part of the point of deploying the technique, Caleb's free indirect style orients everyone's speech and thoughts around his own perspective. His viewpoint subsumes all others, even as it accords them space in his narrative.

Everyone, in short, shall confess *his* truth; as Caleb infamously declares: "I will unfold a tale—! I will show thee [Falkland] for what thou art, and all the men that live shall confess *my* truth!" (314; emph. added). Caleb breaks the boundaries of first-person narrative to provide everyone else's testimony in his own defense. Godwin, meanwhile, cannot so much expose this forensic facet of Caleb's predicament (as he did with criminal biography) as reproduce it and even, as we have seen, use it to expand novelistic form. In this novel the medium triumphs over the message.

One might say, then, that Godwin's "epoch of mind," as he characterized his novel, is in part a result of both capturing and producing the mind of his epoch, a mind that carries within it (or at least within its way of imagining stories) the experience of the world as a series of tribunals that call for individuals' stories. Perhaps this is why when Godwin transports his narrative method into other scenarios and other fictional psyches in later novels, such as *St. Leon* (1799), it never works quite as well. As Henry Crabb Robinson complained of *Mandeville* (1817), "Godwin has no idea of dialogue, and he has confounded dramatic and disquisitional conceptions of character."[29] These objections could easily be made against *Caleb Williams*—except they would miss the point. In *Caleb Williams* Godwin's style has internal justifications. The form of this novel, as well as its content, is a part of the way the novel both exposes and is itself caught up in a justice system that atomizes society into individual, self-justifying storytellers.

Later novelists, such as Dickens and Gaskell, would not replicate *Caleb Williams*'s elaborate and extended construction of this interdependency. They would, however, rely in part on the changes this novel wrought. Godwin's radical novel, originally published as an exposé aptly titled *Things as They Are,* would come to be consumed as a conventional crime novel known simply as *Caleb Williams*. Thus, in the year 1832 Godwin perhaps judged aright the novel as it stood in the year 1832: "And, when I had done all, what had I done? Written a book to amuse boys and girls in their vacant hours, a story to be hastily gobbled up by them" (341). But in the year 1794, he had, at the very least, helped, as Henry Crabb Robinson supposed, to invent the literature that was gobbled up in the 1830s. In particular, he helped inaugurate a new form of crime novel, which would subsequently be reinvented in a subgenre called the Newgate novel. More generally, he established an aspect of novelistic form and a related conception of character which were constitutively entwined with the law court and which would resurface in a number of nineteenth-century novels. *Caleb Williams* was, for one facet of the novel, a landmark case.

CHAPTER THREE

Mary Shelley's Legal *Frankenstein*

M ARY SHELLEY'S *Frankenstein* (1818), so well known as both gothic and science fiction, has never registered as a particularly legal story. So, it may come as a surprise to some readers to realize that Victor Frankenstein— the descendant of "counsellors and syndics,"[1] which is to say lawyers and judges—is a courtroom spectator in the first volume of *Frankenstein,* a defendant in the second, and a would-be plaintiff in the third. In general, this novel's trials, which include the tribunals of Justine, of Safie's father, of Felix De Lacey, and of Victor Frankenstein as well as Frankenstein's final interview with a magistrate, constitute an unnoticed aspect of the novel's underlying structure. With no less than one tribunal per volume *Frankenstein* contains a powerful forensic plot.

That plot can best be understood both as part of Mary Shelley's shifting interactions with the law in 1816–17 (when she was writing her novel amid legal proceedings over the custody of Percy Bysshe Shelley's children) and as part of a larger reflection on the law courts' centrality to social justice and subjectivity, depicted in the work of her parents, William Godwin and Mary Wollstonecraft. In these contexts the familiar issues of birthing and parenting surrounding the relationship between Frankenstein and his human creature return strangely as new, juridical questions concerning custody and family law. These, in turn, reveal a legal *Frankenstein* that helps us to understand the expansive parameters of England's judicial ideology and the corresponding depths of the novel's engagement with the law courts in the early nineteenth century. In surprisingly powerful terms Godwin's daughter recognized the new place of the law courts that her father had tried to overleap.

I

At the end of the first volume of Mary Shelley's novel, Victor Frankenstein returns home from his studies at Ingoldstadt, where he has created the human creature, his homeward journey troubled by the knowledge that his younger brother William has been murdered. Upon his arrival he finds Justine, a servant described as virtually an adopted member of the family, accused of the murder. A distraught Frankenstein attends Justine's trial, and the volume closes with her dramatic courtroom scene and a visit to her in jail by Frankenstein and his fiancée-cousin, Elizabeth Lavenza (also adopted into Frankenstein's family).

Both William Godwin and Mary Wollstonecraft had produced political novels much concerned with legal tribunals, and with Justine's trial their daughter reimagined aspects of both Godwin's *Caleb Williams* (1794), in which Caleb strives in trial after trial to prove the true story of his relations with Falkland, and Wollstonecraft's *Maria, or The Wrongs of Woman* (1798), in which Maria heroically testifies to an unjust court in a trial for adultery and seduction at the end of the manuscript (uncompleted due to Wollstonecraft's death from complications resulting from Mary's birth).

In both Wollstonecraft's and Godwin's novels, rendering a trial means judging the official production of justice itself, and the trial of the aptly named Justine does the same. Like Victor Frankenstein, readers know that Justine did not strangle young William. We share the perspective not of Frankenstein, however, but of Elizabeth, who not only believes in Justine's innocence but also lacks Frankenstein's misplaced confidence that the court's verdict will be just. In contrast to Frankenstein, who has "no fear . . . that any circumstantial evidence could be brought forward strong enough to convict" (75), or his father, who patronizingly advises Elizabeth to "rely on the justice of the judges," Elizabeth alone voices for us the grim fact that justice itself is at stake in this trial: "Alas! who is safe, if she be convicted of crime?" (76).

Mary Shelley's initial point is not to be missed; no one is safe from the unjust contemporary machinery of justice: Justine is convicted. In the courtroom scene damning circumstantial facts triumph over Justine's long, heartfelt plea that she is "entirely . . . innocent" (78). Elizabeth's spontaneous testimony in support of her character falls on deaf ears. As in countless other nineteenth-century novelistic court scenes, the court perilously devalues the knowledge of inner character upon which novel readers thrive. Moreover, as Mary Shelley's focus on the women's attempted defense suggests, the trial and Elizabeth's subsequent visit to Justine's jail cell emphasize where women stand in relation to the all-male production of official justice. Ann Marie Frank has observed many of the essential points: The court "politically disempowered the female voice"; "women intrude on the judicial system and somehow operate outside of judicial prudence and logic"; and "the trial and Elizabeth's visit to Justine in prison following her conviction show how female power . . . recover[s] and replace[s] female experience in a story witnessed and controlled by male voices and male egotism."[2] At the center of the trial Elizabeth's unheeded testimony stands— like the blind, old De Lacey's later altruistic words to the human creature—as one of the novel's fleeting models for moral communication. Implicit in this court scene is Mary Shelley's version of *Maria's* legal critique of patriarchal justice as well as its reflexive depiction of a woman speaking out publicly in court.

At the same time, this initial trial, like *Frankenstein* itself (with its seesawing pursuit between Frankenstein and his human creature), reworks the closed male circuit that Falkland and Caleb travel in Godwin's *Caleb Williams* as well as that novel's emphasis on tribunals as storytelling forums. To expose her male narrators' tragic flaws, Mary Shelley strategically places women on her novel's margins; in the trial scene she quotes only Justine and Elizabeth, briefly shifting the focus to these two. When the court subsequently dismisses these women's collaborative attempt to correct the prosecution's mistaken conclusion that Justine has killed William—when, as Beth Newman explains, "narratives . . . fail to cohere"[3]—responsibility for confronting this miscarriage of justice and narrative truth shifts squarely back to Frankenstein, who wordlessly "rushe[s] out of the court in agony" (80). His fatal silence concerning Justine's innocence contrasts with the women's honest testimony, while his agonized thoughts about his predicament reveal he is misguided and self-obsessed. Ultimately, as

Mary Shelley telegraphs by contrasting Frankenstein's overweening self-pity with Justine's calm acceptance of her fate, the trial that truly makes Justine into a martyr morally convicts Frankenstein, self-canonized martyr. As in *Caleb Williams,* the series of legal scenes which follows only reveals Frankenstein and his human creature to be turning in self-imprisoning circles.

Nonetheless, *Frankenstein* is on its face not a juridical story like *Caleb Williams.* Nor does it seem to be visibly concerned with legalized oppression, like *Maria.* A reader might well believe that, after depicting Justine's trial, the story attenuates whatever judicial slant on its subject was developing. In actuality Mary Shelley meaningfully shifts the law courts to the formative margins, where they help to frame the central story.

We can begin to piece together this shift and its meanings by considering Mary Shelley's immediate context. Approximately a month after she had written Justine's dramatic trial,[4] a Chancery trial for the custody of Percy Shelley's children began to take shape. First, on 15 December 1816 she and Percy learned his estranged wife, Harriet Westbrook Shelley, had drowned herself. The next day Percy wrote Mary from London that a lawyer had advised him he must marry her to regain custody of his two children by Harriet. Shortly thereafter, just before the new year, Mary and Percy married. Harriet's father and sister, however, pressed to retain custody of the children, whom they had hidden away. Thus, in January 1817, in the midst of drafting *Frankenstein,* Mary Wollstonecraft Godwin, lately turned Shelley, found herself a central object in a Chancery suit instituted by Harriet's family (the Westbrooks) in the name of Percy's children. "Said Percy Bysshe Shelley ever since he so deserted his said wife has unlawfully cohabited with the said Mary Godwin and is now unlawfully cohabiting with her and has several illegitimate children by her," accused the Chancery papers of 8 January.[5] Percy protested what he could. In a "Declaration in Chancery," a text that Mary Shelley herself transcribed and revised, he reminds: "Immediately on the death of my late wife, I married the lady whose connexion with me . . . is now to be made the ground of depriving me of my children."[6]

For Mary Shelley this custody case enmeshed her in a battle of conflicting stories in which the domestic sphere pointedly intersected with the public. At issue, as in the novel she was writing, were social and legal definitions of caretaking, marriage, and family, as well as norms of sexual behavior and gender.

As private hearings before the lord chancellor continued intermittently, Mary Shelley completed *Frankenstein*. A judgment was rendered against Percy at the end of March, just two weeks before Mary began correcting her full draft of the novel. When she finished *Frankenstein* two months later, in May, final legal decisions about where the children would go were still being made.

Thus, shortly after introducing a forensic plot that she may have already roughly planned, Mary Shelley found herself embroiled in a legal story. Having begun a novel with a pronounced trial scene recalling those animating her father's *Caleb Williams* and her mother's *Maria,* she confronted a custody case that conjured up even more directly some of the very issues she was raising in *Frankenstein*. On the one hand, the new situation may have engendered meanings and implications for her story which she never intended, causing her to rein in aspects of what was originally to be a more overtly legal novel. On the other hand, the custody case, which would judge her domestic life and literally define her family, might well have expanded and deepened her cross-examination of the legal underpinnings of domestic relations within her novel.

Both alternatives may be partly true. Certainly, Mary Shelley, as the composer of Percy's "Declaration in Chancery," could not have been unaffected by the correspondences between the custody trial and her own novel in progress. Perhaps the most striking parallel arises out of a legal fiction through which little Ianthe and Charles Shelley (ages three and two) are named as the plaintiffs who bring the lawsuit against their father. From the outset Percy Shelley was imagined as the adversary of his children. In the Chancery petition the "infant Orators" demand that "proper persons may be appointed to act as their . . . Guardians."[7] The children echo the human creature's complaint against Frankenstein, suggesting in legalese the breakdown of what Frankenstein himself calls "the duties of a creator towards his creature" (97). They accuse Percy of precisely that which critics have rightly suggested the story of Frankenstein portrays: a "total failure at parenting."[8]

Of course, Percy on trial is hardly another Frankenstein. For one thing the various criminal justice scenes in the novel simply do not compare to Percy Shelley's private custody hearings before the lord chancellor. The custody case also reverses the analogous demands being made for guardianship in the novel. Whereas Frankenstein disclaims his responsibilities for his human creature, Percy, speaking of himself, writes to Eliza Westbrooke that, "if he could ever be supposed to have forgotten them, [he] is awakened to a sense of his duties."[9] He fights for the right to raise "the said Complainants his children," while—in the fiction of the law—the children are "desirous that [they] should not be placed in the custody of the said Percy Bysshe Shelley."[10] As this and other fundamental differences suggest, it is clearly a mistake to think Mary Shelley is either directly alluding to or allegorically portraying the Chancery lawsuit in *Frankenstein*. Rather, like the biographical themes of miscarriage and birth with which her story has become firmly linked,[11] the custody case and the novel are best considered mutually illuminating, thereby avoiding reductive equations such as "Victor equals Percy" and recognizing, instead, Mary Shelley's unfolding, two-way process of making meaning through deranging, amplifying, complicating, and multiplying such connections.[12] *Frankenstein* can suggest Mary Shelley's position vis-à-vis the law; the legal context of the custody case can reveal how *Frankenstein* works; and with this stereoscopic view we may glimpse their interdependence.

Most obviously, the custody trial recasts and exposes questions of affective and familial relations which are explored in *Frankenstein* as juridical. Although *Frankenstein* and the law case are not encodements of each other, they both involve interlocking struggles over questions of "custody" and "guardianship." For instance, Percy's guardianship was specifically challenged because he had rejected the institution of marriage. As Percy explained—and Mary drafted—in the "Declaration in Chancery":

> I understand that it is argued that I am to be rendered incapable of the most sacred of human duties . . . because I have reasoned against the institution of marriage in its present state, because I have in my own person violated that institution, and because I have justified that violation by my reasoning.[13]

Could this violation be Frankenstein's mistake as well? Never mind his later failure to take care of the human creature; should he have anticipated the human creature's "birth" by marrying Elizabeth and establishing the domestic home he would need? The human creature is, after all, another of the illegitimate children whose plight is sympathetically portrayed in eighteenth- and nineteenth-century novels. "Created apparently united by no link to any other being" (125), he is an incarnation of the legal abstraction of *bastard* as *filius nul-*

lius—meaning "no one's son" or "kin to no one."[14] No wonder he warns Frankenstein: "I shall be with you on your wedding-night!" (166). His murder of Elizabeth on their wedding night is not just a quid pro quo for Frankenstein's refusal to provide him with a mate; it resonates as an act of revenge for his own creation without the rights that birth within wedlock confers.

More important, *Frankenstein*'s central story, with its division into characters presenting their narratives, bears the marks of an unofficial legal custody trial. Denied access to legal redress—prejudged as less than human by society—the human creature is able to plead his case only to Frankenstein. So, while the human creature's narrative is partly a forensic attempt to explain his murder of William (as he says: "The guilty are allowed by human laws . . . to speak in their own defence. . . . Listen to me, Frankenstein"), the human creature also pleads his own custody case to Frankenstein: "Listen to my tale: when you have heard that, abandon or commiserate me, as you shall judge that I deserve. But hear me" (96). Initially, Frankenstein does listen and is temporarily persuaded to take responsibility for his creation. Finding "some justice in his argument," Frankenstein concludes that he, "as his maker, owe[s] him" (142). The human creature has, figuratively speaking, successfully argued his rights as Frankenstein's ward, and Frankenstein agrees to end the human creature's complete isolation by making a mate for him.

Frankenstein's later reversal of this decision might suggest simply that he falters in serving out justice. It might also, alternatively, imply that the human creature has doomed himself by framing his tragic bildungsroman as a reasoned, legalistic case. Either way, the pathos of the human creature's unfulfilled, sentimental, domestic narrative has only helped to enlist Frankenstein's patronage momentarily. Ultimately, the human creature has not gained a true guardian. He himself has asked Frankenstein to play, instead, the rational judge, enabling a "justified" Frankenstein to relate with Benthamite coolness that, though he has a duty to his human creature, he has other "paramount . . . duties" that concern "a greater proportion of happiness or misery" (214–15). From this perspective the human creature has, to his detriment, invoked the reasoned, adversarial, narrative mode of the all-male courts—precisely where justice is *not* done in this novel.

And yet Mary Shelley is not merely portraying a narratological or epistemological blunder on the human creature's part. By having him present his story as a legalistic plea, even ending it with oaths and contracts between the two parties, she calls attention to the human creature's and Frankenstein's struggles to negotiate their affiliation without any legally defined guardian-ward relationship. As we will see, the nightmare of relations between the human creature and Frankenstein draws its energy in part from this very lack of a judicial context.

I I

For Mary Shelley in 1817 the general notion that personal relations could not be extracted from their legal contexts, at least not without tragic consequences, could not have been clearer. That very point was being repeated over and over again by the prosecution in Percy's trial, indeed was implicit in the trial itself—and not just because the suit was over the custody of Percy's children. Percy lost the case because he had publicly rejected the laws of matrimony and acted upon that belief, making him, it was argued, an unfit father and making Mary, as Percy's guilty partner in "cohabitation," into that rejection's living proof. Faced with the Westbrooks' lawsuit, Percy would declare to Mary in January 1817, "*My* story is what I have to tell," but "his" story was as certainly, if not as clamorously, hers as well; as Mary would record in her journal the following August: "A letter from Longdill with the masters decision—against *us*" (emph. added).[15]

When the case reached its final stages, the *Morning Chronicle* pointedly summarized its central issues. The lord chancellor had been holding private hearings on "a Petition presented by the relations of the late Mrs. [Harriet] Shelley, for the purpose of her infant children being taken away from the defendant, their father, on the ground of two circumstances": "viz. first the defendant having written a singular kind of book, called Queen Mab, which promulgated the opinion that human creatures should act and live in the state of nature as brutes do, for matrimony was merely an unmeaning ceremony, and certainly by no means binding. The other circumstance was his having cohabited with a woman during the life-time of the deceased, which he still continued to do, and on that account he was certainly not such a guardian as ought to have the care of children."[16]

Leigh Hunt's *Examiner* subsequently protested that Percy Shelley's argument against marriage in *Queen Mab* (1813) was hardly as absurd as that people "should act and live in the state of nature as brutes do" and, in the same breath, rushed to correct the erroneous idea that "the Lady with whom he lives . . . is not his wife."[17] Mary and Percy had married, after all, just before the trial and thereby ostensibly subverted the charge that they did not respect the institution of marriage and would pass their radical view of wedlock on to their children. Mary's views about her own marriage were complex (Godwin, of all people, pressed for it) and muted (she writes in the passive tense in her journal that upon her arrival in London "a marriage takes place").[18] In contrast, Percy insisted the marriage was simply a legal formality done for expedience ("a mere form," "a measure of convenience," "this pretended sanction").[19] Both would quickly learn the marriage had not produced the "magical . . . effects" of solving their legal problems.[20] Instead, as Mary wrote *Frankenstein,* she would be cast as an apostle of Percy's belief, explained by him in *Queen Mab,* that the law had no role in matrimonial relations, and Percy's letters, submitted to the court in evidence, would seem to confirm as much. Both aspects of the case—*Queen Mab* and the letters—are worth considering in detail.

The first piece of evidence, *Queen Mab,* is a radical political poem dedicated to Harriet. It was written and privately circulated in 1813, long before Percy met and subsequently eloped with Mary Godwin. In the poem a fairy queen critiques the world's corrupt ways from a palace among the stars. In a lengthy prose endnote keyed to the phrase "Love is sold," Percy Shelley argues straightforwardly enough that laws should have no jurisdiction over a married couple's love or physical intimacy: "A husband and wife ought to continue so long united as they love each other: any law which should bind them to cohabitation for one moment after the decay of their affection, would be a most intolerable tyranny, and the most unworthy of toleration."[21] Percy's belief was that, since laws cannot enforce affection, separation should be everyone's right in marriage as in friendship.

However just in principle, this view of matrimony was plainly unfair in early-nineteenth-century England, where marriage was perhaps the fundamental, inequitable legal contract defining social relations—for a woman like Harriet, as for most women, marriage was almost foreordained as her career, the measure of her social status, and the primary realm in which she was directed to look for her self-worth. Percy's refusal to recognize "any law which should bind them to cohabitation" may have been equitable in the ideal, but it was lopsided in reality. This asymmetry shows itself even in *Queen Mab*. There Percy may proclaim majestically that "love is free: to promise for ever to love the same woman, is not less absurd than to promise to believe the same creed," but the assumed male (heterosexual) perspective of the sentence betrays the one-sidedness of the viewpoint. It is not that Percy has selfishly forgotten women but, rather, that to devise an ideal for all humanity in the abstract he mentally leaps past both the law's existing injustices and its function as an institution of justice. To Percy breaking free of the artificial shackles created by law seems the paramount problem: "That which will result from the abolition of marriage, will be natural and right, because choice and change will be exempted from restraint."[22]

From *Queen Mab* Percy and Mary's union followed logically as an attempted escape from society's oppressive laws. Theirs was an elopement of the most hackneyed romantic kind: proclaiming that love was not to be bound by law or convention, the passionate pair fled to France (albeit with Mary's stepsister Jane Clairmont along). Such an elopement reenforced the mutually sustaining separation of the personal from the political, private from public—and, specifically, affective relations from legal relations.

Percy thus presented to Mary a critique of marriage which had aspirations resembling her mother's but which had a significantly different approach. Whereas Percy's view is idealistic, his thinking consistent with the utopia-aspiring vantage point of the stars and the inspired, imaginative evocations of his poetry, Wollstonecraft's view is materialist. She develops her critique of marriage in *A Vindication of the Rights of Woman* (1792) out of ethnographic realities, the facts and details of social and mental life, and she writes there in the inquiring philosophical style of rational Enlightenment prose. She goes on to write the novel *Maria* not because the genre allows her to express her utopian imagination but because narrative realism offers the chance to illustrate and explore the processes governing women's contemporary predicament in ways unavailable to a political treatise. Mary Wollstonecraft wanted to change the law, not avoid it. (It is crucial, for instance, that at the end of her novel Maria's protest is read out in a law court.) This difference between Percy Shelley and Mary Wollstonecraft—that Percy's radicalism hoped to transcend mat-

rimonial law, while Wollstonecraft sought to create justice through revolutionizing that law—is one key to understanding the position in which Mary Shelley
found herself placed by the trial as she continued to write *Frankenstein*.

The law case, of course, did not focus on Wollstonecraft, much less on distinguishing between materialist or idealistic critiques of marriage. Percy's "violation," reasoned and acted upon, was all that mattered. Nonetheless, the use of
Queen Mab reframed Mary's life within Percy's philosophy. In a broad sense,
embedded in this custody case was the horrifying and tragic climax to a long-
standing, idealistic notion—loudly propounded by both Percy Shelley and
William Godwin—which called for freedom from the law and the rational self-
government of individuals. Liberation from the institutional framework of the
law courts: it is a relevant context to keep in mind when we turn to examine
Frankenstein and the human creature's relationship from a legal perspective.

But, first, we must attend to the other half of the prosecution's evidence: ten
personal letters, submitted to the court to show Percy explicitly justified abandoning his wife Harriet for a union with Mary. These letters-turned-evidence
quite literally reinscribed Mary and Percy's personal relations as accountable
in court and confirmed "Mary Godwin" as a central character in the suit. (*Godwin,* a multiply charged surname, was used throughout the trial to label Mary
as Percy's mistress.) The letters also illuminate Harriet's position. Percy had
not only refused to consider himself bound to her by matrimonial law but also
had warned her specifically that she defeated herself and was his "enemy" if
she pursued any legal redress. His (past) relationship to her was not subject to
the state's justice system any more than his relationship with Mary was.

Imagine, then, Mary Shelley's feelings in the wake of Harriet's suicide as
the Westbrooks' attorney presented Percy's letters as evidence condemning her
in conventional literary terms as a femme fatale. Through this legal lens Mary
Shelley faced Harriet's posthumous blame—a reproach magnified so enor-
mously for Mary by Harriet's suicide that twenty-two years later she was still
thinking about her life in terms of its "atonement" for the death of "Poor Harriet."[23] Refiguring the most personal of texts within a public legal context, the
Westbrooks' attorney, for instance, repeatedly emphasized a line from one of
Percy's letters which describes Mary as "the lady whose union with [himself]
you may excusably regard as the cause of [Harriet's] ruin."[24] As even this odd
and overdetermined use of *ruin* suggests, the letters were putting sexual free-

dom—what Percy called "immodest & loose sentiments of sexual connexion"[25]—on trial through an absent Mary. The repetition of *cohabit* in an affidavit makes this object manifest: "The Female mentioned or referred to in the said Letters . . . under the name or designation of 'Mary' . . . is Mary Godwin . . . whom the said Defendant Percy Bysshe Shelley in the Lifetime of his said Wife and in or about the middle of the year 1814 took to cohabit with him and hath ever since continued to cohabit and still doth cohabit with."[26] In 1817 Mary Shelley unofficially faced a charge of loose morals as well as an accusation of conspiring to disregard the matrimonial laws that would ostensibly have protected Harriet.

Mary Shelley had no voice or direct avenue of defense in court to respond to such a nonbinding but serious construction of her character and life. We might, however, productively juxtapose the trial's forensic letters with another contemporaneous set of letters turned into evidence: those of Safie to Felix in *Frankenstein*. As has long been noted, Safie's letters are special evidence in this novel. Proffered by the human creature to Frankenstein to "prove the truth of [his] tale" (119) and then similarly by Frankenstein to Walton (207), they mark the novel's philosophical as well as physical center, shaping meaning from its core, just as Margaret Walton Saville, the addressee of Robert Walton's letters (with her significant initials *M. W. S.*), encases the novel. In her letters (summarized for us by the human creature) Safie recounts how she learned from her intellectual mother to seek liberation from mental and sexual enslavement and how after her mother's death she continues to be guided by the "lessons" she learned from her (119). Mary Shelley thus rather plainly conjures up and jumbles together the ghost of her mother Mary Wollstonecraft, *A Vindication of the Rights of Woman,* and herself. (She also reverses the portrayal of "Safie" as a silent, helpless, and objectified woman in John Reynold's *Safie, An Eastern Tale* [1814] and strikes back against the narrow, judgmental portrait of her mother's relationships drawn by Amelia Opie in *Adeline Mowbray* [1805].) Safie's letters have thus rightly been seen as *Frankenstein*'s "feminist core."[27]

In the context of the lawsuit,[28] Safie's letters seem even more deliberately to extol women's sexual independence. As such, they may be read as Mary Shelley's (fictional) counterevidence to her unofficial arraignment in the trial as a wanton woman. At the same time, connecting the fictional letters with the forensic ones reveals Safie's story in a new light: not just Mary Wollstonecraft's and

Mary Shelley's stories but also Harriet Shelley's tragic story may be haunting Safie's. Most obviously, Safie, like Harriet, escapes a tyrannical father by marrying. And, as Harriet had tried to do, Safie would assert her rights as a woman through existing Western institutions: as Safie concludes her letters, her liberation is, amazingly, to come from "marrying a Christian, and remaining in a country where women were allowed to take a rank in society" (119). With ominous naïveté the "Arabian," as Safie is called, ties her emancipation to three institutional frameworks—marriage, religion, and class—through which both Mary Wollstonecraft and Mary Shelley recognized women were oppressed. Wollstonecraft repeatedly insists in *A Vindication of the Rights of Woman* that the repressive practices of "Mahometanism" and the Eastern harems from which Safie has escaped *parallel* the oppression of married women in the West which Safie imagines will provide her with freedom.[29] A European awakening still awaits this Arabian.

Safie's heroism, then, consists in the process of self-enfranchisement she begins, not from her participation in a marriage, however affectionate. Her escape represents an opening, not an end. Right from the day of her arrival in Paris, when her father is thrown into prison and his oppression commences at the hands of the bigoted French justice system, Safie, much like the human creature, is positioned as a stranger to the ways of Western civilization. Fleeing to the De Laceys, Safie finds herself in Italy "utterly ignorant of the customs of the world" (122). Just as Wollstonecraft's heroine Maria must learn from Darnforth's eventual betrayal that it is not enough to replace a tyrannical husband with an attentive lover—that her oppression lies with a larger, inescapable Western society in which unjust sexual relations are legally legitimized and in which married women do not have independent legal status as "persons"—so, too, the Arabian Safie as Felix's "wife" has yet to discover that she has escaped into another institution of female oppression (134).

In fact, Safie's initial marital bliss depends upon the De Laceys' exile by a legal system whose presence might reveal her liberation through marriage to be rather less than "enchanting" (119). Her letters are embedded in the middle of a chapter that begins with the unjust trial of her father, who subsequently purchases his rescue by virtually bartering her to Felix as a wife, and ends with her reunion with Felix in exile after his own unjust trial, the result of futilely "deliver[ing] himself up to the vengeance of the law" after rescuing her father (121).

Safie's letters aspire to freedom amid a raging Western judicial tyranny they fail to confront. Mary Shelley thus entertains the possibility that idyllic romantic and familial relations depend upon escaping society's troubled legal framework, but she also shows how doing so quixotically places women's actual legal position in abeyance (and has that nuclear utopia collapse at the incursion of the outside world, symbolized here by the entrance of the human creature). For Mary Shelley, in the evidence provided by both sets of letters—Safie's to Felix and Percy's to Harriet—lurks the same question that emerged from *Queen Mab,* one that overshadowed the trial and Mary's life while she wrote *Frankenstein:* "Do the law courts have a role in governing personal relations?"

III

If we turn back to the relations between Frankenstein and the human creature, their connection to the law at first seems to be obvious: there is none; the law is irrelevant. On the surface there is nothing but a series of brief interactions with criminal justice resulting from the human creature's murders. Yet it is precisely the irrelevance of a legal framework for their relationship and the inappropriateness of the criminal justice system to the unfolding story which come to animate the legal plot. It is no accident that after Justine's unjust trial, Mary Shelley shifts the remaining two legal scenes—Frankenstein's preliminary committal for Henry Clerval's murder and his final interview with a magistrate—to the fringes of the central story, casting the criminal justice system as an interruption of the ongoing plot. These scenes are less concerned with unveiling the injustice of the legal system than with revealing the inadequacy of the entire Western justice system, civil and criminal, to Frankenstein and the human creature's predicament.

First, Frankenstein's preliminary committal for the murder of his friend Clerval confirms the presence of the justice system but reaffirms that its operations are misplaced. Frankenstein unknowingly lands on the very beach in Ireland where the human creature has murdered Clerval the previous evening and is promptly arrested. When a magistrate, Mr. Kirwin, leads him to view the corpse, Frankenstein, shocked to discover it is his friend, forgets "the trial, the presence of the magistrate and witnesses" and gasps out over the body: "Have my murderous machinations deprived you also, my dearest Henry, of life?

Two I have already destroyed; other victims await their destiny" (173–74). This outrageous confession might seem at first a rather formidable obstacle to proving his innocence. But, in stark contrast to Justine (and consistent with institutionalized male power), Frankenstein does absolutely nothing for his defense and is summarily cleared before trial by a grand jury. The magistrate Kirwin, we are told, arranges everything.

Yet, in doing so, he only exposes just how far the justice system is removed from the real conflict. We are plunged into the details of a case only to have it dematerialize before our eyes. As one reviewer sarcastically complained in 1818: Frankenstein "is taken up by a constable called Daniel Nugent, and carried before Squire Kirwan [sic] a magistrate, and very nearly hanged for a murder committed by the monster. We were greatly edified with the laudable minuteness which induces the author to give us the names of these officers of justice; it would, however, have been but fair to have given us also those of the impartial judge and enlightened jury who acquitted him, for acquitted, as our readers will be glad to hear, honourably acquitted, he was at the assizes of Donegal."[30] But did we really miss another trial scene? The operations of state justice necessarily short-circuit here. From the moment Frankenstein wonders "whether [he] should not declare [him]self guilty, and suffer the penalty of the law, less innocent than poor Justine had been" (176), the narrative moves to extricate him from the possibility that the state might actually provide this dramatic poetic justice and martyrdom, even simply by putting him in the dock for a crime he did not actually commit. Instead, justice is, in theory, vindicated, but readers are left with the unsettling recognition that the larger problem of justice in Frankenstein and the human creature's relationship remains unaddressed by either Frankenstein or the justice system.

Within the episode itself Mary Shelley hints at this problem through a scene that recalls and reverses tensions animating the earlier scene in which the human creature comes to life. After seeing Clerval's corpse, Frankenstein falls ill. When he has again finally "awoke to understanding," returning from "the point of death" (174), he is repulsed by his female nurse's "countenance." Her harsh words for Frankenstein, whom she believes is a murderer, elicit the following hypocritical moralizing on his part: "I turned with loathing from the woman who could utter so unfeeling a speech to a person just saved, on the very edge of death" (175).[31] He is, of course, receiving rather better treatment, with less to merit it, than the human creature did in a remarkably similar predicament. As if to underscore this difference between Frankenstein's and the human creature's treatment, Kirwin immediately adopts Frankenstein's cause as his own, and Frankenstein's father rushes to his side.

The legal proceedings become irrelevant here as the irony of the moral situation becomes clearer: society cradles Frankenstein, in stark contrast to the human creature. But Frankenstein cannot see the contrast, much less connect his situation to the surrounding legal framework in which he might be answerable for his acts. As he leaves the prison, his response to an anonymous commentator's shrewd assessment that "he may be innocent of the murder, but he has certainly a bad conscience" is, as usual, to lament yet again that "William, Justine, and Clerval . . . died through my infernal machinations" (180), without pausing to consider that his conscience might be more productively troubled by his own treatment of the human creature than by the human creature's actions, over which he has no control. In a specifically legal context Mary Shelley suggests that Frankenstein's larger challenge lies in formulating the responsible relationship he has to the human creature.

The law, however, is certainly not going to enforce, or provide the underlying framework for, any sort of guardian-ward relationship for the human creature and Frankenstein in this novel. On the contrary, in its final legal scene Frankenstein tries to enlist the law to execute his human creature. After making a frenzied and guilty-looking escape from the scene of Elizabeth's strangulation by crossing Lake Geneva while everyone is out on a fruitless search for the human creature, whom "most . . . believ[e] . . . to have been a form conjured by [his] fancy" (194), Frankenstein is apparently safe in Switzerland from being charged with her murder in France. Or, at any rate, Mary Shelley makes do with having him insane and vaguely locked up in a "dungeon" for "many months." Everything is thus hazy—"What then became of me? I know not"—for a few paragraphs until Frankenstein returns to his senses (such as they are) and proceeds directly to a magistrate to accuse the human creature of multiple murders. (Mary Shelley thereby not only saves us from another scene in which Frankenstein is a defendant but also enables the story to continue a pattern in which Frankenstein has *different* encounters with the law after each of the human creature's murders.) As Frankenstein recounts: "I repaired to a criminal judge in the town, and told him that I had an accusation to make; that I knew the destroyer of my family; and that I required him to exert his whole authority for the apprehension of the murderer" (196).

The magistrate attends to Frankenstein's story, its first telling, and a version of *Frankenstein*'s central plot, we are informed, is rendered as a "deposition" and a legal accusation (196). The moment is difficult to interpret because we are never quite sure how the magistrate receives this story, but, whether we read the magistrate's generally conciliatory responses to Frankenstein as phony reassurance or genuine acknowledgment and acceptance of his story, Mary Shelley's point seems to be that Frankenstein confronts the fact that the magistrate hearkens to his story and will intervene. Frankenstein, tellingly, blanches. He does not do so—as perhaps one might have hoped—because he realizes the magistrate's willingness to bring the human creature to justice indicates he made a monumental mistake earlier in failing simply to tell the truth at Justine's trial. Rather, as Mary Shelley makes clear, the magistrate's willingness to intervene produces an alarmed and incoherent reaction in Frankenstein because his true agenda is personal vengeance, not justice, and the magistrate exposes it as such.

Frankenstein finds no consolation in the magistrate's promises that he will try his best to ensure that "if it is in [his] power to seize the monster . . . he shall suffer punishment proportionate to his crimes" (198). Proportion, adjudication, his story subjected to judgment: Frankenstein can tolerate none of it. His unjust, predatory desire is that the human creature should "be hunted like the chamois [a goat antelope], and destroyed as a beast of prey" (197). He storms off ranting: "My revenge is of no moment to you; yet, while I allow it to be a vice, I confess that it is the devouring and only passion of my soul." Once again exposed as a martyr largely to his own madness, Frankenstein alone imagines in this scene that "trembl[ing] with excess of agitation" and having "a phrenzy in [his] manner" presents "something . . . of that haughty fierceness, which the martyrs of old are said to have possessed." As he himself remarks, "to a Genevan magistrate . . . this elevation of mind had much the appearance of madness" (198). We may be inclined to agree with the magistrate. Elevation of mind? Frankenstein is enraged here simply by *not* finding the justice system much interested in his personal desires for revenge.[32]

The larger point of this interaction lies in Mary Shelley's placement of the scene at the end of the novel's penultimate chapter. This brief exchange—and not, as is usually assumed, the more notorious moment when Frankenstein vows vengeance by the graves of his family members—truly launches Frankenstein's "wanderings" and his terminal pursuit of the human creature into the wilds of nature. Frankenstein's final act is thus the explicit repudiation of the legal world. We have come full circle from Justine's unjust trial. In this novel the justice system is inept and unjust, but it is nonetheless the last stop on the way out of civilization and society. Mary Shelley dismantles both the traditional, pat image of justice as the product of a civilized society whose social contract keeps at bay a savage, revenge-based state of nature and its inverse conceptualization in which justice is imagined flowing from a utopian, anarchic return to a simple state of nature freed from the corruption of oppressive state laws. As Justine's trial announces at the novel's outset, the justice system is an overflowing source of injustice, productive of impoverished personal relations; at the same time, as the final legal scenes suggest, its absence matters. A paradoxical insight runs through this novel: the justice system can be at once a primary source of injustice and a necessary locus for framing just relations.

The point is not that the human creature and Frankenstein somehow need a Chancery trial to work out their differences and establish equitable responsibilities. The law court is not just a mechanism for settling disputes when they arise but a framework in which all relations are embedded and which produces as well as reflects those relations. The essential problem with Frankenstein and the human creature's relationship is not actually that the human creature is monstrous—or that Frankenstein's treatment of him is monstrous, though in reading the narrative we may, like the characters, continually attempt with varying success to affix blame on one or the other. Rather, as in "The Monster" (1898), Stephen Crane's later Americanized, racialized rewriting of *Frankenstein,* it is the relationship itself that is monstrous, neither fitting nor made to resemble "the various relationships which bind one human being to another in mutual bonds" (117), and that abnormal relationship defines who they are, and who they become, as characters.

It has thus made good sense for critics to argue for reading the human creature's gender as female and his race Other. It would certainly seem true from a legal perspective. The human creature's appearance and accidents of birth mean that he occupies a legal status of less than "person," as did women and slaves (as well as "bastards") during Mary Shelley's lifetime. And these comparisons find their corollary and confirmation in the legalistic fact that the human creature does not have his own name. His narrative may even rightly have a special place in the rise of published slave narratives, such as *The Life of Olaudah Equinao* (1789), in which narrators not only "plead" their "cause" as if on trial but also confirm their humanity in the very act of doing so.[33] With all this in mind, we may perhaps want to extend further the self-conscious critical shift that has taken place in which the term *monster,* which echoes Victor Frankenstein's nomenclature, has been replaced by our current use of the term *creature,* the name he commonly calls himself. For just once in the novel, but conspicuously, the nameless narrator is acknowledged as a "human creature" (an appellation that echoes Mary Wollstonecraft's dramatic declaration that she "shall first consider women in the grand light of human creatures").[34] Predictably, it is old De Lacey, sympathetic and, like justice, "blind" and therefore unable "to judge of [his] countenance," who includes our nameless narrator as a fellow human creature (130).

At the same time, without denying that the human creature may represent a nightmarish abstraction of people struggling for recognition of their full humanity, we must also recognize that he explicitly bemoans the fact that he is the sole member of his species. He is, crucially, not representative of any human group. In this respect his unique relationship to Frankenstein stands not so much for larger unjust legal relations but, rather, fantastically, for the specter of having no legal relation at all to his creator, to other individuals, or to society as a whole. In *Frankenstein* it is in part this failure of the legal system to recognize familial relationships outside of blood or marriage ties adequately which allows Frankenstein and his human creature to fall out of their larger society and descend into an endless spiral of warring relations—precisely what happens in society and through the framework of the pervasive legalistic tribunals in *Caleb Williams.* Without due process the human creature must—like Heinrich von Kleist's Michael Kohlhaas—"wrest justice from the world with his own hands."[35]

In this way *Frankenstein* may all the more effectively be suggesting by way of antithesis the need for those public, mundane, constraining social processes and specifying legal frameworks involved in attaining the abstract "justice" that both Frankenstein and the human creature relentlessly, and futilely, invoke. Any two modern individuals can, as they do, evoke legal process endlessly, appropriating its discourse, but without the stopgap of actual individual rights and actual law courts (with, to put it cynically, a third party's enforcement) that legal discourse may devolve into a fatal power struggle rather than prevent it.[36]

Strangely enough, however, the very depths to which Frankenstein and the human creature sink in this novel may also imply alternate vistas of positive legal relationships. The absolute negation of the human creature's juridical affective relations summons up new, expansive affirmations of legal surrogacy, most obviously a broadening of the legal fictions defining family, which in *Frankenstein,* for example, would specifically refigure both the human creature's and Justine's unjust treatment, to say nothing of the refusal by Walton, the leader of the polar expedition in the frame story, to assent to "a demand [by his crew], which, in justice, [he] could not refuse" (211). If, in order to adjudicate rights and responsibilities between people, the law courts assume an impossibly stabilized matrix of relations, acknowledging only a defined set of permutations to define kindredness, that legal pigeonholing, and not transcendence of it, may create the very conditions of possibility for revolutionizing the affective and familial relations that it partly produces in society and within subjects.[37]

It is not enough, then, to conclude this chapter from a biographical-intellectual perspective, though *Frankenstein*'s legal plot partly makes sense as Mary Shelley's displaced consideration of both Godwin's anarchist faith that justice might spring simply from rational discussion between individuals and Percy's overreaching ideal of intimate relations as above the law (along with the unjust trial that was its result). At a broader level, one in which *Frankenstein* lives as a cultural myth structured by that which it explicitly places on its margins (expressing what it is suppressing), this novel amplifies an ideological, novelistic conception of modern subjects as necessarily—even in their affective and familial bonds—subject to and produced by the law courts. In the anonymous first edition of 1818 readers must have understood the novel's dedication "to William Godwin, Author of Political Justice, Caleb Williams, &c" as a signal that the novel was concerned with a radical, larger enactment of justice in society. In later editions, which identified Mary Shelley as the author, it appropriately emerged that her dedication simultaneously bespoke a daughter's relation to her father.

In 1818 Percy Shelley made a similarly telling comment in praising *Franken-*

stein. Bracketing together Frankenstein's explanation to Walton on the frozen, arctic sea and the human creature's plea to Frankenstein next to a sea of ice, he declared: "The encounter and argument between Frankenstein and the Being on the sea of ice, almost approaches, in effect, to the expostulations of Caleb Williams with Falkland."[38] One might rewrite that comparison by observing that the encounter and argument between Frankenstein and the Being approaches in effect the expostulations of Caleb Williams with Falkland except that it occurs on a sea of ice, removed from all "Things as They Are," a monstrous myth of social relations conducted outside of society, its narrating characters' interrelations and narrative self-justifications floundering without a frame-work—even an unjust one—of legal adjudication for their relationship. Here was a novel about, in part, the structuring power of the law courts in the early nineteenth century, told through imagining their removal.

Victorian Courthouse Structures,
The Pickwick Papers

M ARY RUSSELL MITFORD, writing in June 1837, introduces *The Pickwick Papers* (1836–37) to a friend in this way:

> So you have never heard of the "Pickwick Papers!" Well! They publish a number once a month, and print 25,000. The bookseller has made about £10,000 by the speculation. It is fun—London life—but without anything unpleasant. . . . It is rather fragmentary, except the trial (No. 11 or 12), which is as complete and perfect as any bit of comic writing in the English language. You must read the "Pickwick Papers."[1]

It is no accident that Mitford begins her discussion with the economics of *Pickwick* and ends with the book's changing shape—"fragmentary, except the trial." At the time she writes, *Pickwick* is ushering in a new era in the serialization of novels. With *Pickwick,* for the first time a serial begins drawing on material that an author is producing month by month in order to construct a novel. Previous serialization of novels had proceeded by slicing up novels that had already been published in volume form. Hence, Mitford's news here is about *Pickwick,* but that *Pickwick* itself is news—that is, that a fresh novel is being serialized—is the news behind her news. This is why literary critics rightly continue to turn to *Pickwick* to chart and analyze the dawning of the

Victorian era of serialization in which "a number once a month," which could eventually be collated with its other numbers into a novel, was mass-marketed at a shilling apiece, making for "that beloved Victorian thing, 'a cheap luxury.'"[2] Yet, though these critics have told the historical and economic story of *Pickwick* the book, they have overlooked that the story of Pickwick in itself conveys a story of *Pickwick*.

To look into Pickwick's varied, episodic adventures for the historical and economic story of *Pickwick* becoming Dickens's first novel and Dickens becoming a novelist, and to see in it as well how one of the earliest Victorian novels adapted to the judicial matrix we have seen taking shape in the Romantic era novels of William Godwin and Mary Shelley, we can take a cue from Mitford's letter. Mitford predictably finds that *Pickwick* "is rather fragmentary," but she goes on to single out chapter 34, the "full and faithful Report of the memorable Trial of Bardell against Pickwick," as indeed the most memorable, "complete and perfect" part of the story. For her the trial is a high point of the novel's comic writing, and, as her syntax implies, it contrasts with the story's otherwise "fragmentary" construction. As she senses, the trial marks the transition of Dickens's work from loosely linked narrative sketches into the complexly plotted form of the Victorian novel. *Pickwick*'s visits to the law offices and the law courts are less about legal reform than about the novel's form and the establishment of the middle-class, professional author at the outset of the Victorian period.

I

As is well known, Dickens originally planned a fragmentary form for the "papers." His advertisement heralding the publication (and writing) of *The Pickwick Papers* promises:

> High-roads and by-roads, towns and villages, public conveyances and their passengers, first-rate inns and road-side public houses, races, fairs, regattas, elections, meetings, market days—all the scenes that can possibly occur to enliven a country place, and at which different traits of character may be observed, and recognized, were alike visited and beheld, by the ardent Pickwick and his enthusiastic followers.[3]

From "high roads" to "market days," this list, an unprogrammatic itinerary of sorts, aptly advertises the shape that *Pickwick* initially takes: another series of thinly connected sketches by "Boz." This time, various country places are to be "alike visited and beheld" tourist style, as the passive construction underscores. Dickens does not set out to recount Pickwick's story but, rather, to capture the country "scenes" and by using these scenes, "at which different traits of character may be observed," to describe a range of characters. Pickwick is primarily a device, a body that justifies the roving of Dickens's narrator's gaze rather than a developing, speaking character. Even if the first illustrator and the publishers had not already planned this wandering and almost plotless form (desiring at first only that a cheap writer provide six pages of text each month for four pictures), Dickens originally thought he understood the constraints of producing so-many-pages-a-month that were so soon turned into a published number. He thus concludes his advertisement by collapsing together the form of his text as series, its actual serial mode of production, and the fiction of its production as extracts from papers, announcing that, "From the present appearance of these important documents, and the probable extent of the selections from them, it is presumed that the series will be completed in about twenty numbers" (900).

It is a conflation that at first seems natural. Dickens himself explicitly apologizes in his first preface to the book that the serial mode of production has required him to produce a fragmentary form. In a later preface, however, he recants: "It was observed . . . that no ingenuity of plot was attempted, or even at that time considered very feasible by the author in connexion with the desultory mode of publication adopted . . . [but] experience and study have since taught me something" (43). Beginning with *Oliver Twist* (1837–38), which he commenced while he was writing *Pickwick*, Dickens produced only heavily plotted narratives; therefore, we can deduce with hindsight that this "experience and study" of fashioning an "ingenuity of plot" was gained through the writing of *Pickwick*.

It was in fact in *Pickwick* that Dickens first discovered an extended plot. Early in the writing he wrestled with his story to introduce a progression of the seasons. Eventually, he roughly planned his numbers so that the characters' time corresponded to the month before publication time, thereby strengthening both his own planning and his audience's sense of ongoing participation in

Pickwick.[4] Yet, as James Kinsley notes in his introduction to the Clarendon edition of *Pickwick,* an extended plot does not appear in the novel until the "opening of the affair of Mrs. Bardell, and so (by Dickens's design or discovery) the establishment of a coherent narrative structure."[5] Pickwick might set out to roam aimlessly and innocently through the country, but, when his landlady, Mrs. Bardell, accuses him of breach of promise for marriage, he is forced to return to the city and is there eventually required to visit the courthouse, that most thoroughly urban building, for a trial that enmeshes him in a plot.

The introduction of the trial of Bardell against Pickwick calls forth the extended plotting that comes to characterize and dominate the form of even serialized Victorian novels. Once the "action" (as it is aptly called) against Pickwick for breach of promise of marriage is begun (325), it structures the novel's action. The characters move toward the courthouse as a destination, constructing a trajectory: "It really is your intention to proceed with this action?" (349); "I suppose you've heard what's going forward" (446); "This action . . . is expected to come on" (508); "The trial's a comin' on" (543). At the same time, the introduction of even the potential for a trial retroactively envelops earlier scenes in the new plot. The comic scene in which Mrs. Bardell mistakenly concludes that Pickwick has asked her to marry him becomes both a crime and a beginning, and all the other scenes, both before and after it, change into potential evidence. Suddenly able to return as testimony, these scenes take on a new coherence, as a horrified Mr. Winkle discovers at the trial when he must testify to the "trifling circumstance of suspicion" of "Mr. Pickwick's being found in a lady's sleeping apartment at midnight; which had terminated, he believed, in the breaking off of the projected marriage of the lady in question, and had led, he knew, to the whole party being forcibly carried before George Nupkins, Esq., magistrate and justice of the peace" (570).

Part of the joke here, created by the trial, is that the kindhearted Pickwick can be caught in a plot where none was planned. A Pickwickian "plot," in both the overlapping novelistic and legal senses of the term, is virtually an oxymoron. Nonetheless, for the reader the Pickwick trial does introduce an extended and ongoing plot, one that makes the serial novel akin to the periodical account of a trial in a contemporary newspaper. In particular, it constructs the anticipation of a resolution. For this very reason the final marriages can seem anticlimactic and even irrelevant; the trial has driven the action. The trial plot results in Pickwick's incarceration in Fleet, which is the actual focus of the end of the novel, and it leads finally, only a few chapters before the end, to its own dramatic resolution, when Pickwick makes his final angry payment to the notorious lawyers Dodson and Fogg.

Moreover, the trial of Bardell against Pickwick ushers in a more complicated narrative transformation than simply the introduction of what Kinsley terms *narrative coherence,* which is only plot in its most plodding sense. As the serial becomes a novel, a tension between plot (personified by the lawyers with their machinations) and anecdote (personified by the good-hearted Pickwick) becomes a theme and problem animating the story. A Pickwickian worldview that revels in a fluid and fragmentary life, acknowledging only the temporary unity of vignettes, encounters an opposing (legal-novelistic) ideology in which system and underlying intrigue loom ominously. In the end, when Pickwick finally pays off and is rid of the grasping lawyers Dodson and Fogg, his seeming escape betrays how deeply he has actually become enmeshed in the sort of continuous struggle characteristic of an extended plot. That extended plot only surfaces in the first place because the lawyers threaten a trial at which a Pickwickian plot will necessarily be exposed; or, rather, because Dickens introduces a trial scene that calls forth an extended plot from Pickwick's story. The depiction of a trial spawns a doubling of the story, though it remains part of the story itself, and it conjures up doubles of the plotting author within the text in the shape of the storytelling and scribbling lawyers.

A deconstructive reading might begin at this point: *Pickwick* takes its own representations and even its own authorship as its subject through a displacement. Yet that displacement crucially points us outside of a hermeneutics of textual self-reflection to a Victorian legal world. Dickens is creating *Pickwick* and himself as a novelist against and through his contemporary legal world. This sort of self-fashioning depends on a dialectic in which differences define and maintain each other. *Pickwick* forms part of a history of law and literature in which the *and* in *law and literature* is not, as is still common practice,[6] to be translated into law *in* literature or law *as* literature.

I I

From the first the Pickwick trial foregrounds interpretation. Mrs. Bardell has understandably misinterpreted a conversation with Pickwick; she believes he has proposed marriage, though Pickwick has only been discussing his plans to hire Sam Weller. This initial misunderstanding is compounded when Pickwick's friends arrive just after Mrs. Bardell has fainted into his arms. The comic misinterpretation in this scene is similar to several others in which Pickwick is mistaken for a philanderer or worse—though here (in contrast to a subsequent incident at a women's school) Pickwick has no recourse to corroborating testimony. Everyone within the story doubts him. For the reader, aligned with the omniscient narrator and Pickwick, the case initially does not pose much interpretive ambiguity. Pickwick is innocent, guilty only of his typical naïveté about the possible interpretations of his own behavior. At this point the only question seems to be how or even if this misunderstanding between Mrs. Bardell and Pickwick will be resolved.

It is not until a letter announcing the legal action arrives, bringing new complexity and new characters into this confusion, that the novel's focus begins to shift from the comic quagmire of Pickwick and Mrs. Bardell to the hermeneutics that underlie it. Now forced to review explicitly the fashioning of interpretation at work in the original confusion, Pickwick declares of the situation, "What a dreadful conjunction of appearances! . . . We are all the victims of circumstances, and I the greatest." In the same moment that he recognizes the dangers of misinterpretation Pickwick detects that he is also a victim of misrepresentation—that is, that he is the main character of a plot constructed by the lawyers: "It's a conspiracy, . . . a base conspiracy between these two grasping attorneys, Dodson and Fogg" (326–27). This "conspiracy" is reaffirmed for Pickwick when he visits Dodson and Fogg to inform them of his innocence, as if the matter were still merely a conflict of interpretations. The attorneys, of course, are indifferent. With the introduction of the lawyers, what was merely a dilemma of conflicting interpretations becomes a study in the manipulation of interpretations.

Dickens immediately affirms and explores the complex situation he has introduced through the lawyers. He does so by recreating a version of the larger trial plot in miniature without the lawyers. In scenes sandwiched between his visits to lawyers' offices, Pickwick leaves London briefly for Ipswich; he is back on the road, in the style of the beginning of the book. At an inn he embroils himself in the adventure about which Mr. Winkle will later testify at the Bardell trial: Pickwick accidentally ends up in an elderly woman's bedroom and provokes a misinterpretation that upsets a marriage proposal, initiating talk of a duel. As a result, Pickwick and his friends are brought before the local magistrate for a trial. The scene, as Philip Collins notes, is stock.[7] Indeed, that is the point. Dickens is exposing the difference between depicting a stock, traditional, rural trial held by a justice of the peace in his chambers and the urban, lawyered trial of the London courtroom which he has just introduced into his story. He is imaginatively visiting a Fielding novel, and he finds it wanting. The magistrate trial predictably ends up focusing on the tyranny of Nupkins, his "wash-up" (worship), while Pickwick extricates himself by influencing the judge and not through a scene of retelling. In the magistrate's trial lawyers are out of place, and for Dickens and the reader, their absence reveals their import. Dickens thus affirms through a brief detour back into the country that there is a new order of trial and a new order of representation at work in his depiction of the lawyered London case of Bardell against Pickwick.

What Dickens slowly reveals—first at Dodson and Fogg's law office, then at Pickwick's barrister's office, and finally at the trial—is that the lawyer's profession is not only caught up in manipulating interpretations but is also immersed in writing and reading, in orchestrating discourses, and finally in telling stories for money. Through the depiction of these characters Dickens not only exposes the law profession but also constructs an analogue to his own predicament as author. These lawyers, bent on interpreting and constructing the character Pickwick and his story, are the authors within the novel.

In a general way the depiction of the lawyers registers simply the dismal, psychological underside of producing—at a feverish pitch of work—what John Forster calls the novel's "inexhaustible fun."[8] As Dickens once reminded his publishers when he was behind schedule, "spirits are not to be forced up to Pickwick point, every day";[9] and, even when they are, the submerged cynicism that predominates in his later novels and the economics driving the current labor are still present in the work, cast into the characters of the lawyers.

Hence, as Pickwick tells Sergeant Snubbin, his barrister: "Gentlemen of your profession, sir, . . . see the worst side of human nature. All its disputes, all its ill-will and bad blood, rise up before you. You know from your experience of juries (I mean no disparagement to you, or them) how much depends upon *effect*" (518). Like a grimmer version of Dickens the professional author, the sergeant is indeed concerned primarily with "*effect*"—its production is his "profession." In Phiz's illustration of this moment Sergeant Snubbin is pausing from his work at his writing table; only a forensic wig distinguishes this particular writer as a barrister. Appropriately enough, then, the sergeant responds to Pickwick here by ignoring him and returning to the labor of writing which Pickwick has interrupted and of which he will be the subject. Thus, Dickens creates a foil not only for Pickwick but also for himself as author.

Indeed, Sergeant Snubbin, writing amid dusty "heaps of papers" (515), recalls Dickens's earlier self-representation in the advertisement and in the frame as the story's fictional "editor" who sorts through "multifarious documents" (67) and "voluminous papers" (236). It is also not much of a leap from this sergeant within the novel to the book's dedication to Sergeant Talfourd, an author and lawyer, for his work in parliament on the copyright issue.[10] All are signs that Dickens was struggling to establish for himself and for authors a new professional status and doing so, in part, by looking to the figure of the lawyer.

From the very beginning of *Pickwick* the story has been concerned with Dickens's establishment as a professional author. Dickens creates authorial surrogates in Jingle, a wordsmith who works in fragments; in Sam Weller, who oversees the character Pickwick; and even in Pickwick, who is himself a published author. In the first sentence of this first novel, moreover, Dickens signals that he is concerned not just with an abstract conception of authorship but with the work and professional potential of his own authorship. Dickens writes:

> The first ray of light which illumines the gloom, and converts into a dazzling brilliancy that obscurity in which the earlier history of the public career of the immortal Pickwick would appear to be involved, is derived from the perusal of the following entry in the Transactions of the Pickwick Club, which the editor of these papers feels the highest pleasure in laying before his readers, as a proof of the careful attention, indefatigable

assiduity, and nice discrimination, with which his search among the multifarious documents confided to him has been conducted. "May 12, 1827." (67)

The Genesis-like creation—"the first ray of light"—evoked here points to the fictional professional editor, and not just Pickwick, as the (parodied) creation of every circumlocution and high-flown clause of this first, lengthy sentence. The passage is not creation ex nihilo but ex Dickens. The sentence even turns its own creation inside out: with much comic pomp Dickens conjures both himself as author and his book to life. In other words, this first sentence is a *professional* in-the-beginning-there-was-the-word that proclaims the emergence of the "public career" of a Pickwick that is *Pickwick*—or, rather, of a verbose editor who is at once a parody of Dickens and yet Dickens the parodist. With this traditional novelist's device of constructing a fictional editor, Dickens not only aligns himself with the likes of Walter Scott, but he also constructs his own beginning as a novelist. Thus, as it turns out, we could do worse than to take this first line seriously as an instruction to peruse "the following entry" for "the first ray of light which illumines the gloom, and converts into dazzling brilliancy that obscurity in which the earlier history of the public career of the immortal [Dickens] would appear to be involved"—for the very next sentence, "May 12, 1827," which is the first fictional entry and the putative beginning of the *Papers,* in fact provides an illuminating first ray of light. As Steven Marcus has noted, this date is significant because in May 1827, at age fifteen, Dickens began his "public career."[11] He left school and took up his first job within a middle-class working world. Coming three years after he had been forced to work at the Blacking factory, where his dreams and his (class-based) self-image were rocked, this job marked the beginning of his (middle-class) life plot. Although in *David Copperfield* (1849–50) Dickens returns to the moment more cynically, the commencement of this job nonetheless is appropriately recounted in the title of chapter 23 of that novel: "I . . . choose a Profession."[12]

That profession was the law. In May 1827 Dickens began working as a clerk at the law firm of the solicitors Ellis and Blackmore. His job lasted for roughly the same span of time (from May 1827 to November 1828) that *Pickwick*'s action covers (from May 1827 to August 1828), an amount of time that also roughly parallels the labor-time of writing the novel (which extended from February 1836 to October 1837). Although when he begins *Pickwick* Dickens merely refers to the beginning of his own professional, middle-class career through the persona of a fictional editor, midway through his novel he returns specifically to that beginning in the legal profession as a way of working out the complexity of his own development as professional author.

The lawyers, then, do not simply recall the fictional editor; they take on and refigure Dickens's self-representation as a professional at work, which that fictional editor performs initially. In the introductory advertisement this editor, identified as "Boz," is at once a parodic self-representation and explicitly a working professional: "A gentleman whom the publishers consider highly qualified for the task of arranging these important documents . . . [and who] is at present immersed in his arduous labours" (900). By the end of the novel, however, this fictional editor and his "arduous labours" have disappeared, replaced by a clichéd, heroic authorial voice that addresses the reader from the lofty regions of "art," declaiming that "it is the fate of all authors or chroniclers to create imaginary friends, and lose them in the course of art" (896). The lawyers, meanwhile, are portraying the dirtier work. They are the textual evidence within *Pickwick* that it is also Dickens's fate with this novel to exploit his "imaginary friends" as no one had quite done before as well as to experience his own exploitation, his own professionalization and commodification as author, as part of the precarious beginnings of his success. For, in contrast to even the original fictional editor of the frame, the lawyers are firmly within the story, in which they emphasize—instead of suppressing, as the editor does—the fact that their work of representation is done for money.

The lawyers do not just crucially expose Pickwick's benign and principled world as one of moneyed ease, existing in tension with a grimmer working world in which relations are based on the cash nexus; in doing so, they also point back to *Pickwick*'s own economic underside. Like the lawyers within the novel, Dickens has mercenary designs of his own upon Pickwick. The novel's plot, driven by the lawyers' successful quest for money, uneasily mirrors the book's—and Dickens's own—plot for money. The depiction of the lawyers and their trial does not just usher in the novel's plot: that plot itself is a displaced expression both of the plot of (rather than in) the book and of the author's current life—that is, of Dickens's struggle toward a successful financial and professional debut. There is thus another side to Anny Sadrin's argument that the fragmentation in *Pickwick* reflects the fact that Dickens "had learned from cruel experience that life was unpredictable."[13] By the time he introduces the lawyers Dickens is also experiencing his own "progress," a financial progress. Rather than precluding the creation of an extended plot as Dickens had originally supposed, the serial mode of production which kept him writing as he and *Pickwick* rose to fame and financial success actually generates the novel's extended plot.

The serial consumption of *Pickwick* also plays back into the story's production. Perhaps some of the acidity of Dickens's depiction of the lawyers expresses how difficult it was for him to reconcile his workaday economics and labors with his own and his culture's myths of eternal art and genius. We know that, well before he was finished with *Pickwick*, Dickens hoped that "long after my hand is withered as the pens it held, Pickwick will be found on many a dusty shelf with many a better work."[14] Dickens thus rather searchingly envisioned *Pickwick* as a lasting work of art (the respectable dust on this imaginary shelf is of a different sort than the dust in the lawyers' offices) at the very moment when *Pickwick*'s aura is deriving both from the audience's sense of ongoing participation in a fresh textual amusement ride and from the myth that an entire nation is concurrently consuming the story. Put another way, Dickens wishes that his novel will be consumed in the tradition of expensive volumes in a personal (rather than a lending) library when it is actually selling much more like the celebrated court trials that he used to report for the newspapers.

So, one might say: in the end Pickwick can go free, but only because the lawyers get their fees—as does Dickens. Or is it, rather, the publishers, Chapman and Hall, who, like an echo of Dodson and Fogg, get their fees from *Pickwick?* After all, Dickens was laboring for publishers who, like the lawyers within the novel, also had mercenary designs upon Pickwick. It is tempting to correlate the triangle of author, publisher, and book with a triangle formed within the novel by Pickwick's friendly lawyer Perker, Dodson and Fogg, and Pickwick. This serial novel might be read as a roman à clef of the production of the book itself. Yet the legal world that Dickens depicts should not be dismissed in order to return the text upon itself. Nor should one make a noose out of too-tight correlations between Dickens's biography and the novel's legal world. *Pickwick*'s "lawyer-land," as John Glavin calls it,[15] is an overdetermined

and imaginative displacement of Dickens's varying, contradictory, and complicated concerns. Only as such should this lawyer-land be understood as a topol-
ogy of his specific, but historical, struggle to establish himself as a professional
novelist, fashioning himself and his work.

After all, disparaging depictions of law professionals did not stop Dickens,
who had pursued entrance to the legal profession as early as two years before
Pickwick, from finally becoming a law student in 1839, two years after *Pickwick*
was completed. Of course, he had no intention of practicing law. As he put it:
"I am (nominally, God knows) a Law Student, and have a certain number of
'terms to keep' before I can be called to the Bar; and it would be well for me to
be called, as there are many little pickings to be got . . . which *can* only be bestowed on Barristers."[16] In a single breath, Dickens calumniates the coterie that
he hopes to join, capturing the essence of the whole (failed) attempt: mixed
feelings toward lawyers were bound up with an envy of their professional status and financial security. What seems to matter most in this particular intricacy
in his life and in the imagined world of *Pickwick* is that, unlike authors, lawyers
had a well-defined, middle-class profession. The barristers especially had the
qualifying and disciplinary association of the Inns of Court, official titles, their
own books and journals, unwritten codes of etiquette, attractive aristocratic
pretensions, and, perhaps most important, a centralized and narrow, urban,
professional geography of office, court, and legal district.[17]

This "world of the law," suggests Fred Kaplan, had been for Dickens at
fifteen a newly "fluid, varied world, . . . in which he could move from his clerk's
stool into the streets, into legal chambers, into the law courts, into administrative offices."[18] After a stint as court reporter in which this legal world became
something Dickens represented (as well as being itself an enterprise of representing), in *Pickwick* Dickens returned imaginatively to this lawyer-land in
order to explore the alleys of his own profession as novelist.

III

At the center of the novel's lawyer-land, in which the law offices can recall
Dickens's own writing space, is the courthouse and its trial, in which a story is
told and voices are orchestrated, much as in the novel itself. Here a novelist's

imaginative journey to the urban, physical structure of the court becomes an encounter with another structure for storytelling.

In *Pickwick* the courthouse and courtroom are revealed as building and room in which roles in the production of a narrative are turned into physical positions or sites. Predictably, the only position that matters for Dickens is the lawyers'. Pickwick identifies the parts of the court (Guildhall) when he enters— "That's the witness-box, I suppose?" "And that, . . . that's where the jurymen sit, is it not?" (553). Yet, as his lawyer announces, "Mr. Pickwick himself had better sit by me," and

> the little man led him to the low seat just beneath the desks of the King's Counsel, which is constructed for the convenience of attorneys, who from that spot can whisper into the ear of the leading counsel. . . . The occupants of this seat are invisible to the great body of spectators, inasmuch as they sit on a much lower level than either the barristers or the audience, whose seats are raised above the floor. Of course they have their backs to both, and their faces towards the judge. (553)

This descriptive passage has an echo of Dickens the court reporter. Specifically, however, it goes to extraordinary lengths to situate Pickwick and the lawyers. It is not surprising that Phiz chose to illustrate this description (558). In his picture Phiz leaves out the rest of the courtroom entirely, and yet the illustration, showing Sergeant Buzfuz as he makes his case against Pickwick, is nonetheless completely appropriate. The trial centers on Sergeant Buzfuz, the tale-telling barrister, as he relates a plausible—or at least Dickensian—account of Pickwick's actions.

As Sergeant Buzfuz performs his story about Pickwick and Mrs. Bardell, he incorporates quotations and even interpolates letters, accompanied by their interpretation. Much of the humor throughout the chapter springs—after the fashion of Robert Surtees's comic trial of his character Jorrocks[19]—from the ridiculous portrait of Pickwick "the serpent" (560) which the Sergeant goes to comic extremes to construct; or, rather it springs from the ridiculous textual double of the character Pickwick which Dickens produces through the words of his authorial Sergeant character. Dickens the author takes a step back and reveals his mastery over the creation of Pickwick and his story by creating a character who presents an opposing characterization of Pickwick within *Pickwick*. Authorlike, the barrister produces character.

Indeed, Mr. Weller has warned earlier in the novel that the trial will be about the construction of character:

> Now I s'pose he'll want to call some witnesses to speak to his character, or p'haps to prove a alleybi. I've been a turnin' the bis'ness over in my mind, and he may make his-self easy, Sammy. I've got some friends as'll do either for him, but my adwice 'ud be this here—never mind the character, and stick to the alleybi. Nothing like a alleybi, Sammy, nothing.
> (543)

Unfortunately, as Sam tries to tell him and the narrator points out, an alibi is inadmissible in this civil case. In a larger sense, however, Mr. Weller rightly points out that "Verever he's a goin' to be tried, my boy, a alleybi's the thing to get him off" (544)—that is, that, without the absolute denial of proving Pickwick to have been bodily elsewhere and therefore part of another plot, the novel's trial hinges upon the art of representing Pickwick's character. The difference here is more subtle than it might first appear. Dickens emphasizes through Mr. Weller that the issue in this trial is not whether Pickwick is the proper subject but, rather, how his character can be constructed in different ways. Mr. Weller's lament after the trial is telling: "I know'd what 'ud come o' this here mode o' doin' bisness. Oh Sammy, Sammy, vy worn't there a alleybi!" (577). The "mode o' doin' bisness" has depended largely upon the construction of character, part of the mode of business of its author. The trial that introduces the extended plot also turns out to be inseparably focused upon the construction of character.

The trial scene even plays off and calls attention to the author's ability to create characters. In the depiction of the trial the defending barrister's speech is summarily quashed: "Serjeant Snubbin then addressed the jury on behalf of the defendant; and a very long and a very emphatic address he delivered, in which he bestowed the highest possible eulogiums on the conduct and character of Mr. Pickwick; but inasmuch as our readers are far better able to form a correct estimate of that gentleman's merits and deserts, than Serjeant Snubbin could possibly be, we do not feel called upon to enter at any length into the learned gentleman's observations" (575). Dickens's direct address to "our readers" here explicitly betrays the otherwise tacit parallel between himself and this sergeant; there is no need for the Sergeant to go over the part Dickens has already performed better for the reader.[20] Thus, though Dickens parodies the lawyers for their "excellent ideas of effect" (556), he does so only by way of casting them into parallel authorial and narratorial roles. Pickwick becomes a character in the barrister's story as well as a character in Dickens's; the barrister's position presents a warped version of Dickens's position as author; the narrative becomes reflexive.

It is the trial that creates this reflexivity. If at first *Pickwick* is primarily a record of details, speeches, characters, and even scenes of misinterpretation, then after the introduction of the trial all these representations are potentially and explicitly to be re-presented. Then, in the court scene itself, the story's original representations, even the characters, explicitly become objects of representation. Nowhere is it clearer that, as J. Hillis Miller suggests, Pickwick, who sets out as "the spectator," "becomes himself a spectacle."[21] Nowhere is it clearer that *Pickwick* represents a world in which character is itself a representation. The process of representation which is the trial imagined within the novel brings out the novel as a reflexive process of representation.

In particular the trial reflects the fact that the story has become a sort of Tower of Babel of competing voices. Before the trial the introduction of the character Sam Weller most clearly shifts the narrative toward a novelistic state in which no single language, including the narrator's, exclusively possesses or dictates this fictional world: Sam Weller has a voice of his own. The omniscient narrator's voice, though still authoritative, from then on competes with the story's other voices. Hence, in the depiction of the trial the narrator stands against the representations made by the Sergeant and beside the voice of Sam Weller. As Bakhtin suggests of the novel in general, "the 'depicting' authorial language now lies on the same plane as the 'depicted' language."[22] The introduction of Sam Weller, however, only divides the text into self-authorizing voices. The trial then figures this state within the narrative. It reveals the paradox that the novel's potentially boundless polyglossia is nonetheless contained: the law court demarcates the achievement of the novel as the orchestration of speaking people and forms of speech, and it enfolds this achievement into the world it is portraying.

Still, we must remember that the trial here is relentlessly depicted as a mean ploy for money and disparaged as such. In a sense the trial has been a trial of the lawyers themselves.[23] Dickens thereby creates and distinguishes the ethical dimensions of two different sorts of work of representation. A novel is not a trial; Dickens is not, after all, a lawyer.

Yet it would also be a mistake to think the lawyers in *Pickwick* are simply villains. Pickwick might sympathetically proclaim his judgment that "they are great scoundrels" (512), but the novel persistently reveals Pickwick's failure to comprehend that his moral high ground is erected upon his wealth and leisure-class status and that money has become increasingly important to maintaining his enchanted world. This is most obvious when the lawyer Perker protects Pickwick. He once scolds Pickwick: "If you *will* take the management of your affairs into your own hands after entrusting them to your solicitor, you must also take the consequences" (512). Perker is a guardian, and thus he is much like Sam Weller, with whom he conspires to overcome Pickwick's "obstinacy" in order to spring Pickwick from Fleet prison. Perker's presence registers the ambivalence and complexity with which the novel actually presents the lawyers beneath Pickwick's fiery condemnation. Thus when Pickwick calls them "great scoundrels" he must ignore the sensible defense of Perker, his own lawyer: "That's a matter of opinion, you know, and we won't dispute about terms; because of course you can't be expected to view these subjects with a *professional eye*" (512; emph. added).

In the end Pickwick can only furiously dismiss Dodson and Fogg after finally paying them off. The male world of Pickwick's homosocial camaraderie, which orbits around an almost absent set of female ciphers who culminate in Mrs. Bardell, must finally give way to another male world, one that might be called a homoprofessional association. As Pickwick bows to the lawyers' control, he fails to see the significance of his own payment, which indicates at least his inability to remain aloof from the professional and financial world of the lawyers. No wonder Pickwick's final dismissal of Dodson and Fogg, though sympathetic, is clearly childish and, worse, rooted in class snobbery and a simplistic view of the effects created by his own wealth: in outrage over their "insolent familiarity," he calls Dodson and Fogg "Robbers!" no fewer than five times (847). Even if his display is not considered an overreaction to the "easy terms" he has actually gotten in the affair (a payment of roughly a hundred and fifty pounds, which Perker remarks "is nothing to" Pickwick [754]), Pickwick's insults are not just actionable by the libel laws of the day (as Dodson and Fogg angrily retort but mysteriously never pursue); the insults are also—it is more important—explicitly hurled in spite of his "friend Perker's wishes" (847). After this loud denouement, then, the actual complexity of the situation is quietly revealed when Pickwick turns to Perker and announces: "Well, now, . . . let me have a settlement with you." Laughing, Perker slyly responds: "Of the same kind as the last?" (848). Here Perker again points up what Pickwick cannot admit—that the counsel on his side is not much more or less of a villain than the opposing lawyer. The lawyers are all employees, all professionals.

At this point Pickwick can only ridiculously go on to insist on a world in which money is absent even as he is handing it out, replying to Perker: "Not exactly, . . . I only mean a pecuniary settlement. You have done me many acts of kindness that I can never repay, and have no wish to repay, for I prefer continuing the obligation" (848). The narrator pointedly continues, underscoring the financial world behind Pickwick's adventures, even as it is cast as perfunctory business: "With this preface, the two friends dived into some very complicated accounts and vouchers, which, having been duly displayed and gone through by Perker, were at once discharged by Mr. Pickwick with many professions of esteem and friendship" (848). A productive misreading here might recognize that Pickwick's only professions are indeed "esteem and friendship." The more important point is that after Pickwick lambastes the lawyers Dodson and Fogg, the trial plot quietly concludes on the opposite note, with Pickwick placidly sorting out finances with the lawyer Perker, "two friends." In fact, Perker continues to appear in the final scenes as a jovial advisor who, authorlike, knows the characters "a great deal better than [they] know [themselves]" (854–55). After revealing Pickwick's dismissal of the lawyers as simplistic, the novel signals a benign view of their profession.

All of this is underscored when, interspersed with the final scenes with the wealthier characters, another lawyer emerges to play a large and friendly role for the Wellers. This lawyer, Mr. Pell, a self-described "professional man" (869), helps to settle Mrs. Weller's will, the novel's final legal affair. At first, because the matter of executing the will has no direct connection to the legal plot that has preceded it, this part of the novel's ending seems tacked on. It may even appear to be a return to the fragmentation of the beginning. The matter of the will makes sense, however, in terms of the imaginative work that the legal plot has thus far performed, for the successful settling of Mrs. Weller's will produces the same final (imperfect) comfort with the legal profession among the working-class characters which has been produced among the gentrified and middle-class characters.

Thus, as a result of this episode, in a novel notorious for its disparagement of lawyers, Phiz's final sketch is nevertheless strangely fitting: Sam, his father, and their friends raise their glasses in a toast to a lawyer. Pell's response to this toast sounds like Dickens imagining his own potential response at one of the business dinner celebrations of *Pickwick*'s success: "Well, gentlemen, . . . all I can say is, that such marks of confidence must be very gratifying to a professional man. I don't wish to say anything that might appear egotistical, gentlemen, but I'm very glad, for your own sakes, that you came to me: that's all. If you had gone to any low member of the profession, it's my firm conviction, and I assure you of it as a fact, that you would have found yourselves in Queer Street before this" (873). It would have been an apt thought for Dickens as he finished *Pickwick,* at least, for both within and without the novel there has been a successful negotiation of lawyer-land.

As is so often the case, however, at the same time that a resolution is established, the narrative tension ostensibly being resolved reaches its straining point. The final affair of Mr. Weller's inheritance produces some of the novel's most disingenuous and inconsistent moves. Mr. Weller's final decision concerning his newfound wealth is "that it ain't o' no use to me. I'm a goin' to vork a coach reg'lar" (882)—that is, that the best thing this sharp, working-class character can think of to do with his money is give it away as fast as he can to the richest character he knows. When the story veritably screams the message of harmony between classes which the relationship of Sam to Pickwick has affirmed and created throughout the novel, the question is how it ever got to quite this pitch.

An answer—and a more profound twist in the representation of the working-class Mr. Weller's character—lies just before this scene, in the legal shenanigans. Mr. Weller's inheritance is paradoxically less important as money (which he cannot unload too fast) than as the novel's vehicle for representing the idea that even working-class identities are the harmonious subjects of the civil courts. That is, the deus ex machina is the money that Mr. Weller inherits, not because it equalizes already pleasant class relations but because it transports Mr. Weller, Sam, and several other almost anonymous working-class characters into the propertied arena of the civil courts in the novel's final scenes.

It is hardly necessary to show that Mr. Weller is content with his lot, since this is something the reader already knows. Instead, with Mr. Weller's inheritance the novel shows that he, too, must negotiate the same civil legal world to which Pickwick has just bowed. Sam stops Mr. Weller from burning the will that names him "eggzekiter" (executor), even though, as Mr. Weller points out, the affair is only between himself and Sam. As Sam informs his father, the will "must be proved, and probated, and swore to, and all manner o' formalities." In response to this information Mr. Weller conjures up the only court he is familiar with which figures money: "Ve'll have this here, brought afore the Solvent Court directly." Sam, ever the canny mediator between classes, then admonishes that Mr. Weller has "Old Baileys, and Solvent Courts, and alleybis, and ev'ry species o' gammon alvays a runnin' through his brain" (867). Yet Mr. Weller, of course, only knows the grim side of the law: civil law is largely for the propertied; criminal law mostly affects the poor. His "conviction that the Old Bailey was the supreme court of judicature in this country, and that its rules and forms of proceeding regulated and controlled the practices of all other courts of justice whatsoever" likewise makes sense (544). In marked contrast to Pickwick, Mr. Weller's problem is not that he feels the law is petty but just the opposite. In the final adventures of Mr. Weller class harmony is signaled in part by banishing the specter of the Old Bailey. All the characters are finally embraced by the middle class as the juridical subjects of their civil courts. The fairy-tale ending is not Weller's inheritance but his presentation at civil court.

The strange logic of *Pickwick* lying behind Weller's inheritance is that, though the central legal plot has realistically left out the working class, in order to have his ending provide resolution Dickens must imagine a codicil in which his working-class characters successfully negotiate the civil courts. It is as if Dickens makes a conflicted attempt to depict classlessness, though his fiction is best characterized by its attention to class. Yet concluding *Pickwick* with an imaginative cancellation of working-class concerns makes sense in a multitude of ways in light of the class anxiety operating behind the scenes upon Dickens himself. His own uneasy entrance into the labors of middle-class professionalism cannot help but find its way into this novel. *Pickwick* is producing Dickens as much as he is producing it, and this particular ending reveals just how over-determined the lawyers and civil courts have become for him and for this story.

Almost immediately Samuel Warren's *Ten Thousand a-Year* (serialized in *Blackwood's Magazine* from 1839 to 1841) confirmed the larger resonance of the creative intersection Dickens had discovered in *Pickwick*. *Ten Thousand a-Year* capitalized directly on *Pickwick*'s forensic structuring. Indeed, with its own "memorable action of *Doe on the demise of Titmouse* v. *Roe,*" Warren's story fed Victorian readers more elaborate legal detail and plot than any Dickens novel would ever dare. At one point, for instance, Warren interpolates a learned authorial "Note *concerning the law* of ERASURES *and* ESTOPPELS," and at another he reflexively imagines how a character (intriguingly named Mr. Pip) successfully "make[s] the interesting facts of the [newspaper's report of the Titmouse] case the basis of a new novel."[24] Here, as in its more famous self-comparisons to mirrors, was one of the Victorian novel's new favorite recursive, self-generating equations, which had so helped Dickens to see himself and his work.

IV

Why would Dickens find the courthouse a particularly apt place to explore the intersection of the form of the novel and his own middle-class professionalization? The answer does not lie in the history of law reform in the 1830s, which would seem to be an obvious context for *Pickwick*. Although Dickens has often been pictured as a crusader for legal reform, his legal scenes, in the last instance, are not attempts to intervene in politics or policy. *Pickwick* is not a novel with a purpose, a *roman à thèse,* any more than is *Bleak House,* which Dickens lamely defended for its anachronistic attack on a reformed and reforming Court of Chancery. For one thing, as we have seen, the legal forensics of *Pickwick* are freighted with other meanings, such as Dickens's own concurrent professionalization. Dickens is a novelist, and so perhaps the best way to describe him and his imaginative legal milieus is to say that, under the influence of experiences close to home, he "metamorphosizes" what he sees. When Dickens imaginatively traverses and creates a "world of law," he turns not so much to the abstract concerns, debates, and issues of contemporary legal

F I G . 3. Alfred Waterhouse, competition design for the Royal Courts of Justice. Royal Institute of British Architects, Library Photographs Collection

reform as to the palpable places, the human participants, and the daily relations and work of the legal world he has experienced. Hence, the sort of law reform which matters here is, in part, simply the actual production of both criminal and civil courthouses as central, city buildings. When in *Pickwick* Dickens finds that the study of the justice of the peace represents the eighteenth century and its style, he sets out to explore the new forum of the urban courthouse and legal district and his own era's style. In this way *Pickwick* belongs to the new age of the lawyered, urban courthouse.

It is no coincidence, then, that when Dickens was imagining *Pickwick*, other Victorians were imagining the most impressive courthouse ever built in England, the Royal Courts of Justice. They were moving in synchrony. As Dickens was writing his novel, the architectural debate and planning of London's immense Royal Courts were just beginning. Unlike *Pickwick*, the production of the Royal Courts subsequently took the greater part of the Victorian period. (The cathedral-like courthouse on the Strand finally opened for civil cases in

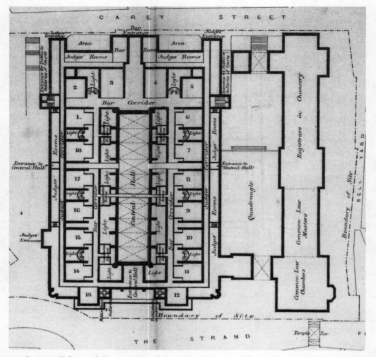

FIG. 4. George Edmund Street, *Royal Courts of Justice: Block Plan: Shewing the Courts, Judges' Rooms & Corridors, Bar Rooms & Corridors, Public Entrances, Etc.* Public Records Office, MPI 1/489

1882 and is still in use.) But by the 1830s the law courts had come to be seen as deserving a central, urban building in their own right, one to rival even parliament's palace.

The law courts had come a long way from their old place in Westminster Hall. There, as J. H. Baker notes, the superior courts had neither been closed off from a "throng of suitors, lawyers, shopkeepers, cutpurses [pickpockets] and sightseers in the body of the hall" nor divided from each other by screens until the eighteenth century.[25] (Only in 1739 were the Courts of Chancery and the King's Bench even placed on raised and enclosed platforms.)[26] When the nineteenth century began, courthouses, and not merely court spaces in parish town halls, were for the first time being built in significant numbers, and the Victorians eventually crowned this transformation of the modern cityscape with the Royal Courts of Justice. I think one unfulfilled conception of the courthouse done by Alfred Waterhouse as part of a design competition held in the 1860s particularly captures the sort of magical, symbolic place being imagined (see fig. 3).

As David Brownlee's study *The Law Courts* recounts, the Victorians also theorized the designs for the modern courthouse. This codification primarily involved the establishment "of wholly separate circulation patterns for the different types of people who might have business in the building."[27] The resulting maze of concentric corridors, typically circling around a central public hall, carefully built the trial's particular division of labor (such as judges, jury, and lawyers) into the courthouse space. Figures 4 and 5 illustrate the resulting complex, multilevel design of differentiated rooms, passageways, and entrances. The explicit object of this "principle of separation throughout the entire building" was, as Brownlee explains, simply administrative—to smooth the move-

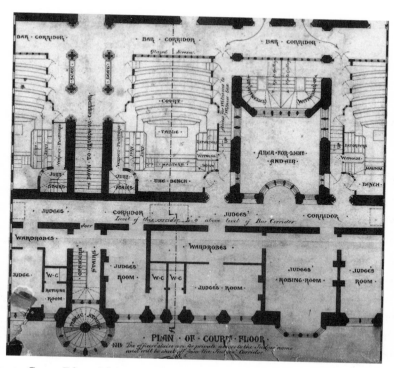

FIG. 5. George Edmund Street, *Royal Courts of Justice: Details of Common Law Courts.* Public Records Office, Work 30/2235

ment and functioning of the "legal professionals."[28] The shaping of the court-house building was part of the rise of the immense Victorian administrative machinery. Driving this particular architectural bureaucratization was the rise of middle-class professionals—specifically in this case, the rise of the middle-class lawyers, who had begun their surge in the previous century.

The Victorians eventually constructed the Royal Courts of Justice in a most pragmatic place: at the heart of the legal district, amid the centers of journalism and printing. The courts were not in the location on the Thames embankment which had been championed, in part, on aesthetic grounds. And, as Brownlee observes, they were not where they had been at "the beginning of the nine-teenth century, [when] the superior courts themselves were clustered in the vicinity of the royal Palace of Westminster . . . where their location reflected their origin as an extension of the King's personal judgment."[29] Neither were they any longer scattered, as they had been to a certain extent during the dec-ades of planning and building. Instead, they were erected in a single, gigantic building in the legal district, a short distance from the Central Criminal Court, which handled criminal cases (having replaced the Old Bailey in 1834). The move, like the designs of the courthouse, underscored the fact that the courts were firmly in the hands of middle-class professionals.

Caught up in this history is *Pickwick,* written just as "the discussion of the architectural component of law reform began in earnest in the 1830s"[30]—that is, with the lawyers in the midst of a solidification of the justice system which would signal their professional, middle-class control by literally reshaping the London landscape. Thus John Glavin can write aptly of *Pickwick* that it "wit-nesses the early nineteenth century's crucial transfer of male hegemony from an earlier to a later form of capitalist ideology, from a culture of 'commercial hu-manism' to the ideology of administration: lawyer-land."[31]

It need only be added that, in this trip through lawyer-land, the story of *Pickwick* also tacitly explores a novel-land. Dickens invests in this lawyer-land a displaced version of the story of *Pickwick* and of his own debut as a novelist, and, at the same time, he discovers in the Victorian legal world an answer to what he and his novel might be. *Pickwick* brings us news from the law courts of both a new middle-class, professional role for the author and a new Victorian structure for the novel.

CHAPTER FIVE

Mary Barton's Telltale Evidence

ELIZABETH GASKELL'S first novel, *Mary Barton* (1848), climaxes in a trial scene. John Barton, Mary's father, has assassinated a factory owner's son to protest the lethal conditions suffered by workers in Manchester. Jem Wilson, however, is mistakenly put on trial for the murder, which is attributed to a romantic rivalry over Mary between himself and the factory owner's son. At the heart of the novel is Mary's heroic trip to Liverpool, where she must find the only witness who can prove an alibi for her beloved Jem and then, secretly knowing her father is guilty, undergo the prosecution's examination at Jem's trial.

As even this brief summary suggests, the court scene explicitly unites the story's two major strands, interweaving class politics and romance. But it is clearly a mistake ever to think of these strands as separate, as if the tale could be divided between them, and "John Barton," the novel's working title, somehow separable from "Mary Barton," the novel's final title. Each functions as a palimpsest of the other. From the beginning of the story Gaskell intentionally juxtaposes personal and political, individual relations and socioindustrial ones, insisting on their inseparability and carefully plotting a story organized toward their crossover. Indeed, this intersection is Gaskell's stock in trade. Her later novel *North and South* (1854–55) contains a similar, climactic crossover scene

on the threshold of a factory owner's home, symbolically bracketing him between domestic and public spaces already cross-pollinated.

Mary Barton, then, raises the question of why, and how, the law court works
as this pivotal space in Gaskell's first story. As Hilary Schor has suggested,
Mary's public appearance as a witness in court illuminates Gaskell's own gendered public debut, reflecting a woman writer's confrontation with authorship
and authority.[1] Yet even Schor's shrewd explication provides only a hint of the
extent to which the law court, itself a tempered battleground for class conflict,
organizes this reflexive and purposeful story. This Victorian novel exemplifies
the difference between merely depicting a trial within a story and using the law
courts as an epistemological, cultural presence through and against which the
novel develops. Without ignoring *Mary Barton*'s very specific concerns—with
evidence, with testimony, and with contemporary Chartist politics—I want to
suggest that we can see in Gaskell's novel how the broader forensic literary history whose development we have been exploring across key novels may also
work within a novel.

I

In *Mary Barton* Jem Wilson's gun—the murder weapon—is the courtroom
exhibit that nearly hangs him. The gun (borrowed by John Barton) is the one
"found on the scene of the murder,"[2] and the prosecution produces it in court,
where Jem's grief-stricken mother reluctantly identifies it. Yet a more incrimi-
nating piece of physical evidence which would expose John Barton as the murderer circulates in this novel before the trial. The story of its suppression
reveals how Gaskell is striving to wield her novel as something like physical evidence of the dire situation in Manchester, effacing the borders between narrative, narrator, reader, the very book in the reader's hands, and the "real" world
in which her fiction exists.

Right from the opening of the novel, Gaskell's narrator calculatingly links
her fictional story to her readers' reality. So, you, the reader, must not be fooled
when, in the midst of describing the countryside outside Manchester in the
novel's first paragraph, Gaskell's narrator seems artlessly to interject the following comment addressed directly to "you": "You cannot wonder, then," says the
narrator, "that these fields are popular places of resort at every holiday time;

and you would not wonder, if you could see, or I properly describe" (2). This announcement might appear at a glance to be a clumsy admission of authorial inadequacy, but it is really quite the opposite. Having established her third-person omniscient narrator, Gaskell begins to stage an explicit engagement with the way that omniscient novelistic narrator creates a separation between her text and reality. The *I* and *you* call attention to that separation even as they mark the introduction of Gaskell's "engaging" narrator, who works "to bring together the worlds within and outside the fiction," as Robyn Warhol has argued.[3]

Using the special effects enabled by this self-referential narrator, Gaskell begins to plant some evidence. First, she carefully manipulates the way the novel handles the only two complete and lengthy texts that are incorporated into her story from outside sources. Both interpolated texts—a Manchester song and a poem by a radical—are, like the novel itself, artistic pieces concerned with the grim conditions of the working class, but, otherwise, they initially seem to have little to do with the story. As it turns out, what matters is not their specific message but the development of the relations between Gaskell's narrator, her reader, and the text which is constructed through their insertion.

As readers often notice, the narrator initially misleads her readers by titling the insertion of the Manchester song "The Oldham Weaver." A character has just called it "Th' Owdham Weaver," and Gaskell's contrasting title plays upon the reader's expectation that she will silently standardize the English of the worker's song. The text, however, goes on to render the song in the (difficult-to-read) vernacular. Gaskell thus distinguishes the workers' powerful dialect as an authentic language. (This lesson resonates throughout the novel in, for example, the authorizing of dialect words by footnotes. Gaskell, as Gillian Beer observes, presses "her middle class readers to *hear* and pay attention to living working class speech.")[4] In the midst of this prearranged jolt to her readers one also finds a seemingly frank and spontaneous commentary by her self-referential narrator introducing "you," the reader, to the song and announcing its re-inscription for us:

> "Margaret, thou must let Mary hear thee sing. I don't know about fine music myself, but folks say Marget is a rare singer, and I know she can make me cry at any time by singing 'Th' Owdham Weaver.' Do sing that, Marget, there's a good lass."

With a faint smile, as if amused at Alice's choice of song, Margaret began.

Do you know "The Oldham Weaver"? Not unless you are Lancashire born and bred, for it is a complete Lancashire ditty. I will copy it for you.

THE OLDHAM WEAVER

I

Oi'm a poor cotton-weyver, as mony a one knoowas,
Oi've nowt for t' yeat, an' oi've worn eawt my clooas, (37)

As Warhol points out, the text of this song is framed by reminders from the narrator that reading writing is what "you" are doing. The narrator's book-conscious declaration "I will copy it for you" not only recalls the moment of writing but even points to the "copy" in the reader's hands. Likewise, after the text of the song the narrator, concerned with the reception of the song's dialect, explicitly instructs the reader on how to read it: "To read it, it may, perhaps, seem humorous; but it is that humour which is near akin to pathos" (39). Less obviously, and more important, these reminders by her self-referential narrator, which amount to an explicit announcement of this first copying of a text, are tacitly preparing "you," her reader, for the next insertion of an outside text.

A bit further on in the novel the insertion of a poem by a radical appears within the story without similarly explicit commentary from the diegetic narrator, who merely relates that Job Legh "read aloud a little poem of Samuel Bamford's'" (127). The footnote is, however, Gaskell's. Identifying the source as *Passages in the Life of a Radical* with a laudatory comment, it corresponds to the narratorial explanation concerning the "Lancashire ditty" that was produced for the first insertion. Here, instead of addressing the reader from within the story, an editorial persona adds the secondary information. With the explicit discussion of the insertion of the text removed from the story, Mary's father asks a telling favor after Job recites the poem:

"Amen!" said Barton, solemnly and sorrowfully. "Mary! wench, couldst thou copy me them lines, dost think?—that's to say, if Job there has no objection."

"Not I. More they're heard and read the better, say I."

So Mary took the paper. And the next day, on a blank half sheet of a valentine, all bordered with hearts and darts—a valentine she had once suspected to come from Jem Wilson—she copied Bamford's beautiful little poem. (129)

This moment recalls the copying of the Lancashire song, the first insertion, which went on between narrator and reader—"I will copy it for you." Here, however, the copying goes on within the story. The reader is out of the frame, and the narrator follows the conventions of an ordinary omniscient narrator in a nineteenth-century, realistic novel and simply records the copying of the poem onto "the paper," "a blank half sheet of a valentine." This copying of a radical's poem onto a valentine has thematic resonance in a novel that insists both on the scarcity of goods for workers and the intersection between the political and the personal. Yet, for the moment, the detail of the valentine paper is like other material, realistic details provided by an omniscient narrator. It resides in a zone of silently observed background. At this point in the novel this piece of paper is something like the seemingly irrelevant presence of a barometer in Flaubert's narrator's description of a room, whose very irrelevance, as Roland Barthes argues in "L'Effet de Réel," creates the artistic illusion that reality is being directly reproduced.[5]

Gaskell, however, is wary of producing this sort of realism. We might compare, for instance, the moment when she first describes a room. There her self-referential narrator pointedly introduces a moment of self-conscious doubt about how to describe a certain type of table: "Opposite the fire-place was a table, which I should call a Pembroke, only that it was made of deal, and I cannot tell how far such a name may be applied to such humble material" (13). Such gentle intrusions make sense in this novel. Gaskell's concern, after all, is to raise her reader's awareness of the details of a part of this material world, and the novel otherwise conventionally separates and contains this material world in a sort of semiconscious, omniscient narratorial background. So, throughout the novel the narrator intermittently reminds the reader that she acts not as a distanced, hovering, omniscient, observing eyeball but as an active, eye-level describer of a real world.

More subtly and powerfully, however, Gaskell also weaves the reader's awareness of this material world into the story line. Specifically, the damning evidence of the assassination is the return of this "blank half sheet of a valentine" that has otherwise been unconsciously copied. Appropriately, Mary's aunt Esther, who has been called the "surrogate" narrator of the story,[6] first rediscovers this paper at the scene of the murder:

> Suddenly . . . she became aware of something white in the hedge. All other colours wore the same murky hue, though the forms of objects were perfectly distinct. What was it? It could not be a flower. . . . A frozen lump of snow . . . ? She stepped forward to examine. It proved to be a little piece of stiff writing-paper compressed into a round shape. She understood it instantly; it was the paper that had served as wadding for the murderer's gun. (274–75)

After the slow, dramatic materialization of the paper, Esther recognizes it "instantly" as gun wadding, but neither she nor the reader knows the evidence is a scrap of the valentine-poem paper. Although Esther rightly sees that the fragment of Mary Barton's name on the paper would surely involve Mary in the case, she mistakenly concludes that Jem Wilson is the murderer because Mary's name is in his handwriting. Esther does not realize that the paper itself implicates the murderer, not the writing on it, which only identifies the paper. She is enmeshed in a confusion over the relation of the text (what the words say) to its material existence (the handwriting seems to identify the piece of paper as Jem's).

In this state of turmoil Esther brings the paper to Mary, who will finish the "task of unravelling the mystery of the paper, and the handwriting" (284). She, along with the reader, completes the process of self-consciously recognizing it. As the narrator announces:

> I must tell you; I must put into words the dreadful secret which she believed that bit of paper had revealed to her.
> Her father was the murderer!
> That corner of stiff, shining, thick, writing paper, she recognised as a part of the sheet on which she had copied Samuel Bamford's beautiful lines so many months ago—copied (as you perhaps remember) on the blank part of a valentine. (286)

The paper continues its materialization in this passage. Mary discovers the stuff of the paper, its materiality as "stiff, shining, thick, writing paper." She must even fit it together with its other half, which she finds in her father's coat pocket, so that the letters on the paper are meaningful not as letters but as ink splotches, some of which have predictable shapes: "Yes, it fitted; jagged end to jagged end, letter to letter; and even the part which Esther had considered blank had its tallying mark with the larger piece, its tails of *y*s and *g*s" (287). At the same time, the self-referential narrator ("I must tell you; I must put into words") not only oversees the shift of the paper from its original existence in the narrator's province into the characters' consciousness ("she recognised . . ."), but also even into the reader's consciousness ("as you perhaps remember"). Gaskell thus forges a series of connecting bridges for her readers: taking a part of the narrative's material reality which had been a semiconscious background detail, she explicitly maneuvers it into consciousness.

Moreover, this "tell-tale paper" (289), the valentine turned radical poem turned gun wadding, tacitly doubles for another telltale paper; we have taken a step forward from the interpolation of other, actual aesthetic, political works ("The Oldham Weaver," Bamford's poem) and arrived at Gaskell's novel itself. The paper's trajectory might even seem to chart a condensed inversion of the telos of the story (wrongly but commonly) conceived of as moving from the politics of the factory workers' material conditions to the sentiment of Mary's personal romance. The paper, however, like the novel, resists categorization. Although the valentine–poem–gun wadding adds significations to Mary's revelation, it primarily moves her to act. Recognition of this piece of paper precipitates Mary's conversion into an active heroine; from this point until almost the end of the novel the story essentially recounts Mary's heroic struggles to protect both her father and her lover. More to the point, the narrator immediately links this moment of Mary's transformation to the reader's own conscious behavior. "Oh! I do think that the necessity for exertion, for some kind of action (bodily or mentally) in time of distress, is a most infinite blessing," the narrator exhorts (288), beginning the novel's longest and most didactic speech to the reader. As this address reveals, Mary's recognition performs in the relation between character and narrator the recognition that Gaskell hopes to invoke in her reader. Both telltale papers are part of a material world; both call for reaction, not just rumination.

Gaskell is writing with a nineteenth-century conception of her novel as a material work in her reader's hands, not as a bodiless text. (As Roland Barthes explains, "The difference is this: the work is a fragment of substance . . . the Text is a methodological field.")[7] And her concern is that her almost-immaterial words be connected to the material reality in which they exist and persist. The novel's connection to "your" own physical conditions while reading this story, right down to the book in our hands, plays a part in Gaskell's attempts to check the reader who might otherwise put her novel down with a self-satisfied sigh. Gaskell thus somewhat paradoxically raises her book's materiality as an idea represented in her text.

In so doing, she is not particularly concerned with the materiality of the text the way we often think of it today—the actual specifics of the surface of her work, such as the paper quality or the typeface. We are not really to worry about those severed tops and tails of *y*s and *g*s. Rather than actually manipulate her physical book, Gaskell uses her story to raise consciousness of its textual materiality. Here is how she depicts paper and font bearing meaning when Mary receives a subpoena: "Many people have a dread of those mysterious pieces of parchment. I am one. Mary was another. Her heart misgave her as she took it, and looked at the unusual appearance of the writing, which, though legible enough, conveyed no idea to her, or rather her mind shut itself up against receiving any idea, which after all was rather a proof she had some suspicion of the meaning that awaited her" (301). In this moment the material form of the message outdoes the message itself—the words—in delivering meaning. Gaskell, however, is portraying, not actively shaping, this materiality. She has both Mary and the narrator, with the reader in tow as well, move immediately to the fearful "idea" to which the font and type of paper point.

In contrast, Job will depict the problem of paying too much attention to the physiognomy of the text when he identifies this paper as a summons. He delightedly "turn[s] the parchment over with the air of a connoisseur" (302), ignoring the frightening and specific idea—that Mary will have to testify, that the trial is really going to occur—indicated by the appearance of this legal paper and typography. Gaskell thereby models for her own readers the notion that texts are part of the material world through Mary's response but also warns through Job's reaction that merely wallowing in the surface of the text's physical reality risks missing the point.

In a similar way Gaskell registers her novel's material production throughout the story. Through casual and infrequent interjections by the writing narrator (for example, "Very different to this lovely night in the country in which I am now writing." [290]), Gaskell vaguely points to the actual composition of her novel. Her intent is not to call attention to the economic or physical conditions of the novel's production, as, for instance, George Gissing does in *New Grub Street* (1891), but, again, to anchor her words in the material reality of her reader's world. For Gaskell her novel, like the paper evidence, is a bridge between words and the material world in which they exist.

The book in Gaskell's reader's hands is not simply a mimetic description of horrific working-class conditions; it is a (missing) piece of evidence connected to those conditions. It tells the real story, like the telltale paper within the novel which will never appear in the courtroom. And, just as the depicted physical paper accrues evidential meaning by being brought within the purview of the law courts—Mary "could swear to the paper anywhere" (286)—Gaskell's book has already metamorphosized through the legal trial it has yet to depict, defining for itself an evidentiary role in the determination of justice in class relations. Like all evidence, the book speaks "for" or "against." It informs, and in informing its purpose is served. Ultimately, within the story Mary "carrie[s] the paper down-stairs, and burn[s] it on the hearth, powdering the very ashes with her fingers, and dispersing the fragments of fluttering black films among the cinders of the grate" (289). This assiduous annihilation of the paper reminds us that it is physical evidence that can perform the unique act of condemning her father. But at another level—Mary will now be an active heroine—it emphasizes that the knowledge the physical paper evidence imparts is not an end in itself; it drives action.

Just what that knowledge is only becomes clear in light of another, different scrap of paper with which Gaskell has captivated her reader and constructed a paper chase. This other, multivalent piece of paper receives a dramatic and detailed introduction, worth quoting at length, when the factory owners meet with the striking workers:

> While the men had stood grouped near the door, on their first entrance, Mr. Harry Carson had taken out his silver pencil, and had drawn an admirable caricature of them—lank, ragged, dispirited, and famine-stricken. Underneath he wrote a hasty quotation from the fat knight's well-known speech in Henry IV. ["No eye hath seen such scarecrows."]

He passed it to one of his neighbours, who acknowledged the likeness instantly, and by him it was sent round to others, who all smiled, and nodded their heads. When it came back to its owner he tore the back of the letter on which it was drawn in two, twisted them up, and flung them into the fireplace; but, careless whether they reached their aim or not, he did not look to see that they fell just short of any consuming cinders.

This proceeding was closely observed by one of the men.

He watched the masters as they left the hotel (laughing, some of them were, at passing jokes), and when all had gone, he re-entered. He went to the waiter, who recognised him.

"There's a bit on a picture up yonder, as one o' the gentlemen threw away; I've a little lad at home as dearly loves a picture; by your leave I'll go up for it."

The waiter, good-natured and sympathetic, accompanied him up-stairs; saw the paper picked up and untwisted, and then being convinced, by a hasty glance at its contents, that it was only what the man had called it, "a bit of a picture," he allowed him to bear away his prize. (216–17)

Like the other, this piece of paper registers the complexity and intersection of seemingly different worlds. Before the worker, so carefully watched by the "sympathetic" waiter, retrieves it, the "letter" turned to a "caricature" has become paper itself, which is not even destroyed after it is torn, twisted, and thrown (almost) into the fire.

The persistence of this paper, with its representation of the callousness of the employers, will be fatal. At a meeting of the trade union the picture circulates and horrifies the working men, who see even their starvation parodied. John Barton gives a speech that calls for vengeance, and the paper recirculates once again:

A number of pieces of paper (the identical letter on which the caricature had been drawn that very morning) were torn up, and *one was marked.* Then all were folded up again, looking exactly alike. They were shuffled together in a hat. The gas was extinguished; each drew out a paper. The gas was re-lighted. Then each went as far as he could from his fellows, and examined the paper he had drawn without saying a word, and with countenance as stony and immovable as he could make it.

Then, still rigidly silent, they each took up their hats and went every one his own way.

He who had drawn the marked paper had drawn the lot of the assassin! (223–24)

This piece of paper, the "marked" piece, the ripped-up letter-picture from which the men draw lots, is the paper that should have served as gun wadding: the assassin, after all, self-consciously walks away with it.

Why the substitution of one piece for another? One answer might be that through the substitution Gaskell signals an exchange of papers, the literal replacement of one representation with another. The domestic valentine turned into a poem, which recognizes the plight of the poor, replaces a (business?) letter turned into a callous depiction of the workers. Given that the valentine–poem becomes gun wadding, that switch would seem to run against the grain of this novel's social conscience, except perhaps as a warning of what might happen if the signs on that paper (indicating the humanity of the workers, their protest against their lot) are ignored. Perhaps the most that can be said in the way of solving the exchange is that the different papers originally circulate in the two separate linguistic and material worlds of prosperity and poverty, Benjamin Disraeli's "two nations." The crossing over of middle-class representations is thus depicted as inevitable (paper persists) and dangerous to her middle-class readers. They would do better to pay attention to the working-class's representations, lest they become the paper for gun wadding. Yet even this oversimplifies. The transformation of paper into evidence insists on the presence and technology of paper itself, whether used as the almost-invisible background for ink, torn up to draw lots, packed for gun wadding, or burned. As these pieces of paper move and change use, portable, recyclable, disposable, and more, they exceed traditional ideational symbolic solutions. The pieces of paper, instead, call forth a response—a deadly response in the case of the letter–caricature–token and ultimately a lifesaving response in the case of the valentine–poem–gun wadding. Gaskell gently corrals her readers forward with two overdetermined, imaginary pieces of paper and ink in her struggle against the limiting paper boundaries of the novel as a form.

In *Mary Barton,* then, Gaskell's telltale paper book is a facet of the form of her art which she can turn into content. So, while the art of her novel succeeds when her readers close off the outside world and become entranced by her story, they must also paradoxically open themselves up to that outside world in absorbing her art. The catalyst for this process is Gaskell's evocation within her story of the epistemology of the law court, which allows her to transform paper and ink into evidence and creates the novel's complex and political self-reflection upon its own link to reality. As I mentioned earlier, even before we reach the central trial scene, this story is tacitly guiding our reading of it in terms of the law court as another framework for true, and not fictional, stories—in this case, as one in which objects testify. The trial will draw this design out even further.

II

Readers of the novel will recall that after Mary Barton burns the paper evidence she realizes she must not only protect her father but also rescue her lover, Jem, who is wrongfully accused but will not incriminate her father. Recognizing that Jem "must have been somewhere else when the crime was committed; probably with some others, who might bear witness to the fact, if she only knew where to find them," she sets out to find out if "an *alibi* . . . might mean the deliverance she wished to accomplish" (291).

In the text the word *alibi* always appears in italic type, as it customarily did throughout most of the nineteenth century, to indicate its status as a foreign, Latin word. Aligned with Mary, the reader may also begin to see this italicized *alibi* as extrinsic, suggesting the "elsewhere" not just of the accused but of the courtroom itself. For Mary her physical journey to the courtroom turns into a trip toward the courtroom as an alternate space of storytelling. The "alibi" is the real story that Mary strives to ensure is told in court, while for the reader the novel at this point becomes the story of reconstructing an alibi—a story about the makings of a forensic story. Later this alibi will barely materialize in the court scene. The reader is told merely that Jem's cousin Will Wilson "told the story you know so well" (389). In part its ghostly presence in court reflects that the fact that this alibi is, like all alibis, a kind of antistory, a story canceling another story. Also, however, as "the story you know so well," the alibi points us straight back to the novel, like the fleeting echo of a novel listening to itself through the court.

In a larger sense this legal inflecting of her speech, in which the court acts like an echo-chamber, serves as one of the primary ways Gaskell fashions this novel. Unlike Dickens, who discovers the forum of his novel in part by depicting the forum of the court, Gaskell puts this relationship to work, drawing attention to the boundary between courtroom and novel. Her trial scene is certainly not merely about the suspense of awaiting a verdict; to the horror of some readers the chapter title proclaims: "THE TRIAL AND VERDICT—'NOT GUILTY!'" (372). Instead, it complicates the goal Gaskell has claimed in her preface of trying "to write truthfully" (xxxvi). "The truth, and the whole truth" (379) of the courtroom obviously represents a different means to truth than that of the novel, and, specifically for Gaskell, the depiction of a trial scene offers a parallel, but different, space of representation which productively throws into relief the formal and stylistic boundaries of her novel as verbal act and artifice.

The beginning of *Mary Barton*'s trial scene sets the stage. The narrator initially draws a straightforward comparison between the reader and the courtroom spectators: "The circumstances of the murder, the discovery of the body, the causes of suspicion against Jem, were as well known to most of the audience as they are to you, so there was some little buzz of conversation going on among the people" (376). But in this "little buzz of conversation," consisting of a series of anonymous quotations, the courtroom spectators can only shallowly speculate on the characters' physical appearances. The narrator then returns to voice and sympathize with the reader's actual disjunction from the court spectators: "Poor Jem! His raven hair . . . was that, too, to have its influence against him?" (377). As in Dickens's depiction of Fagin's trial in *Oliver Twist,* the narrator constructs the reader's perspective by contrasting it with that of the courtroom spectators' purely visual perspective. Unlike Dickens, however, Gaskell has first carefully pointed out the similarities between reader and spectator. This strange shift from defining the reader as essentially another courtroom spectator to defining the reader in opposition to the courtroom spectators emphasizes the differences between the two spaces of storytelling, exposing both the novel's and the court's limits. We are made aware of two interlocking views of the story. Gaskell can thereby point to what she sees as a truth that lies beyond the conventions structuring either of their generic limits—or, rather, she can harness these limits to express her meaning.

At the trial Mrs. Wilson's testimony concerns exactly this sort of limit, the problem of the courtroom's concept of the "whole truth." When she must incriminate her son by identifying his gun, she dramatically asks him, "What mun I say?" He replies, "Tell the truth, mother" (378). Mrs. Wilson concludes, however, by protesting the codes of representing "truth" in the courtroom: "'And now, sir, I've telled you the truth, and the whole truth, as *he* bid me; but don't ye let what I've said go for to hang him; oh, my lord judge, take my word for it, he's as innocent as the child as has yet to be born. For sure, I, who am his mother, and have nursed him on my knee, . . . ought to know him better than yon pack of fellows' (indicating the jury . . .) 'who, I'll go bail, never saw him before this morning in all their born days'" (379).

Because the reader knows Jem is innocent, Mrs. Wilson's humorously accurate accusation that the jury "never saw him before this morning" carries some weight. By extension the reader must acknowledge her protest against the methods the court uses to arrive at the truth. Most obviously, Mrs. Wilson objects that she has been forced to articulate words invested with someone else's aim— "the whole truth, as *he* bid me; but don't ye let what I've said go for to hang him." Gaskell thus has Mrs. Wilson expose the seemingly passive, descriptive process of witnessing as consisting of speech acts, even as she calls attention to the distortions imposed by the question-and-answer truth-telling format of the court.[8] By then having Mrs. Wilson swear figuratively and tragicomically that "[she]'ll go bail" at the very moment she protests the court's rules, Gaskell further gently puts us in mind that those rules are filters for reality even outside the court and that truth does not just depend on context but carries its contexts with it.

Gaskell goes on to portray Will Wilson, the final witness, in opposition to Mrs. Wilson. Will understands the rules of the courtroom only too well. He cannot be stopped until he has assumed the role of a narrator in the court, meaning (for Gaskell) that he is "telling his tale in the witness-box, the legitimate place" (387). He replies to the lawyer's accusation that he is a paid witness by pointing more accurately to the lawyer as the one being paid to talk. Returning impudence for impudence, as Job, who also understands the unwritten rules of the court, has earlier advised Mary to do (302), Will clears Jem. In contrast to Mrs. Wilson, Will is able to use his words to good effect. Yet, although Will's words change the court's verdict, bearing out the power of testimonial evidence to effect material change, his testimony has been orchestrated by the love and work of Mary and only establishes the local facts.

Gaskell makes it clear that Will has merely conformed to the trial's procedures, a man manipulating the male-controlled space of the court. He has used words to convey necessary facts. Mrs. Wilson has provided heartfelt caring. According to the novel, each alone is finally inadequate. Mary's confessional words of love for Jem, spoken aloud to the court but directed to Jem (who does not yet know she loves him), combine the two; she provides both a surprising truth in the court and the long-awaited revelation of the novel's romantic plot. Although Mary's testimony has little bearing on the verdict—as a lawyer says, her "evidence would not be much" (311)—it stands as the centerpiece of the trial scene and the novel, framed between these two depictions of different approaches to the court, both of which focus on the court's rules of storytelling.

Unlike either Mrs. Wilson or Will, Mary neither rejects nor adapts to the courtroom's rules. This independence is not surprising; her journey to the courtroom has been a willful self-construction as heroine. As her earlier dramatic boat ride suggests, she has literally and metaphorically fought her way against the tide. At the trial, her testimony, expected to be a mere public repetition of the known, of so-called reality, disrupts the conventional plotting of reality anticipated by her audience. The narrator explicitly warns us that this disruption is approaching: "Old Mr. Carson felt an additional beat at his heart at the thought of seeing the fatal Helen . . . for you see it was a fixed idea in the minds of all, that the handsome, bright, gay, rich young gentleman must have been beloved in preference to the serious, almost stern-looking smith, who had to toil for his daily bread" (380). The courtroom spectators here may have their individual perspectives, but these perspectives are all blinkered by formulaic assumptions ("the fatal Helen," "a fixed idea"). Gaskell presumably sees the same predicament in her own audience, and Mary's testimony can thus both model and make real the type of speech act which Gaskell envisions her novel to be for her audience.

Just as Gaskell situates her book vis-à-vis material evidence, gaining pressure and meaning from its prooflike presence, she here promotes a similar channeling of her novel through testimonial evidence. Mary Barton's legitimate establishment of herself (albeit reluctantly) as a heroine to the public at the trial represents, within the novel, what the novel is attempting to do for *its* public. In this respect Hilary Schor quite rightly sees that Gaskell meaningfully places Mary in the role of narrator: Mary, like the author Gaskell, negotiates becoming a public figure and gives evidence for a differently plotted reality. In Schor's view, however, the court operates simply as a convenient mirror, the metaphoric equivalent of depicting a woman writing a novel. In reality the uneven parallels between the courtroom and the storytelling of the novel enable Gaskell not only to reflect on herself as author but also to imbue her novel with a testimonial form, as serious and "real" as that which might be told in court.

Indeed, one way to understand the onset of Mary's delirium after her testimony is as a dramatization of the logical breakdown that occurs when Gaskell mixes together two different narrative epistemologies—the law court's and the novel's. The result is a crisis of narration. First, in an odd moment the narrator herself abdicates, declaring: "I was not there myself; but one who was, told me" (381). Immediately thereafter, as a reflection not of her weakness but, rather, of the heroic communicative power she has expended on the stand, Mary becomes delirious: "Mary never let go her clutched hold on the rails. She wanted them to steady her, in that heaving, whirling court. . . . [I]t was such pain, such weary pain in her head, to strive to attend to what was being said. They were all at sea, sailing away on billowy waves, and every one speaking at once, and no one heeding her father, who was calling on them to be silent, and listen to him" (385).

As Schor has noted, Mary's physical reaction in the courtroom recalls her earlier trip up the river to catch the sailing ship departing with Will Wilson; in the court she experiences a ship full of narrators steering in different directions on a linguistic ocean. Moreover, if the day before she was grimly heroic (enduring, for instance, a young boy's condescending wish to show off the town's stock exchange in the midst of her frenzied chase after Will's boat), now her story is blandly recast as a clichéd romance novel within the court: "A gallant tar brought back from the pathless ocean by a girl's noble daring" (388). The key to Mary's madness, and perhaps even the narrator's strange absence, may lie in this multilayered overlapping of novel with court: a certain wobbliness arises when those incompatible enframings of this story confront each other head on.

More important, however, what this way of seeing the central trial scene particularly brings out is how at this moment the novel and the trial overlap as storytelling forums that both hinge upon—and here come unhinged by—the suppression of another, truly absent narrator: John Barton, "her father, who was calling on them to be silent, and listen to him" (385). It is a central juncture. For both novel and law court their claims to truth telling turn out to be built on the suppression of John Barton's self-justification of the assassination he has committed.

I will come back to this crucial suppression in a moment, but for now we may observe that in the trial scene, the oppressive secret knowledge that her father has committed the murder and has a very different story to tell about it makes some sense of Mary's complicated, demented "repetition of the same words over and over again": "I must not go mad. I must not, indeed. They say people tell the truth when they're mad; but I don't. I was always a liar. I was, indeed; but I'm not mad. I must not go mad. I must not, indeed" (387). Presumably, Mary "must not go mad" in part simply because if she does she might accidentally reveal her father as the murderer. On another plane, however, Mary plunges us here into all-too-sane questions about the truth-telling properties of speech with which the trial has been concerned. Like the mad Caleb in the original ending of *Caleb Williams*, Mary has abandoned the parallel distinctions that suggest truth opposes lies as reason opposes madness. She points out that these binaries are easily and commonly reversed, aligning truth and madness: "They say people tell the truth when they're mad." Pursuing this logic, however, Mary strangely rejects the possibility that her madness will bring out the truth with the words *I don't* by declaring she "was always a liar." Her words are ambiguous but meaningful in the aftermath of her performance as the novel's narrator. One formulation, that she tells the truth by lying, recalls Gaskell's own project, her "truthful" documentarylike fiction making. The other, that truth telling requires a coherence and sanity that involve a lying, unfaithfulness to reality, touches on the axiom coiled within all realistic novels: not that they tell the truth by lying but that lying, that fiction making, is always a part of telling the truth.

In terms of the unfolding formal concerns about novelistic speech and evidence, testimonial and physical, Mary's mental whirl after her testimony in court thus represents something of an overheated climax. In terms of the plot, however, it tolls the downbeat after the novel's climax, signaling the beginning of the story's denouement. Mary's breakdown after her testimony in the trial marks her finish as the novel's active heroine. From then on she cedes control to the male characters. In fact, as portended by the anonymous male spectator at the trial who ostensibly informs the suddenly absent narrator of what happened, the novel's focus also shifts to its potential effect upon its audience of male industrial management, and Gaskell wraps up for them the question of class justice, still unaddressed by this trial after its official legal conclusion.

In a rather blunt manner the novel goes on to show a figurative conclusion to the trial by depicting how Mr. Carson, the factory owner, discovers and judges the truth about his son's murder. Focusing on Mr. Carson, the only developed middle-class character besides the narrator, the scene shifts to his mind as the real judge's chambers, with the novel becoming a kind of higher court of appeals. Where are those characters who represent the working class, Mary and John Barton? John Barton is soon dead, and as Raymond Williams correctly declares of the ending, "All are going to Canada; there could be no more devastating conclusion." Yet it is not, as Williams continues, that "a solution within the actual situation might be hoped for, but the solution with which the heart went was a cancelling of the actual difficulties and the removal of the persons pitied to the uncompromised New World."[9] This novel intentionally gives the reader some healing closure for its ground-down working-class heroes and their sad story but not for the situation in Manchester which produced it, where nothing is yet settled. This didactic novel does not offer solutions; it aspires to create (middle-class) readers who have formed a judgment based on the evidence of working-class oppression it presents.[10]

In a conspicuous step-by-step sequence Mr. Carson walks through the production of this judgment. After Jem's trial he implacably determines to begin legal proceedings against the dying John Barton, despite Barton's voluntary confession to him and tearful plea for forgiveness. Witnessing an incident of forgiveness between children of different classes in the street in which the police are pointedly avoided—"Nurse won't call a policeman, so don't be frightened" (434)—Mr. Carson returns home and rereads "the Gospel." The narrator then reports succinctly: "He shut the book, and thought deeply" (436). Having seen a model for behavior and been moved by his reading, Mr. Carson changes his mind and forgives John Barton, who dies in his arms. Gaskell thus presents Mr. Carson's verdict, and by extension her reader's, as dependent upon the observation of exemplary behavior and a shift from recognizing the meaning of a text to acting upon that meaning. She illustrates, with an almost religious tract–style clarity, the construction of sympathy for the working class which the earlier part of her book has presumably stirred in her reader. The process completes in a final tribunal scene that takes place, appropriately, in Mr. Carson's library. There he is turned from his cross-examination of Job and Jem, as they testify about John Barton and his difficulty with the masters, toward an empathetic judgment that extends his support to the workers as part of his own interest. Having modeled how reading can elicit sympathy (and, one might add, represented a physical book taking its effect), Gaskell figures the power of testimonial words to transform social positions and material relations. One speech act leads to another, and improvements, we are told, are subsequently produced by the "short earnest sentences spoken by Mr. Carson" (458).

The narrator's earlier advice to the reader—"it is for you to judge" (26)—turns out to be, not surprisingly, disingenuous. Mr. Carson presents the judgment for which *Mary Barton* is striving to be evidence. But what is interesting about this ending as a pronounced extension and resolution of the legal trial is that at the close of the book we discover that even the seemingly incidental realistic depictions of working-class life of the beginning are to be connected to the story's central depiction of a law court, as if the court scene somehow quietly but meaningfully neighbors every event and detail told. During and after the climactic trial scene it becomes clear that the trial is not simply a scene in this novel; it is more like the scene *of* the novel, inflecting the entire speech act Gaskell wishes to perform by threading the novel back through the law courts. In purely formal terms a sustaining interplay between the novel and the law courts underlies Gaskell's construction of her novel such that—to borrow Michael McKeon's apposite description of dialectical relations—"'unity' and 'difference' are kept simultaneously before our eyes."[11] This novel is meaningfully like and unlike the law courts it depicts, as Gaskell specifically constitutes our reading in terms of evidence and testimony.

This formal structure, moreover, makes historical sense. For the novel thereby actively participates in the contemporary Chartist movement with which it is concerned. This connection may not be immediately obvious to readers today: Chartism, the world's first working-class movement, now most likely conjures up images of crowds, of organized marches on parliament like the one John Barton attends, and of massive signed petitions calling for the six-point political charter to be accepted, not of trials. But in the decade before this novel's publication the trials of Chartists garnered the same sort of electric attention as their meetings and protests. For *Mary Barton's* contemporary readers the story's central trial would have registered directly with John Barton's Chartist and trade union politics.

When Gaskell addressed mistaken accusations from an upset family that she had fictionalized the story of an actual murder, she naturally and pointedly assumed precisely this context for her novel. Writing apologetically but firmly to the family that she "had heard of young Mr. Ashton's murder at the time when it took place; but . . . knew none of the details, nothing about the family, never read the trial," she adds: "It's [*sic*] occurrence, and that of one or two similar cases at Glasgow at the time of a strike, were, I have no doubt, suggestive of the plot, as having shown me to what lengths the animosity of irritated workmen would go."[12] The Glasgow trials to which she refers were those of cotton spinners, whose trade union struck in the winter of 1836–37, amid widespread starvation. The trial of their strike leaders for the murder of a blackleg worker was a key early catalyst to the Chartist movement: the first trial seen as a national concern.

By 1848, when *Mary Barton* was published, the history and identity of Chartism would be indissociable from its legal trials. In 1839 a large number of court cases followed on the conviction of Joseph Rayner Stephens (a Lancashire preacher against the New Poor Law) which marked the onset of a judicial disciplining of the Chartist movement. As Dorothy Thompson recounts: "By the autumn of 1839 nearly all the leaders of Chartism were either in prison or on bail awaiting trial."[13] While Chartist protests produced leaders and resulted in trials, trials themselves generated protests and brought leaders into national focus. At the beginning of 1840 those deemed responsible for the Newport uprising were tried (sentenced to death, they were later transported). Shortly thereafter, trials of ordinary participants in the movement became ubiquitous. Thompson reports that in 1842 "more people were arrested and sentenced for offences concerned with speaking, agitating, rioting and demonstrating than in any other year [of the nineteenth century]."[14] This mass movement passed through the law courts. Asa Briggs computes that, "taking the years from 1839 to 1848 as a whole, more than 3,500 Chartists were tried (some of them more than once)."[15] This staggering number includes Chartism's leader, Feargus O'Connor, who dramatically defended himself in trials for seditious libel in 1840 (which he lost) and seditious conspiracy in 1843 (in which he prevailed).

Briggs comments: "For the authorities . . . the trials were more than instruments of repression: they opened a window on Chartism, enabling an assessment of the extent of the 'Chartist threat.' For the Chartists themselves, the trials provided an opportunity for self-justification."[16] It is precisely this two-way view through the law court which is denied in *Mary Barton*. John Barton is *not* legally tried for his political assassination. No wonder Mary deliriously imagines in court there is "no one heeding her father, who was calling on them to be silent, and listen to him." Instead, the novel steps in, as it were, to both provide a window on the working classes and render their testimony.

The false accusation that Jem has committed the murder removes John Barton's charged political trial back to the homes of those concerned, allowing specific, private individual relations to intervene in abstract class animosity, just as the trial itself explicitly brings ordinarily private relations into the public realm of which they are already part. Thus, Mr. Carson, the factory owner whose son has been murdered, enters sympathetically into the Chartist John Barton's personal experience and vice versa, making them "brothers in the deep suffering of the heart" (431). Master comforts workman in a deathbed reconciliation scene; end of novel. What Gaskell pointedly has not done is rehash another polarizing Chartist or trade union trial.

As a result, the novel may seem to provide a superficial, apolitical answer to the vivid economic distress it initially evokes. A deathbed reconciliation may appear a fanciful resolution to an otherwise unresolved, real-life class conflict. We know and understand that the problems plaguing the working class in Manchester are part of the industrialization of England. Some economic change to the contemporary laissez-faire capitalist system might help; in *Mary Barton* we seem to get, as Raymond Williams respectfully despairs, "the characteristic humanitarian conclusion": "Efforts at improvement and mutual understanding."[17]

This economically oriented view, however, misapprehends the politics of *Mary Barton* in its time. From the perspective of the Chartists, as Gareth Stedman Jones has argued, the causes of their distress were essentially *political*, not economic.[18] The Chartists overwhelmingly saw themselves as living at the end of a long history of governmental tyranny. From eighteenth-century Enclosures Acts depriving the poor of their livelihood to the aid afforded southern paupers to migrate to northern industry, they were at the mercy of a state that controlled the economy, not at the mercy of industrial economic forces whose power centers the state simply reflected. Moreover, since the 1832 reform act the middle class had direct political power. The working classes were now for the first time isolated in their official disenfranchisement. Their Charter and protests were thus directed, in a long-standing English radical tradition, against the ruling state. The Charter calls for reform of parliament and, most important, for the vote for the working classes. Yet, by the time Gaskell was writing *Mary Barton,* the possibility of changing government was clearly a lost cause. The petitioning of the House of Commons had failed signally: in 1839 the House voted 235 to 46 against considering the petition; in 1842 the vote was 287 to 49; and in 1848, the year of the novel's publication, its possibility was simply ridiculed. If Gaskell sought justice for the working classes, she would have to outflank purely legislative politics. Besides, Benjamin Disraeli had already expertly told the parliamentary-political story of trade unions and Chartism in *Sybil* (1845).[19]

Gaskell thus seized upon a different political side to the story: the judicial. Her novel does not sidestep John Barton's trial; it absorbs and redirects its political energies. By the end of the novel John Barton may not have publicly explained the political and social dimensions of his act, but the novel has in ways he never could. Moreover, by engaging an epistemology of witnessing throughout her story and placing the narrative arena of the court at its heart, Gaskell gains as a fundamental premise of her novel the notion that part of the political problem lies at the level of language and storytelling. The depicted trial centers a novel that, as Catherine Gallagher has shown, works hard to expose how "contrasting narrative forms" become "conventional ways of organizing reality," political ruts.[20]

At the same time, the novel's judicial framework, with its pervasive trope of witnessing and providing evidence, is of a piece with the Chartist agenda itself. Chartist leader Bronterre O'Brien opened an early discussion of petitions (in this case one concerning the 1834 Poor Law) as follows:

I would recommend that instead of petitioning for a mere repeal of the Act, we should petition—

"THAT THE POOR OF ENGLAND SHALL BE HEARD BY COUNCIL AT THE BAR OF THE HOUSE OF COMMONS, AGAINST THE LATE TYRANNICAL AND INHUMAN ENACTMENT, MISCALLED THE POOR-LAW AMENDMENT ACT."

A petition of this sort, accompanied to the House by 200,000 people, and headed by all the popular leaders of good repute throughout the country, would be worth ten thousand petitions of the ordinary kind. Mr. Feargus O'Connor, who first suggested the idea to me, would make a capital counsel on the occasion. Few are better acquainted with the feelings of the poor and with their legal rights as subjects.[21]

O'Brien asks not for majority votes and divisions but to testify and to prove his case.

We can hear the same epistemology of the law court undergirding *Mary Barton*'s political history: "So a petition was framed, and signed by thousands in the bright spring days of 1839, imploring Parliament to hear witnesses who could testify to the unparalleled destitution of the manufacturing districts" (97–98). Gaskell's novel's political edge lies in providing such testimony to the conditions of the working classes. Nor, as we have seen, does she present this evidence naively. Truth within this novel is understood as a constructed thing, not an a priori category. As Gaskell commented to Mary Ewart in 1848: "I wanted to represent the subject in the light in which some of the workmen certainly consider to be *true,* not that I dare to say it is the abstract absolute truth."[22] We must not be misled because the novel's witnesses to working-class struggles, including the narrator as well as the characters, appear ingenuous: Gaskell's presentation, if sometimes heavy-handed, is ultimately percipient. But this is not surprising: the realism of Victorian novels is as patently designed as the physical organization of the law courts.

III

Always the open-eyed realist, Gaskell weaves into *Mary Barton* a self-consciousness about the law courts' historic import to her literary project, showing just how her novel fits into that larger marketplace in which the materials of state justice are transformed into print products. At several points in the story a minor character, Sally Leadbitter, provocatively declares that Mary Barton— and by implication *Mary Barton*—is produced from and by the trial the novel depicts. Predicting the effect of the trial, Sally says, "Really, Mary, you'll turn out quite a heroine" (324). Even more sharply, she informs Mary after the trial: "You can't hide it now, Mary, for it's all in print" (421).

The "print" to which Sally Leadbitter refers is actually the newspapers. What Dickens's Mr. Pickwick only imagines when he laments that through "the reports of the trial in those confounded papers" strangers "have heard all about" him is true in *Mary Barton* (543). The newspapers turn Mary into a heroine. As Sally Leadbitter jealously reports, "Why! it was in the *Guardian*,—and the *Courier*,—and some one told Jane Hodgson it was even copied into a London paper. You've set up heroine on your own account, Mary Barton." Only a "miserable notoriety," however, is actually produced by the press accounts of the trial (422), and Sally's understanding of Mary's situation is, we learn, dulled by her newspaperlike view: having "looked [Mary] over and over (a very different thing from looking her through and through) . . . would make Sally into a Gazette Extraordinary the next morning" (323–24). In contrast, readers are, we understand, seeing Mary "through and through." Gaskell's reasoning in relation to the depicted trial is plain enough: having admitted a parallel between the newspapers and her novel, she stakes out the alternative to the newspapers which she sees her novel providing.

She similarly registers the presence of criminal broadsheets that the conjunction of novel and newspaper have all but replaced. Shortly after "the idea of Jem on the gallows, Jem dead, took possession of Mary" (268), Mary Barton and *Mary Barton* stumble quickly past "halfpenny broadsides, giving an account of the bloody murder, the coroner's inquest, and a raw-head-and-bloody-bones picture of the suspected murderer, James Wilson" (269). As a preoccupied Mary Barton's indifference to the broadside hints, this textual doppelgänger is more inadequate than even Sally's newspapers. The criminal broadsheet's momentary intrusion merely confirms its irrelevance. It marks what the novel is not. (*Mary Barton* assumes what Caleb's extended encounter with "The Wonderful and Surprising Adventures of Caleb Williams" established.) In Gaskell the broadsheet is only a reminder of the still-lingering presence of gallows literature, and that genre's concern with the violent physical movement leading to its criminal subject's dramatic bodily death—"bloody . . . bloody"—powerfully contrasts with *Mary Barton*'s avoidance of the bloody assassin's scene. "Let us leave him," announces the narrator when John Barton sets out to commit the murder (233).

Neither reference to competing forms of publication, newspapers or criminal broadsheets, is in itself very important to Gaskell's story. Rather, their presence suggests how novels often recapitulate in their contents the established literary-historical relationships of which they are a product. Earlier ideological narrative paradigms, such as that of the gallows broadsheet, not only persist alongside newer developments in actuality; they show within the historical memory of the novel as well. Gaskell's text can be read as a record of transition as well as a part of the evolving, knotted history of the crime novel. (This way of looking at novels is an implicit part of the approach I have taken throughout this book.)

Important for us, then, Gaskell's novel also records a new threat to its governing juridical narrative paradigm: police detective fiction. The police are first mentioned by John Barton early in the novel as an unfamiliar and modern presence (9). Later, they are the focus of a brief episode in which a disguised detective easily tricks poor Mrs. Wilson into identifying her son's gun. The "officer of the Detective Service" walks away disappointed that his sleuthing skills have not been tested: "he liked an attempt to baffle him" (261). Mrs. Wilson has simply, trustingly answered his questions. It is a sad scene that at once unmasks the aims of the new policing authority and the sort of narrative perspective Gaskell feels they epitomize. Gaskell herself decodes it for us as such, writing damningly of the detective's "pleasure in unravelling a mystery, in catching at the gossamer clue which will guide to certainty. This feeling, I am sure, gives much impetus to the police. Their senses are ever and always on the qui-vive, and they enjoy the collecting and collating evidence, and the life of adventure they experience; a continual unwinding of Jack Sheppard romances, always interesting to the vulgar and uneducated mind, to which the outward signs and tokens of crime are ever exciting" (258–59). Not only is the possibility of treating John Barton's crime as a mystery to be solved repugnant to the politics of the novel; the very form of detective fiction, then just murkily emerging, is here summarily condemned. Just as we may see the novel is neither gallows literature nor newspaper, we also could not go further wrong than to label Mary a detective or this crime story an early detective novel.[23]

Better to notice—as we did with *Pickwick*—the explicit way that *Mary Barton* is historically situated vis-à-vis the Victorian law courts. Indeed, a reader might well ask why the central episode in a novel subtitled "A Tale of Manchester Life" involves a journey to a Liverpool courthouse. The simple answer is that, given the novel is pointedly of documentary-level realism, for such a serious crime Jem must be tried at the assizes, and Manchester did not yet have its own assize court. Liverpool was its assize town. Had Jem's trial taken place roughly two decades later, it would then have been properly set in Manchester—specifically, at the Manchester Assize Courts, one of the most famous and important law courts constructed in the Victorian era (see fig. 6).

Called unabashedly "the best law courts in the world" by the *Times*, the design by Alfred Waterhouse was the forerunner of the Royal Law Courts in London, discussed in the previous chapter.[24] Using innovations developed by John Soane, Harvey Lonsdale Elmes, and Charles Barry, Manchester's Assize Courts first successfully realized the architectural specialization of the courthouse's circulation around the participants in court procedure.[25] There were separate entrances, corridors, and rooms for each role, and roles were often further subdivided by gender and specific subclassifications (such as defense and prosecution). No less than ten doorways led into each courtroom, including, as Waterhouse reported to the Royal Institute of British Architects, "two doors on the upper floor leading to the ladies galleries above; one for the judge from his retiring-room; another for the grand jury; another for the common jurors, connecting their box with their retiring room; another for the barristers; another under the Bench, and not shewn on the ground plan, for witnesses; another for the more respectable portion of the public and those having business at the Courts, and two others opposite the Bench for the 'greasy' public."[26] Prisoners came up from communicating cells below each court directly into the dock. Such a courthouse design physically organized the participants' segregation and convergence as the narratological epistemology of the judicial process dictated (see fig. 7). Trial narratives were not produced within this space; they were a part of it. Here was the solidification of a juridical architecture—a structured set of interrelations for storytelling—which novels had been and were increasingly shaped against.

FIG. 6. Alfred Waterhouse, *Manchester Assize Courts: View from the South,* from *Papers Read at the Royal Institute of British Architects, Session 1864–65.* Courtesy of the Frances Loeb Library, Graduate School of Design, Harvard University

In *Mary Barton* this new age of courthouses has not yet arrived in Manchester, but already the physical legal terrain has changed dramatically. If Jem's trial had been set merely a decade or so earlier, Mary and the other characters would ostensibly have had to confront a much different situation. They would have had to travel by carriage, cart, or foot (there being no trains) to Lancaster, which was then Manchester's assize town, and there the trial would have been held in a much different venue: Lancaster Castle, which was, and still is, very much a castle. As suggested by the 1827 painting *The Castle with the Arrival of Prisoners,* this ancient fortress, with the town spread beneath it, bespeaks the approach of criminals or petitioners to a ruler for judgment (see fig. 8). Notice that the crowds are located outside in this picture, as in the days of the scaffold, and the anonymous artist has even drawn a wooden warehouse crane (on the edge of the scene) which seems evocative of a gibbet. In the long era of this sort of courthouse assize festivals and hangings eclipsed trials. By the nineteenth

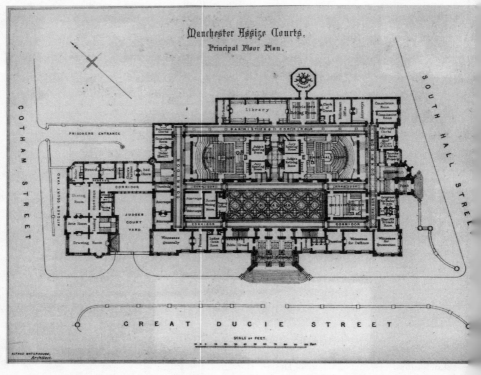

FIG. 7. Alfred Waterhouse, *Manchester Assize Courts: Principal Floor Plan,* from *Papers Read at the Royal Institute of British Architects, Session 1864–65.* Courtesy of the Frances Loeb Library, Graduate School of Design, Harvard University

century this courthouse was outdated in all sort of ways, not least for being combined with a prison. As the populations of Manchester and Liverpool exploded, it became increasingly inconvenient for these towns to use Lancaster for their assize sessions, and Liverpool, where Mary goes, began holding assizes in 1835.

Mary Barton thus takes the train, her first ride on one, to Liverpool (on the famous Liverpool and Manchester line, whose opening in 1830 marked a beginning of passenger rail travel) and finds it "crowded by attorneys, attorneys' clerks, plaintiffs, defendants, and witnesses, all going to the Assizes" (332). Mary's arrival at the train station in Liverpool—"and now they were in the tunnel!—and now they were in Liverpool" (334)—actually places her directly opposite the massive construction site for new law courts being built *there* to accommodate its new designation as a town where assize sessions were held. The town had laid a symbolic stone for the new central building on 28 June 1838, the day of Queen Victoria's coronation. Although the dating of the novel's story can be slightly confusing, if Mary arrives sometime in or shortly after 1842, as seems likely, then demolition of the buildings on the site would have commenced.[27] The final edifice built—St. George's Hall (which, contrary to original plan, ultimately incorporated a hall for music and public meetings in addition to the assize courts)—would not be completed until 1855.

So, when we learn in *Mary Barton* that for Jem's trial "the judge, the jury, the avenger of blood, the prisoner, the witnesses—all [are] gathered together within the building" (373), this building would have been the temporary and inadequate quarters being used for the assizes: the Sessions House, Chapel Street. We are thus located physically, as well as symbolically, amid the fresh construction of law courts. And, because Mary Barton's journey to the story-

FIG. 8. *The Castle with the Arrival of Prisoners* (1827), artist unknown. By permission of Lancaster City Museums

telling space of this law court—"their awful place of rendezvous" (373)—intersects so deeply with this novel's own architecture and, more broadly, with the blueprints for this wing of the house of fiction, it is perhaps also worth recognizing that this forensic novelistic form, in turn, grew up in the midst of the physical reshaping of the nineteenth-century cityscape around central courthouse buildings.

CHAPTER SIX

The Newgate Novel and the Advent of Detective Fiction

IN THE 1830S AND 1840S a literary controversy raged over the depiction of criminals in novels. William Makepeace Thackeray shuddered "for the public, whom its literary providers have gorged with blood, and foul Newgate garbage." "Let your rogues in novels act like rogues, and your honest men like honest men; don't let us have any juggling and thimblerigging with virtue and vice, so that, at the end of three volumes, the bewildered reader shall not know which is which," he cried.[1] Ever since Edward Bulwer had published *Paul Clifford* in 1830, taking a highwayman for his hero, and two years later sympathetically told the story of a near-murderer in *Eugene Aram,* the question of how novels should portray criminals had become an intensely scrutinized public issue. One result would be an identified school of fiction, the Newgate novel.[2]

These Newgate novels were not, as one might think, much concerned with London's infamous Newgate prison and its gallows. Three of the criminals most famously depicted by Newgate novels (Paul Clifford, Eugene Aram, and Dick Turpin) never even stayed in that prison. Nor were the Newgate novels identified primarily by a general concern for imprisonment or capital punishment. Rather, their Newgate name derived from reviewers and satirists who accused novelists of elaborating unhealthily on the genre of the *Newgate Cal-*

endar, that is, on anthologies of criminals' lives (a number of which were named the *Newgate Calendar*) and similar popular collections of state trials, such as George Borrow's *Celebrated Trials, and Remarkable Cases of Criminal Jurisprudence* (1825). Newgate novels portray actual figures found in these books or imagine characters who seem to have crept from their pages. And, most important, according to the contemporary critics wielding references to "Newgate," these novels inadequately condemned the outlaws they depicted. As an advertisement for Thackeray's anti-Newgate novel *Catherine* (1839) explained, these "popular fictions . . . made heroes of highwaymen and burglars, and created a false sympathy for the vicious and criminal."[3]

This chapter returns to the era of this Newgate controversy, during which both *Pickwick* and *Mary Barton* were published. It focuses on two novels central to the unfolding Newgate debate, Edward Bulwer's *Eugene Aram* (1832) and Charles Dickens's *Oliver Twist* (1838). These novels powered a social and formal crisis worth rethinking in terms of the larger contemporary juridical literary context we have been exploring (and to which *Pickwick* and *Mary Barton* belong). It is no coincidence that the most influential Newgate novels depict climactic trial scenes: it is almost a signature of the Newgate form. In line with a forensic narrative paradigm focused on the criminal's viewpoint and defense, for the first time in English fiction omniscient narrators extensively entered the perspective of guilty criminal protagonists. The result would be something of a culmination to the novel's juristic transfiguration in the early nineteenth century (whose later effects we may trace particularly in Eliot's *Adam Bede*) and also, subsequently, the provocation of a new, opposing paradigm for narrating crime: the detective mystery.

I

The first Newgate novel, Bulwer's *Paul Clifford,* culminates in the trial of its title character. At this trial William Brandon, the very man who falsely accused Clifford of the theft of his watch seven years earlier, precipitating Clifford's career of crime, is now his judge. Armed with this fact and a sense of how "circumstances make guilt,"[4] Clifford's defense speech is a lengthy protest against the criminal justice system. Denouncing publicly the legal institution he holds responsible for making him a thief, the accused accepts his doom and roundly

accuses the court, "revers[ing] the order of things" (401). The mishmash of
critiques he levels, from his original wrongful conviction to the law's protection
of the rich, partly inveighs against those "errors in our penal institutions"
which Bulwer raises in a preface (vii). Yet it is his heroic speech itself—"the
boldness and novelty of the words" told in a "deep and firm voice" (395)—
which confirms he is not to be slotted into the conventional role of villain and
registers Bulwer's larger aim. Not only are Clifford and other criminals produced by circumstances (meaning society in general and the criminal justice
system in particular), but, by nobly saying so, Clifford underscores that there
is no absolute divide between criminal characters and virtuous ones.

Bulwer melodramatically fixes the trial to support this case. The overambi-
tious and corrupt judge Brandon learns from a message delivered in the middle of the trial that Clifford is his son. There will be no easy dismissal of the
central criminal character in this novel. As Bulwer demands rhetorically of his
readers in a preface: "Compare . . . the hunted son and the honoured father,
the outcast of the law, the dispenser of the law—the felon, and the judge; and,
as at the last, they front each other, one on the seat of justice, the other at the
convict's bar, who can lay his hand on his heart and say, that the Paul Clifford
is a worse man than the William Brandon?" (xi).

Bulwer's problem was how to narrate this collapsed distinction between
"the outcast of the law" and "the dispenser of the law" without seeming to sympathize with immorality. Leaving aside the stir caused by *Paul Clifford*'s side-
light of contemporary satire,[5] the moral outrage dogging this novel's wild
success arose from its portrayal of the delinquent Clifford. A guilty criminal
protagonist justified his wrongs by laying them at the feet of society, and it was
unclear what perspective the novel provided on this situation or even what the
character's own thinking was. Epitomizing this opacity is a rare moment when
Bulwer finally opens "more of [Clifford's] secret heart" (199). In the long
speech that follows, Bulwer lacks any defined narratorial voice or authorial
presence distinguishable from Clifford, who rants: "To those laws hostile to
me, then, I acknowledge hostility in my turn. Between us are the conditions of
war. Let them expose a weakness—I insist on my right to seize the advantage:
let them defeat me, and I allow their right to destroy." Seeming merely to con-
cur in his hero's self-defeating, personal duel with the legal system, Bulwer
brought down upon himself much righteous fury from the critics. In 1848 he

parried with an impatient footnote: "The author need not, he hopes, observe, that these sentiments are Mr. Paul Clifford's—not his" (200).

But what were "his" sentiments? Without a consistent narratorial voice or silent-but-guiding authorial presence, Bulwer creates a novelistic hybrid, the criminal-hero, without the framework for assessing him which the third-person narrative accompaniment implied. From the first, the Newgate novel's critics thus paradoxically protested not only the new extended use of an omniscient narrator to explore and share a criminal character's perspective but also the inadequate performance of this omniscient narratorial perspective. On the one hand, Thackeray would damn Bulwer's Newgate novels outright for "false sympathy," and, on the other, John Forster could complain that Bulwer depicts a "man of crime . . . in whom the limits between good and evil are scarcely marked throughout with sufficient clearness and precision" when precisely "upon these points there should be no possible doubt, for they imply the extreme danger of suggesting a false sympathy with crime."[6]

As Bulwer himself recognized in an 1848 preface, *Paul Clifford* had broached a new novelistic treatment of transgression but, in doing so, his novel "rather deals with the ordinary surface of human life, than attempts, however humbly, to soar above it or to dive beneath" (xi-xii). The philosophical examination of the "solitary human heart" (xii) which was crucially missing from *Paul Clifford* would explicitly become the intended key to his next and most influential Newgate novel, *Eugene Aram*. The third-person narrator in this novel straightforwardly announces: "It is not only the history of his life, but the character and tone of Aram's mind, that I wish to stamp upon my page."[7] The well-known tale Bulwer chose to rework for his story is certainly conducive to excavating the psychology of its protagonist. Eugene Aram is an educated and generally humane man who rationalizes participating in the murder of a despicable character, afterward leads a scholarly, contemplative life for years, and finally (and famously) fabricates an ingenious court defense.

As in *Paul Clifford*, a sensational trial scene focused on the criminal's defense marks *Eugene Aram*'s denouement and reflects its formal structuring around a criminal's viewpoint. Asked "the thrilling and awful question—'What he had to say in his own behalf?'" Aram claims innocence and delivers that "remarkable defence still extant, and still considered as wholly unequalled from the lips of one defending his own cause" (360–61). In Aram's multifaceted speech we learn—as we do as well in its version in the *Newgate Calendar*—of the likelihood of finding any old skeleton in a hermitage where the murdered body was found; of how his poor health prevented his participation in the murder; of the fact that his law-abiding "life contradicts this indictment" (362); and so on. This courtroom defense is not a straightforward rendering of his views, as Paul Clifford's is. Readers know full well that Eugene Aram is equivocating. This novel follows Aram's struggle to live an ordinary, harmless life after his grim crime—a story more than half-located in Aram's inner thoughts.

In so doing, *Eugene Aram* not only established the powerful new Newgate genre; it also laid out the stakes of the controversy surrounding it. We get a sense of these stakes from the strange position of Aram in his trial scene. As we learn after Aram is convicted (despite his defense), he has fabricated his case for absolute innocence largely in order to protect those who would be crushed to discover him guilty in any degree. He has not merely defended himself in the trial; he has constructed, and maintained, himself through his defense as a virtuous character. It is a performance for others: "*Their* eyes were on me; *their* lives were set on my complete acquittal, less even of life than honour;—my struggle against truth was less for myself than for them." His "defence fulfilled its end"; his fiancée, Madeline, whose health deteriorates during the suspenseful months awaiting Aram's trial, dies shortly after his conviction "without distrusting the innocence of him she loved" (390). (Her death in turn partly frees him to confess.) At his trial Aram has both protected Madeline and denied his guilt in the murder, in this, too, proving himself that potent literary mixture of hero and criminal whose existence Thackeray bewailed.

More important, Aram has performed, as Bulwer's novel does, for an audience holding their literature to a simple dual philosophy in which a villain is a villain and a hero absolutely pure. The trial thus restages within the novel the literary pressures acting externally upon Bulwer. While critics claimed the public must be protected from blurred visions of vice and virtue, the novel conceived as a mirror of reality was expected to represent precisely this contradiction in some of its criminal characters. Aram's trial captures the overarching tension animating the Newgate novel: Eugene Aram must suppress the crime to be accepted as a man; the Newgate novel teaches that the man must be accepted though he has committed a crime.

We might even see the trial—as illustrated by the frontispiece to the Stan-

F I G . 9 . Frontispiece to Edward Bulwer Lytton, *Eugene Aram: A Tale* (London: Richard Bentley, 1833). Courtesy of the Department of Special Collections, Young Research Library, UCLA

dard Edition of *Eugene Aram* (see fig. 9)—as itself a frontispiece to the form of the Newgate novel. In the engraving a pure woman (Madeline, Aram's betrothed, in her wedding gown) is pictured in a conventional pose of concerned adoration for her noble hero in the dock. But this hero is guilty, not just technically but morally. Appropriately, then, he is triangulated (each is spotlighted) with the woman and the judge: to the woman he appears on a pedestal, while the judge who will condemn him looks down upon him. From our perspective Eugene Aram occupies an intermediate space, a middle position between the condemning judge and the worshiping woman which in this context suggests his actual admixture of altruistic heroism and self-seeking criminality. Likewise, Aram's upright carriage and open stance signify neither self-possessed guiltlessness nor swashbuckling bravado. As we readers know, the situation is more complex—including, in part, the continuation of his proud attempt to transcend his past crime. And we alone understand this situation; notice that, in contrast to the other figures (both in their appearance to us and in their views of Aram), we see Aram from head to toe: we know him whole, as it were. We look on this criminal protagonist from a third-person perspective, but in that perspective it is his story that dominates and matters to us.

At stake is a question of representing criminals, hinged upon the telling of the criminal's story, a peformance metonymically connected back to the trial scene (even though in this case it is, paradoxically, precisely Aram's inability to tell his tale in court which reveals his bigger story). In the frontispiece the court spectators transform what might merely be a picture of Aram into one that reflects upon his representation; we watch Aram being watched. Within the story the representation of the criminal character is similarly at issue in the trial but in a historic literary sense. Aram's defense speech runs for five pages (361–66), with barely any narratorial commentary, in essentially direct quotation of the *Newgate Calendar*.[8] A footnote, for instance, simply refers us for further information to "his published defence" (363). Yet we are hardly back in the *Newgate Calendar*. Rather, this novel inverts the earlier Newgate Calendar representation of Aram. The omniscient perspective of Bulwer's novel has aligned us with Aram's perspective, in stark opposition to the *Calendar*'s, which at best sanctions only a reader's horrified fascination. In the novel readers must attend to Aram's defense not merely, as in the *Newgate Calendar*, for its renowned ingenuity, the cleverest of attempts to evade the gallows, but as an extension of Aram's inner struggle, an unfolding psychosocial conflict.

As a result, this founding Newgate novel must be distinguished from those of William Ainsworth, whose two major Newgate fictions, *Rookwood* (1834) and *Jack Sheppard* (1839), really do simply hit upon romantic criminals (a dashing gentleman highwayman and an escape artist) and in fairy-tale fashion erect them as racy popular heroes. Bulwer aimed to explore criminal characters as part of a tangled psychological and social mix. In this Bulwer saw himself as a successor to William Godwin. Unlike Godwin in *Caleb Williams*, however, Bulwer related his radical refiguration of his Newgate tales through an authorial, omniscient narrator. Casting a criminal as protagonist in a third-person narrative—thereby doing for the English novel what Stendhal's *Le Rouge et le noir* (1830) did for the French—Bulwer crystallized a new narrative form in two gathering stages: in *Paul Clifford* he first postulated that external circumstances produce a character as criminal, and in *Eugene Aram* he unveiled a criminal character psychologically.

Little surprise that Bulwer trumpeted *Eugene Aram* as the most successful of his Newgate novels, boasting in a preface: "If none of my prose works have been so attacked as EUGENE ARAM, none have so completely triumphed over attack. It is true that, whether from real or affected ignorance of the true morality of fiction, a few critics may still reiterate the old commonplace charges of 'selecting heroes from Newgate,' or 'investing murders with interest'; but the firm hold which the work has established in the opinion of the general public . . . [indicates] it belongs to that legitimate class of fiction which illustrates life and truth" (xv). Yet, persistently attacked for *Eugene Aram* and his other Newgate novels, Bulwer nonetheless felt compelled to produce elaborate published defenses for them in the form of lengthy prefaces and eventually even a standalone booklet, *A Word to the Public* (1847). Bulwer's discussion of *Eugene Aram* in this small book is typical and revealing. Ostensibly, he reappears as author to explain his novel to his readers. *A Word to the Public* advises that in *Eugene Aram* "the moral consisted in showing more than the mere legal punishment at the close" and is to be found in the way Aram's crime transforms his life into a lived secret, imprisoning him within himself: "The knowledge of the bar between the minds of others and his own, deprived the criminal of all [the various possibilities for happiness]."[9] His novel's emphasis of Aram's internal struggle has itself been part of its moral lesson.

Yet, at another level, Bulwer's answer to his critics lay not in the actual explanations that he gave for his stories but in the addition those explanations made to his novels' form. These appendages—in constructing a supervising, expository third-person narratorial perspective—struggled to satisfy a perceived shortfall in the original narrator's perspective on its central criminal character. *A Word to the Public* and the prefaces were attempts to construct that seemingly missing objective view that would mark "the limits between good and evil . . . with sufficient clearness and precision." We might even say that the follow-up moralizings Bulwer produced for his Newgate novels reveal just what his narrator had needed to lay aside in the first place to enter into a sympathetic exploration of his criminal protagonists: a distancing, judgmental narratorial perspective and tone, still being broadcast by the various *Newgate*

Calendars.[10] In a post-Austen era, however, the novelistic narrator could no longer be attached to a narrative after-the-fact, like a verbal splint. Especially by the 1830s, the narrator of a realistic novel was not expected to stand at the side of the story and direct but to weave together the third-and first-person perspectives, building up the reader's perspective from within. That was what Bulwer's narrator and the Newgate novels in general were pioneering in their omniscient treatment of criminal characters; there also was the source of dissatisfaction.

Certainly, the results were clear enough to some critics: Bulwer's omniscient narrator's "false sympathy" endangered readers, the law-abiding public, everyone, by misleading them into a false sympathy for criminals. Thus, in the anti-Newgate novel *Catherine* Thackeray is obsessed with the Newgate novel's ability to make an audience "expend [their] sympathies on cutthroats, and other such prodigies of evil!"—*Catherine* itself is his "endeavour to cause the public . . . to hate them."[11] This focus on the reader arises in part from the special effect of the Newgate novel's omniscient third-person narration: relating a story from an overseeing point of view which not only follows a criminal character closely over time and through changing circumstances but also enters into the criminal's inward viewpoint, the Newgate novels were inevitably beginning to construct their readers' perspective on the outlaw from within the narrative, much as scenes painted with perspective construct a controlling viewpoint from which to look at them.

By contrast, the narrative of first-person crime fiction, such as *Moll Flanders* (1722), represents to readers the relation of the storytelling criminal to him- or herself, and—though readers may certainly be cued by the narrative in all sorts of ways about how to evaluate the depicted criminal character—they must fashion any omniscient, third-person perspective themselves. Newgate fiction threatened because it began to blend the psychological immediacy and living closeness of such first-person narratives into its omniscient view of a leading, criminal character. Bulwer would commonly stipulate that such feeling attention to a character's inner perspective is a primary function of the novelistic narrator. "It is the notable convenience of us narrators to represent, by what is called *soliloquy,* the thoughts—the interior of the personages we describe. And this is almost the master-work of the tale-teller," he declares in his last Newgate novel, *Lucretia* (1846).[12] "The description of *feelings* is also the prop-

erty of the novelist. The dramatist throws his feelings into dialogue,—the novelist goes at once to the human heart, and calmly scrutinises, assorts, and dis-
sects them," he argues in "On Art in Fiction," citing Godwin as a model.[13] At
the heart of the controversy surrounding Bulwer's Newgate novels was their
capacity to provide readers with an authoritative distance on the depicted criminal character and move them explicitly across that distance into communion
with these most liminal of society's members.

There was ultimately no question of upholding naive myths of stable subjectivity, despite Thackeray's cry to "let your rogues in novels act like rogues."
For the Newgate novel to gain acceptance it required a stabilizing "moral" narrator through which the narrative could portray a panorama of plastic individuals confronting and being shaped by a rapidly changing society and picture
in that panorama even society's criminal characters as leading figures. George
Eliot would perhaps most successfully create this narrator, transcending the
Newgate controversy Bulwer provoked and fulfilling the aims Bulwer had
sketched in his theoretical prefaces and pamphlet. Her novels explicitly provide precise guidance for the relations between crime and morality, an enlargement of the realm of narratorial identification to those considered beyond the
pale and an ethic for readers which upholds the extension of sympathy to all.
Although *Felix Holt* would present her most dramatic trial scene (and contain
a passing reference to *Eugene Aram*), Eliot's first novel, *Adam Bede* (1859)—
widely received as a leap forward in the moral capacities of the novel—presented the social and formal resolution to the Newgate controversy Bulwer
sparked.

Written long after the first Newgate novel but only a dozen years after *A
Word to the Public, Adam Bede* may at first appear anti-Newgate in form: it severely assesses its central criminal character, Hetty Sorrel, the shallow, vain
farm girl, seduced and impregnated by the local squire, Arthur Donnithorne.
Hetty abandons her baby and is justly charged with infanticide; her confessor,
Dinah Morris, the self-possessed Methodist preacher whom Adam Bede must
learn to love in place of Hetty, is clearly the heroine of this novel. Nonetheless,
Eliot's narrator frequently sees Hetty's seduction and rejection through Hetty's
point of view; she emphasizes that this viewpoint, like Hetty's predicament as
a fallen woman, is socially produced and not just the result of individual flaw;
and, finally, she explicitly demands, both through Adam Bede and her narra-

tor's prescriptions, her reader's sympathetic understanding for both Hetty and Arthur as well as the other characters. In these ways Eliot's novel negotiated the literary terrain previously trod by the Newgate novels.

The chapter describing Hetty's criminal trial encapsulates just how Eliot's narrator productively maneuvers around the issues animating the Newgate controversy. Eliot finesses the old question of "false sympathy" by focusing on Adam focusing on Hetty. The law court is not wrong to condemn Hetty, but, as Adam indicates, the proper moral response is to feel with her and for her, acknowledging that individual guilt, like individual evil, is impossible in a world in which "men's lives are as thoroughly blended with each other as the air they breathe."[14] This explicitly moral perspective, which governs *Adam Bede,* relies on being in a stabilizing tension with the law courts as a complementary scene of justice. As long as the law courts punish individuals properly, Eliot's narrator can call collectively for moral sympathy. This neat balancing act between the law courts and the novel eluded a more explicitly reform-minded Bulwer, who could only theorize what Eliot would perform.

Writing that "it is precisely those offences which society cannot interfere with, that society requires fiction to expose," Bulwer insists that the moral mission of the novel is to relay characters' internal states: "Fiction . . . strikes through the disguise, lifts the mask, bares the heart, and leaves a moral wherever it brands a falsehood."[15] Yet it is Eliot's narrator, not Bulwer's, who successfully takes up this charge of didactically relaying her characters' internal states. Here, for instance, is her description of the unconscious mental state of Arthur Donnithorne:

> Was there a motive at work under this strange reluctance of Arthur's which had a sort of backstairs influence, not admitted to himself? Our mental business is carried on much in the same way as the business of the State: a great deal of hard work is done by agents who are not acknowledged. In a piece of machinery, too, I believe there is often a small unnoticeable wheel which has a great deal to do with the motion of the large obvious ones. Possibly, there was some such unrecognised agent secretly busy in Arthur's mind at this moment— . . . The human soul is a very complex thing. (172)

And here is a similar moment provided by Bulwer's narrator in *Lucretia:*

[Olivier Dalibard] rarely communed with himself; a sort of mental calcu-
lation, it is true, eternally went on within him, like the wheels of a destiny;
but it had become a mechanical operation—seldom disturbed by that *consciousness of thought,* with its struggles of fear and doubt, conscience and
crime. . . . He did not face his own soul; his outer life and his inner life
seemed separate individualities, just as, in some complicated state, the
social machine goes on through all its numberless cycles of vice and
dread, whatever the acts of the government, which is the representative
of the state and stands for the state in the shallow judgment of history.
(178–79)

Despite some striking shared descriptions of the mind's capacity not to know
itself, there is a fundamental distinction between the two passages. In *Adam Bede*
Eliot's narratorial commentary is standard fare. In *Lucretia* Bulwer's analysis
is much, much less common. Indeed, Bulwer's narrator's description of the
difficulty of conveying his character's mental state may be seen as an elegant
excuse for not doing so, while Eliot's narrator's analysis forms part of a continuous, microscopic engagement in assessing her depicted characters' minds. It
is through the accretion of such perceptive and preceptive commentary that
Adam Bede establishes the explicit narratorial perspective that Bulwer leaves
only half-adumbrated.

When Eliot spells out the morality of portraying characters who were neither clearly villains nor heroes in chapter 17 of *Adam Bede,* she can thus do so
from an authoritative, rather than defensive, position. The shift in tone from
Bulwer is subtle but crucial. Internalizing the controversy confronted in Bulwer's various prefaces, Eliot begins by imagining a "fair critic" of her work who
rehashes the dull demand Thackeray made twenty years earlier: "Let your most
faulty characters always be on the wrong side, and your virtuous ones on the
right. Then we shall see at a glance whom we are to condemn, and whom we
are to approve" (221–22). As Eliot's confident opposition to this critic suggests,
her basic crime plot in *Adam Bede*—originating from her Methodist aunt's
empathetic account of a condemned woman—robustly defined itself against
the same censures that had plagued the Newgate novels. No wonder Eliot de-
cided not to tell her publisher the story line. As she relates in a journal entry,
she "would not have it judged apart from [her] *treatment,* which alone de-

termines the moral quality of art."[16] She fully understood the contemporary
moral requirements placed on this form of crime fiction, and Bulwer had paved
the way for this understanding, propounding prophetically in *A Word to the
Public:* "It is the treatment that ennobles, not the subject. . . . Art can . . . con-
vert into poetry the most lofty, the homely image of the girl condemned for
infanticide."[17]

In 1860 Bulwer wrote of Eliot: "I know no female author with such grasp of
character, such deep cuts into secret recesses of the heart, such ease and power
of language."[18] That formal achievement should be seen against the backdrop
of Bulwer's best-selling Newgate novels and his published attempts to defend
their achievement, much as Eliot's historical novel *Romola* (1863) has been
related to his *Rienzi* (1835). *Adam Bede* may justly have become famous as a
treatise on the way "our deeds determine us, as much as we determine our
deeds" (315), but, to the author who wrote in 1886 that "after all, the true religion of Fate has been preached by George Eliot, when she says that our lives
are the outcomes of our actions,"[19] we might respond that it was Bulwer who
articulated in *A Word to the Public* that novels show how "our conscience is our
oracle, our deeds shape our fate."[20] It was he who, quoting John Fletcher, provided this *Adam Bede*–like epigraph to *Eugene Aram:* "Our acts our angels are,
or good or ill, / Our fatal Shadows that walk by us still." Eliot extended Bulwer's
efforts to reshape the novel's treatment of transgression rather than, as Frederick Karl suggests, "set[ting] herself quite firmly against anything that might
smack of . . . Bulwer-Lytton."[21]

The point here is not just that Eliot was influenced by Bulwer's Newgate
novels and his theoretical concerns to an extent often forgotten today. Rather,
both Eliot and Bulwer were part of a shift in early Victorian crime fiction which
first coalesced around the Newgate novels. (Even Mary Shelley tried her hand
at writing one in the unsuccessful *Falkner: A Novel* [1837].) The linchpin of this
moment in literary history was the depiction of leading criminal characters'
perspectives through a novel's omniscient third-person perspective. The Newgate novel refigured the censorious and distancing omniscient perspective on
criminal characters still being promulgated by the *Newgate Calendar*. The related magisterial tone of such eighteenth-century omniscient narrators as Henry
Fielding's in *Tom Jones* would from then on resonate as intonations of a past
age. Developing Godwin's approach in *Caleb Williams,* the Newgate novels of

the 1830s and 1840s again retried the characters of the *Newgate Calendar,* but this time they imagined for them the sort of omniscient form of defense which the lawyers had begun actually to provide in court. For readers this double perspective, like the bifocalization of observing and attending to a criminal's defense in a trial, allied an authoritative viewpoint on society with the criminal's own.[22]

By the end of the nineteenth century diverse authors—such as Thomas Hardy in *Tess of the D'Urbervilles* (1891) or Oscar Wilde in *Dorian Gray* (1891)—would rebel against such intrusively "moral treatment" of criminal protagonists, casting it as straitlaced and priggish. But they took for granted the ideological and technical work that had gone into constructing an omniscient narrator whose perspective was allied with that of their depicted criminal protagonist. By confirming that narrative form, their predecessors had done much in their own time to revolutionize literary and cultural understandings of crime. There also would emerge a starkly alternative approach to narrating crime, one that repudiated the juridical Newgate form.

I I

Perhaps more famously than any other Newgate novel, Charles Dickens's *Oliver Twist* takes up the type of criminal characters previously relegated to the *Newgate Calendar* and reimagines their lives from a sympathetic omniscient perspective. We catch a glimpse of the lineaments of this literary reconfiguration at the beginning of the second volume of *Oliver Twist.* Oliver, confined again with Fagin's gang of pickpockets after having been recaptured by Sikes and Nancy, reads a book: "He turned over the leaves. Carelessly at first; but, lighting on a passage which attracted his attention, he soon became intent upon the volume. It was a history of the lives and trials of great criminals; and the pages were soiled and thumbed with use. Here, he read of dreadful crimes that made the blood run cold."[23] Oliver is reading a *Newgate Calendar,* and Dickens goes on to evoke its hair-raising contents in some detail. Its relevance to his predicament is as obvious to Oliver as, in a more textual way, it is to the reader, and, terrified, Oliver prays that he will not become like the criminals about whom he reads. (Later Master Bates will comically worry about precisely the opposite when he despairs that the Artful Dodger's feats will not be properly celebrated by the *Newgate Calendar* because he has been indicted merely for petty theft [295].) Oliver's horror that his life might be worthy of being in a *Newgate Calendar* (like the worry that the Artful Dodger's will be kept out of it) registers with the reader metatextually, calling attention to the novel *Oliver Twist*'s relation to the *Newgate Calendar*.

Oliver's brief scene encapsulates the relationship between Dickens's Newgate novel and the *Newgate Calendar* in a variety of ways, not least by showing that the novel cannibalizes and reflects upon this other crime genre. Most important, however, Dickens has Nancy, a prostitute and member of Fagin's criminal coterie, silently and compassionately overhear Oliver's prayer to be "rescued from his present dangers" (130). As a literary figure, she signifies the difference between the *Newgate Calendar* Oliver is reading and the Newgate novel he is in.

In part this difference is simply that Nancy, though a criminal, acts heroically. She will reluctantly carry through with fetching Oliver for Sikes, but after this moment she will be instrumental in saving him from the dangerous underworld of which she is a part. When she next appears, she will discover Fagin's secret arrangement that makes Oliver worth one hundred pounds to him and will begin to investigate (and eventually altruistically to expose) this shadowy subplot in which Oliver's half-brother Monks schemes to keep Oliver from his inheritance. Nancy's story—in which she herself fatally becomes a storyteller—will, as Hilary Schor has traced, ultimately collapse the initial opposition between herself and the novel's ostensible heroine, the maternal gentlewoman Rose.[24] By helping Oliver and paying for it with her life, Nancy will come to represent, at least to Thackeray, one of *Oliver Twist*'s most egregious depictions of a heroic criminal character: a "white-washed saint," he calls her.[25] Dickens is, as Thackeray will elaborate further on Nancy in a later article, "giving us favourable pictures of monsters."[26]

Actually, Dickens's omniscient narrative carefully constructs its sympathetic perspective toward Nancy, maneuvering readers into a position from which they must imagine and share in her outlook simply to follow the story line. In her scene alone with Oliver, Nancy tells him to lower the light because "it hurts [her] eyes," and we suspect she is about to cry; our suspicion is confirmed when she "thr[ows] herself into a chair, with her back towards him," and begins "wr[inging] her hands" and "rock[ing] herself to and fro; . . . uttering a gur-

gling sound" (130); we further realize she must brace herself to take Oliver to
Sikes when we are twice told by the narrator that she is "affecting" her casual
demeanor (131). Her obscured behavior is not very difficult to understand, but
the point is that the reader must put it together: Nancy's viewpoint and experience are completed in the reader's mind. The textual illusion that the character has an active inner state, a conscience, is depicted by showing the fleeting
signs of its suppression. To understand Nancy's behavior the reader must enter
that inner state, imagining that Nancy pities Oliver, that she is responding to
his prayer to have someone rescue him, that she now has divided loyalties and
must act contrary to her wishes and hide her intentions. We readers supply
the free indirect discourse that the narrator, all-knowing but not all-telling, is
plainly withholding.

This device through which we must read Nancy's behavior as a front for
her actual perspective also arises from our larger understanding of the way in
which her character is developing. Introduced with caustic sarcasm as one of
two "very nice girls indeed" (55), Nancy enters the plot as a prostitute who
sadistically masquerades as Oliver's protectress, dressing up respectably and
pretending to be his sister, the better to track and kidnap him. But Dickens subsequently has her internalize the protecting role she has parodied. When Oliver
is attacked by Sikes's dog and beaten by Fagin, Nancy struggles to save him:
"Ha! ha! my dear, you are acting beautifully," Fagin nervously observes, trying
to discount her defense of Oliver on the original terms (103). But the narrator
has already established that Nancy is not feigning her outrage at their treatment
of Oliver and will indicate repeatedly that she is performing for Sikes and
Fagin, staging, for instance, a ruthless criminal bravado—"an air of defiance"
(125)—which she does not feel.

The moral terms of her behavior shift. "Is the Nance of the first volume the
same Nance that we find in the third?" a critic disapprovingly inquired in 1840.[27]
She is not supposed to be. Nancy's character unfolds as "a contradiction"
(lxv), as Dickens calls her in his 1841 preface (responding to Thackeray). In
seeing through Nancy's dissembling, we do not see the "real" Nancy: the real
Nancy—her allegiance split between Oliver and her comrades—dissembles because she has become a character divided. By the end of the novel the omniscient narrator has attuned readers to Nancy's ongoing inward "mental struggles," and at the opening of chapter 44 the narrator seamlessly slides into

relaying and assessing Nancy's thinking directly and at length, specifying the "wanderings of [her] mind" now that she has agreed to meet Rose Maylie and partially betray the trust of her underworld confederates (301).

From a Foucauldian perspective all the prying into Nancy's mental state may look like an extension of the novel's disciplinary regime: this narrative provides both an omniscient mastery of the criminal world and, as D. A. Miller suggests, a cordon sanitaire firmly separating the middle class from the delinquents.[28] But, historically, the moral valences of the representation of the criminal characters' consciousnesses in *Oliver Twist* indicate anything but normative surveillance. Whether appalled or accepting, contemporary readers record a connection being forged with the depicted criminals which critiqued or even threatened middle-class authority. *Familiarizing* was the recurring verb used to name the introductory, familial sort of intimacy they felt was created with the criminal characters. While within the novel Nancy's meetings with Rose confirm the absolute separation this story draws between the two of them and, more broadly, between the hallowed middle class and the criminal underworld, no such separation has been granted to the implied middle-class reader. On the contrary, the narrator connects the reader to Nancy's perspective in marked contrast to Rose's overly simplistic sympathetic encounters with Nancy. Rose betrays a distancing perspective that walls out Nancy as "lost" (274), and she goes blank at the possibility that she might find in her underworld a "home" (316). The middle-class reader being produced by this Newgate novel understands differently.

After Nancy's brutal murder, an event that marks the beginning of the end of the criminal circle, Dickens presses the Newgate form she embodied toward its moral and formal limits, as if for Dickens her removal set loose the spirit of her treatment. In three of the novel's final six chapters the omniscient narrative perspective heightens the ongoing psychological delineation of—and aligns the reader's perspective with—two of the most unequivocally vicious and inexpiably guilty of the leading criminal characters, Sikes and Fagin.

Establishing a perspective that seems to hover above the entire city, chapter 48, "The Flight of Sikes," opens after Nancy's murder with an omniscient declaration: "Of all bad deeds that, under cover of darkness, had been committed within wide London's bounds since night hung over it, that was the worst" (323). The narrator then immediately swoops down to the troubled Sikes cooped up with Nancy's corpse in a view that blurs the initial omniscient perspective into Sikes's. Four of the next five paragraphs, describing Sikes in the presence of Nancy's body, follow a pattern of building toward exclamatory statements—for example, "God, how the sun poured down upon the very spot!" (324)—clarifying that the ongoing objective description is also subjective perception. Sikes's view, including the expressions of horror, is shared with the narrator's. Not only does the reader enter into Sikes's responses, but also his responses are depicted as if he is looking at his work from without and is aghast at what he has done. For the rest of the chapter Sikes will flee from himself as much as from detection, and the reader, aligned with the narrator, observes and accompanies him in this psychological flight. Sikes is not redeemed—part of Dickens's point is that his act has isolated him irrevocably from society—but the narrative form follows his experience of this isolation.

This formal approach generally continues in Sikes's next and final chapter, in which he returns to London and hangs himself while trying to escape a pursuing mob, and also through the penultimate chapter of the novel, in which Fagin is tried and sentenced to death. The representation of crowds and spectators further emphasizes Sikes's and Fagin's exile from society and pronounces a difference between the reader's and society's perspectives. As the critic R. H. Horne objected in 1844 to Sikes's final chapter: "Our sympathies go with the hunted victim in this his last extremity. It is not 'Sykes [*sic*] the murderer,' of whom we think . . . it is for that one worn and haggard man with all the world against him."[29] Much the same might be said about Fagin's condemnation in a "court . . . paved, from floor to roof, with human faces," in not one of which "could he read the faintest sympathy with himself, or any feeling but one of all-absorbing interest that he should be condemned" (358). Although Dickens clearly condemns Fagin (in disturbing, anti-Semitic terms), we are nonetheless *with* Fagin, as we are with Sikes. In fact, in this trial—itself a predictable culmination to the series of chapters which concludes this Newgate novel, with the usual trial scene understood from the guilty prisoner's viewpoint—the representation of Fagin's perspective verges into interior monologue. At this extreme of the Newgate form the omniscient perspective almost merges with the internal, first-person perspective of the depicted criminal character, prompting Elizabeth Barrett Browning to comment in 1842 that "Charles Dickens has meditated deeply & not without advantage upon Victor Hugo," taking "the Jew's condemnation-hours in Oliver Twist" from Hugo's *The Last Day of a Condemned Man* (1829): she heard the first-person voice of a criminal's spilling thoughts depicted in Hugo's novel intensifying in new ways in Dickens's third-person description of "The Jew's Last Night Alive."[30]

This ending follows naturally enough from a story that, according to Thackeray, inappropriately interests the reader in a whole crew of criminal characters: "The power of the writer is so amazing, that the reader . . . must follow him whithersoever he leads; and to what are we led? Breathless to watch all the crimes of Fagin, tenderly to deplore the errors of Nancy, to have for Bill Sikes a kind of pity and admiration."[31] When he evokes the "power of the writer" to "lead" readers, Thackeray worries about the Newgate novel's construction of a perspective aligned with the criminal, not just virtuous rogues. This omniscient alignment, the core of the Newgate form, which returns it repeatedly to the scene of criminals' trials understood through their eyes, is pushed to its extreme at the end of *Oliver Twist*. Readers became, and still often become, caught between a narrative valorizing Oliver's success in terms of norms sanctioned by middle-class authority—Oliver must escape the criminals—and a narrative that persistently "leads" the reader to side with those made outcast by these norms and that authority. At the end of the 1830s, when the Newgate genre was well established, *Oliver Twist* presented a Newgate novel that was at once a deepening of the form yet also centrally conflicted about it, much as society was. As readers can still sense today, in cornering its criminal characters, this novel corners itself.

To extricate his story from its narrative impasse Dickens belatedly focuses on the character Monks. Like the trapdoor with which the story and the illustration by Cruikshank associate him, Monks providentially provides the narrative with a villain who, because he is not also a victim, the middle class can blamelessly triumph over in the end of the novel. With Monks's entrance into the story, a new, vigilante policing regime springs into action. Literally "kidnapped in the street" by the "authority" of Mr. Brownlow (331), he undergoes a process of forced confession at the end of the novel in which Mr. Brownlow relentlessly unveils his knowledge of the true story and Monks's machinations.

Interleaved with the final chapters on Sikes and Fagin are thus starkly different chapters that revolve around Monks. As the omniscient narrator most fully enters into two of the most guilty characters' preoccupations, Dickens provides alternate chapters that more firmly than ever divide the criminal world from the middle class, to which it stands in continuously interacting opposition. The deathward journey depicted in "The Flight of Sikes" is interrupted by a chapter in which Mr. Brownlow captures and exposes Monks's activities: "Monks and Mr. Brownlow at Length Meet." We return for the final chapter on Sikes, who hangs himself. In the next we are back with Mr. Brownlow, who completes his clinical account of Monks and crimes past: Mr. Brownlow is "Affording an Explanation of more Mysteries than one." Then the story proper ends with Fagin's trial and last days alive. (An epilogue details what happens in the future to the characters.) Dickens thereby staggers the explication of his complicated inheritance plot—"Your tale is of the longest," observes Monks to Mr. Brownlow (334)—with chapters unfolding the fates of Sikes and Fagin. In terms of a deeper narrative structure, at the end of *Oliver Twist* two very different formal paradigms, both involving the narrator's omniscient perspective, alternate: Dickens counterbalances the power of an omniscient perspective to explore the criminal's viewpoint with its power to pursue the criminal's crimes, to *detect* the criminal.

And *Oliver Twist* can feel like an incipient detective story. The pattern is familiar: the real police, Bow Street Runners Blathers and Duff, enter the novel midway through, only to be displaced by amateur sleuths who track down the real criminal and conclude the story with dramatic finger-pointing. Mr. Brownlow undergoes a metamorphosis into a detective figure, rather suddenly finding, as one contemporary critic would object, "unwearied zeal in tracing out the intricacies of a complicated plot, and determined activity in pursuing a murderer to his last haunt of refuge."[32] In the wake of the more than one hundred and fifty years of detective stories that began in earnest in the decades after this novel, Mr. Brownlow's final unmasking of Monks and explanation of the novel's mysteries appears at once absolutely clichéd and, to a historian of detective fiction such as Ian Ousby, "sketchily and hastily" done.[33]

Yet in its time, understood as a contradiction to the Newgate paradigm at work in the novel, the detectivelike conclusion to *Oliver Twist* appears less about the emergence of literary detection than about a repudiation of narratorial alignment with the criminal's viewpoint, which that detection conventionally involves. It is no artistic failure that Monks's character is one-dimensional, nor is it accidental that his responses—scowling, stammering, defying, cowering—are all gauged solely to provide appropriate reactions to Mr. Brown-low's melodramatic unveiling of his villainy. The narratorial perspective on Monks's character closes down the reader's alignment with his viewpoint, just as Monks's minimal and hazy extended portrayal does not provide any contextualizing environment in which he might become understandable.

At the end of the novel Monks speaks at length, only to mouth Mr. Brown-low's speeches. Whenever he falls silent, Mr. Brownlow simply takes up "the thread of the narrative" himself (352), "speaking for him" (351). Instead of his own story, Monks provides the beginning of Oliver's, or, more accurately, the middle-class characters literally write that story for him, make him speak the gist of it aloud, and ascribe his name to it, an author without authorship. In police parlance he talks. His, the criminal's, story is only relevant as it answers the gaps in the victim's story, as in detective fiction generally. It is in this specific sense that we can understand Robert Tracy's general point that, with the arrival of Monks, "the struggle for Oliver [becomes] the struggle about which kind of novel he is to figure in."[34] The question of "false sympathy"—the contemporary litmus test for identifying a Newgate novel—simply does not apply to the story Monks portends. Inexplicable as the epileptic fits that finally kill him in a foreign prison, Monks hints how detective fiction stems from producing criminal characters who are denied a self-justifying perspective in the midst of other self-justifying perspectives. In this narrative form the criminal is conventionally treated impersonally, stereotyped, objectified, depersonalized—to use an adverb and a handful of verbs that self-aware Victorians themselves coined for a calculating machine view of people magnified in their time.

III

The split form at the end of *Oliver Twist* suggests that the beginnings of detective fiction in the 1840s and 1850s would not have been seen merely in terms of the detective; it was also centrally about unseating the narrator's omniscient alignment with the criminal's perspective, which was particularly at issue in the Newgate form.

This closing down of the criminal's perspective is visibly at work in the first classic detective story in English, "The Murders in the Rue Morgue" (1841), written by the American Edgar Allan Poe (himself an avid student and critic of

Dickens). The murderer in this story turns out to be an orangutan, and the solution to Poe's mystery depends on M. Dupin recognizing that a voice over-heard lacks speech and that the crime scene lacks human consciousness and conscience. This criminal is archetypically "alien from humanity"[35]—not a madman, even, but an animal. Moreover, Dupin's recognition is part of his power to read off the mind as if it were a puzzle, a kind of living crossword that intersects with external stimuli instead of a locus of character, a feat he demon-strates in the opening by elaborately reconstructing the long chain of thought of the person with whom he has been walking down a Paris street. From its beginnings the mystery genre thus figured the detective as one who expertly "gets inside the mind of the criminal," abrogating the *narrative's* entrance into the mind of the criminal. We must turn upside down the intuitive notion that detective fiction does not allow us to share in the criminal's mind because do-ing so would spoil the solving of the crime. Rather, the depiction of crime as a mystery to be solved grows out of the narrative's refusal to apply to its depicted criminal character the novelistic techniques that Newgate fiction demonstrated could powerfully allow entrance into that character's perspective and mental state.

In England, where the detective as the center of a genre of mystery fiction did not emerge clearly until the end of the century (and only then did Poe's Dupin start to be cloned in earnest), the import of the criminal's consciousness was at first even more clearly directly at issue. Nowhere is this more evident than in Wilkie Collins's novel *The Moonstone* (1868), a work much discussed as one of the earliest full-length English detective novels. Rachel Verinder's re-sponse to the theft of her Moonstone diamond sets the stage: she becomes im-penetrable, locking herself in her room and refusing to talk to anyone about the theft except to warn them off investigating it. This behavior—"conduct" de-scribed by Collins in the preface as the "foundation on which [he] ha[s] built this book"—will eventually lead the detective Sergeant Cuff to accuse "Miss Verinder of deceiving [them] all, by secreting the Diamond for some purpose of her own."[36] Predictably enough, the detective places the crime with the one character whose inner state is seemingly cloaked from his surveillance. Cuff lacks the community's "knowledge of her character" (163), which, as Rachel's mother tells him, guarantees her innocence. As readers know as well, Rachel's closed-mouth stance is not hiding her inner self but, paradoxically, displaying it: Rachel's "fault"—one that the novel will not condone—is that she "never asked your advice; never told you beforehand what she was going to do; never came with secrets and confidences to anybody," though, crucially, "with all her secrecy, and self-will, there was not so much as the shadow of anything false in her" (52–53). Ironically (because he himself is similarly secretive), Cuff's mistake is not to recognize in Rachel's behavior an actual transparency of character.

The novel's lesson, as D. A. Miller has shown, is that detecting omniscience resides not with Cuff, who is dismissed from the novel until its conclusion, but rather with the community, which monitors itself.[37] In order to solve the mystery, however, the community must struggle just like Cuff to see into its own members' minds, only now the obstacles are a drug-induced stupor and a case of amnesia. Most obviously, Rachel's suitor, Franklin Blake, must laboriously uncover that, under the influence of opium secretly administered to him, he unknowingly removed the diamond from Rachel's boudoir (and Rachel has seen him do it). Reconstructing and reenacting Blake's unconscious actions and bringing him fully into the understanding of the community ultimately overshadows even the pursuit of the criminal, Godfrey Ablewhite, in this story. To the elaborate exhibition of Blake's lost consciousness add the further necessity of making legible the delirious ramblings of Dr. Candy, who has lost his memory, specifically the fact that he has slipped Blake a dose of opium to help him sleep. This detective story does not isolate and pin down a guilty criminal and thereby retroactively construct everyone else, even society itself, as essentially innocent;[38] it methodically exposes the essential see-through accountability of everyone but the true thief. Collins's mystery ultimately hinges upon overcoming a series of obstacles that prevent the characters' consciousnesses from becoming transparent to one another and to the reader, thereby establishing their innocence.

The Moonstone's structure as a series of first-person narratives in which the characters tell "the story of the Moonstone in turn—as far as [their] own personal experience extends, and no farther" (8) would seem to bypass neatly the question of representing Ablewhite's consciousness: the characters simply don't know whodunit. Actually, the narrative form sets in motion the same logic operating within the story: in order to solve the mystery after Cuff departs, the characters must reciprocally reveal their individual intelligibility, which merges into an omniscient perspective marking their innocence. As Miller has argued, *The Moonstone*'s limitation to a series of first-person perspectives does not stymie an overarching objective and omniscient view. We know precisely what happened and how the varied personal viewpoints refract those happenings. When the characters, finally, cooperatively generate an omniscient overview of the situation and of themselves, the criminal is defined by his absence and opacity: Godfrey Ablewhite is the sneaky one who failed to truly participate. Whereas Nancy's deceptions in *Oliver Twist* construct the illusion of a character with inner depth and involve the reader in her mental state and situation, Ablewhite's performative ruses make him look reprehensibly hollow. In a jugglery of content with form which underlies the historic emergence of detective fiction generally, the narrative's failure to align, Newgate-style, with the criminal's perspective becomes the criminal's refusal.

In a literary context up in arms about "sympathy" for the criminal, instead of resolving the problems plaguing the Newgate form, detective fiction took shape as a withdrawal from it. Indeed, the detective story is a palimpsestlike overwriting of the Newgate form: it repasses over the crime to discover its absent perpetrator, whereas the Newgate novels trial-like represented both crime and perpetrator. No wonder Thackeray's attempt to write an anti-Newgate novel in *Catherine* failed. His extended narratorial alignment with his vicious heroine became just that: an alignment. "Catherine," he confessed, "was a mistake all through—it was not made disgusting enough . . . you see the author had a sneaking kindness for his heroine, and did not like to make her utterly worthless."[39] Most tellingly, as Sheldon Goldfarb has pointed out, he gave her a motive for her crime, a psychological component completely missing from *The Annals of Newgate,* from which he drew his story.[40] Moreover, he was mistaken in thinking he simply needed to make his story more "disgusting" to create an effective antidote to the Newgate novels. A wholly different approach was called for. Better to observe people from behind a glass partition, as Dickens's life insurance investigator would explain in the story "Hunted Down" (1859). From that perspective rogues could be reinstated as rogues. As Dickens's detective-narrator frigidly reasons: "There is no greater mistake than to suppose that a man who is a calculating criminal is, in any phase of his guilt, otherwise than true to himself, and perfectly consistent with his whole character. . . . Do you think that if he had [the crime] on his conscience at all, or had a conscience to have it upon, he would ever have committed the crime?"[41] All lawbreakers conveniently become psychopaths.

Narrative techniques for representing consciousness, such as free indirect discourse, only become modes of surveillance in a literary context, premised, as detective fiction is, on the equation of a character's transparency with innocence and opacity with guilt. (Therein lies the wonderful ingenuity of Agatha Christie's mystery *The Murder of Roger Ackroyd* [1926], in which the murderer turns out to be the Watson figure who narrates and writes the story, his self-reticences and occasional vaguenesses necessarily providing some of our most important clues.) Ultimately, the Newgate novel's omniscient representation of a criminal's consciousness may have a place in the rise of modern panoptic and discursive forms of power, which operate through instead of over subjects, but we should distinguish both historically and formally between Newgate and detective fiction, especially in their contrasting uses of omniscience to align readers with or withdraw them from the depicted criminal's perspective. This does not necessarily imply a return to a Whiggish view that Newgate novels "humanized" their criminal characters in line with the enlightened progress of civilization. Rather, what occurred was that a long-standing novelistic affinity for the trial scene gelled in the early part of the century, and, while that intensification of the novel's juridical form gave rise to a new focus on the criminal's defense story, at the same time it helped provoke detective fiction as a new literary genre, possessed by the very different bureaucratic and professional policing perspective upon crime and the criminal's story.[42]

In short, English detective fiction should be understood as a reaction both to the emergence of an identifiable narrative genre—the Newgate novel—and, more generally, to the larger juridical narrative paradigm of which the Newgate novel formed a part. Charles Dickens's *Bleak House* (1853) notably exemplifies the branching off of the two literary strands, famously shifting between the Chancery case of *Jarndyce v. Jarndyce* and the first major English police detective character, Inspector Bucket. The narrative motor of the sensation novels of the 1860s—especially Wilkie Collins's *The Woman in White* (1860), in which the law courts explicitly shape the novel's structure—also might be partly understood as a complex interplay between these two formally and historically different literary strands. In a reductive historical shorthand we might say that, in addition to ideologically acclimatizing citizens to the new, permanent, and professional police presence established by Robert Peel's Metropolitan Police Act of 1829 (followed by the creation of a Detective Department in 1842), early detective fiction encodes within itself a shift from an era when, in terms of both the processes of justice and narrative form, the Bow Street Runners were marginal in comparison with the law courts.

It makes historical sense, then, that English detective fiction would consolidate as a stand-alone genre only in the century's last few decades. The year 1887 was an annus mirabilis: the English edition of Fergus Hume's *Mystery of a Hansome Cab* (1886) became a best-seller of historic proportions and Arthur Conan Doyle introduced Sherlock Holmes in *A Study in Scarlet* (1887). At least from then on, the paradigm of the mystery genre has predominated in crime fiction. It has spawned innumerable subclassifications (psychological, suspense, puzzle) and led to attempts at definition (mystery story versus detective story), most of which, as Julian Symons rightly warns, do more to perplex and falsify than illuminate crime fiction.[43] But the Newgate novels (and by extension other, related early nineteenth-century juridical novels, such as *Caleb Williams*) ought not to be thought of as a subclassification of detective fiction.

Nor should earlier crime novels be treated, as has been common practice, as places to excavate primitive traces of the detective. On the contrary, as even the early fiction about police detectives suggests, before detective fiction a different formal paradigm prevailed. Thomas Gaspey's *Richmond; or, Scenes in the Life of a Bow Street Officer* (1827) and the English translation of Eugène-François Vidocq's *Mémoires* (1828–29) both recount in detail how the life of a criminal evolved into that of a detective, emphasizing the detective's connection to, and even sympathetic understanding for, the criminal's perspective. These detectives are closer to roguish thief takers in the mold of Jonathan Wild than to the latter-day Poirots or Marples who solve mysteries.[44] So, while Anne Humpherys is quite right to call for historians of detective fiction, including myself, to stop focusing on the same tired texts (meaning *Bleak House, The Moonstone,* and those of Sherlock Holmes) and begin "serious analysis of the dozens of other texts that contributed to the shape of this enduring and problematic figure,"[45] it would be a mistake to set out on more searches for detectives before the 1840s.

That we continue to do so only confirms that the advent of detective fiction really did succeed in obfuscating the Newgate form it was partly repudiating—

at least in terms of our histories of crime fiction. This is not to suggest that after detective fiction the law courts have been dismissed as a central structuring component of the novel. On the contrary, they become a common feature of the English novel, grounded firmly in the sort of vital incorporations of the law court into the novel which we have been exploring in this book. Taking Bulwer's perspective—and looking forward to *Adam Bede* and on and outward to Fyodor Dostoyevsky's *Crime and Punishment* (1866) or such later American novels as *Billy Budd* (1891), *American Tragedy* (1925), *Native Son* (1940), and *Lolita* (1955)—the Newgate novel's historic contours as a subgenre were not lost but, instead, thoroughly enfolded into the novel as usual. Its essential status may even make it a too-visible assumption of the genre's shape to seem worth historicizing. And that, in turn, may suggest to us just how constitutive the early nineteenth century's juridical reformation was for the novel.

Conclusion

I N   T H E   1 8 9 0 S   Robert Gemmell Hutchison reimagined Abraham Solomon's 1857 painting *Waiting for the Verdict*. For us Hutchison's painting,
titled *Awaiting the Verdict* (fig. 10), offers a glimpse of the evolving tenor of the
novel's juristic structuring later in the century, again allowing us to envisage in
its narratival tension a novelistic story that is counterpoised, and tethered, to its
representation in court.

Hutchison's painting immediately suggests the arrival of a Hardyesque
modernism: its realism is much grittier and darker than Solomon's. The family
is fragmented instead of unified. No person looks to another. The child in the
foreground is stupefied, not sleeping innocently. An idealized domestic sphere
has crumbled. Everyone is older. All are urban denizens, instead of country
people, as in Solomon's painting. No windows brighten this scene, and the gas
lamps that are present seem not even to be light sources. The picnic basket
(barely visible) sits to the right side on the floor instead of tucked beside the
older woman. Glasses and a jug of water are provided by the state. A No Smok-
ing sign rudely intrudes, somehow adding to our sense of the family's burden,
though they themselves seem oblivious to it. And, instead of a legal clerk writing in the background, as in Solomon's painting, Hutchison has substituted a
sign posted beside the door, which reads:

Instructions to Witnesses
The Witness to be Examined Are [*sic*]
    Injoined
To Answer to the Questions put
    to them
To Speak ALOUD and in DISTINCT
TERMS So that the Court & JURY
may at once hear their ANSWER.
        by Order
         of the Court

Hutchison thus introduces into his painting a modern cynicism about authority and language. Instead of weaving the family's story into that of the court's, the textual signifiers mark disconnection. The very fact that we can

FIG. 10. Robert Gemmell Hutchison, *Awaiting the Verdict* (1890s). The FORBES Magazine Collection, New York © All rights reserved

read the words on this sign emphasizes that a dingy wall has been constructed and brought forward, whereas in Solomon's picture the law courts were down a lit passage, stretched back through a series of arches. Now perspective is flattened, and the even balance of the story of a family against the background of the court curtly eliminated. Nor do any human figures bridge these two spaces, connecting them, as in Solomon's painting. And, most important, in sharp contrast to Solomon's painting, the door leading to the court is shut.

Hutchison's depiction signifies the arrival of an era of self-declared modernist angst, in which individuals, their perspectives isolated and fragmented, struggle with the overwhelming and impersonal sociopolitical organizations that collectively they have produced. It also provides a barometer of how the narratival tension, with its juridical literary axis, captured in Solomon's painting continued to thrive through the second half of the nineteenth century and beyond. More than ever there would be novels telling stories that seem to belong metaphorically to the court's waiting room, its *salle de pas perdus* (hall of lost steps), where fiction could rival the court even as it incorporated the court's energies and architectonics. From the perspective of English literary history the later Victorian period is filled with novels explicitly trying to map themselves in profound, or at least creative, ways against a trial scene. A short list of interesting examples not elsewhere mentioned in this book might include Dickens's *A Tale of Two Cities* (1859), Anthony Trollope's *Orley Farm* (1862), Henry Kingsley's *Austin Elliott* (1863), Charlotte Yonge's *The Trial* (1863), F. G. Trafford's *George Geith of Fen Court* (1865), Charles Reade's *Griffith Gaunt* (1866), Mary Elizabeth Braddon's *An Open Verdict* (1878), Maxwell Grey's (Mary G. Tuttiett's) *The Silence of Dean Maitland* (1886), H. Rider Haggard's *Mr. Meeson's Will* (1888), William Black's *Highland Cousins* (1894), and Walter Besant's *The Orange Girl* (1899).

In this book I have tried to mark the development in the first half of the nineteenth century of such later generative intersections with the law courts. More generally, I have tried to suggest and sketch the outlines of a moment when I believe some particular historical formal developments in the novel helped make the genre into one of the most significant forums for complex judgment of modern times, shaping the novels that followed. Without, I hope, oversimplifying a long and complex history of imbrication between literature and law, I have tried to show more clearly, for the novel as a genre, what it might mean—both historically and formally—to think of a trial that is depicted in a novel as a scene beside and through which the novel has positioned itself, in much the same way that we may link the gallows to criminal biography or a crime scene to detective fiction. In these final pages I will first recap and then briefly extend this exploration by returning to two key early-nineteenth-century Scottish works.[1]

The historical trajectory of the novel outlined here is perhaps best summed up by the first chapter of Walter Scott's most famous story about a trial, *The Heart of Midlothian* (1818). At the beginning of Scott's story, instead of delivering "a new number of an interesting periodical publication" to Peter Pattieson, a mail coach accidentally overturns and delivers, instead, its male passengers: two lawyers and an old client just out of jail.[2] One of these witty and easygoing lawyers, Mr. Hardie, proposes after a recuperative dinner at a nearby inn that the Edinburgh prison known as the "Heart of Midlothian" should have its "Last Speech, Confession, and Dying Words." This at least would be better than another novel, he opines:

> Whatever of guilt, crime, imposture . . . and unlooked-for change of fortune, can be found to chequer life, my Last Speech of the Tolbooth [the prison] should illustrate with examples sufficient to gorge even the public's all-devouring appetite for the wonderful and horrible. The inventor of fictitious narratives has to rack his brains for means to diversify his tale, and after all can hardly hit upon characters or incidents which have not been used again and again, until they are familiar to the eye of the reader, so that the development, *enlèvement*, the desperate wound of which the hero never dies, the burning fever from which the heroine is sure to recover, become a mere matter of course. . . . The end of uncertainty . . . is the death of interest; and hence it happens that no one now reads novels. (20–21)

Scott would obviously seem to be having a laugh at the novel here at the outset of his own. So used up is the genre already, we should return with a vengeance to producing those old and true criminal biographies, those gallows-colored accounts of "last words." He thereby teasingly promises, and deflates, his novel's originality, while he also good-humoredly mocks his "all-devouring" novel-reading audience and sends himself up as an author who "has to rack his brains" for a new plot twist. This joke is clear enough. What's puzzling, however, is the position of the lawyer speaking.

Having contemptuously declared that "no one now reads novels," he is immediately and comically unmasked as a zealous novel reader: "Hear him, ye gods!" says his friend; "you will hardly visit this learned gentleman, but you are likely to find the new novel most in repute lying on his table" (21). We are confusingly forced to realize that it is Mr. Hardie, not just Scott, who has his tongue in his cheek. As the wisecracking lawyer continues to press jovially for something as good as a collection of Scottish criminal trials he talks at length about producing, which he is sure is better than any novel, it gradually becomes clear that the metafictional joke here is not, after all, on him as a character in a novel, or even on the other characters who enter into the banter, but somehow primarily on *Scott*. And, at some point, this facet of the whole underlying sweep of the first chapter bursts on the reader like a punch line: all its extended, convoluted, pseudo-allegorical fun house mirroring of the novel's production casts Scott, the living author, as the absent but hapless object of its jesting.

It is in this way that we must understand the talk of the literary value of a Scottish collection of *Causes Célèbres* which eventually leads these two lawyers and a prisoner to recount the "narratives of remarkable trials" which form, we are told, the source of the entire subsequent tale (26). All is not witty, self-referential commentary planted by a controlling author but, rather, the reverse: an unfurling of some of the controlling historical frames that here comically propel author and novel. Out of scorned gallows literature and an imagined collection of Scottish state trials arises this early-nineteenth-century novel. Thus, Scott, progenitor of the Victorian novel and inventor of the historical novel, shows his own novel to be invented by literary history. We should—this book has been arguing—productively rethink our own history of crime fiction along Scott's lines: placing, as he does, the compelling paradigm of the law courts as an organizing force differentiating the novel from criminal biography most clearly before the advent of detective fiction, a narrative form Scott would not live to see.

Some of the theoretical implications behind such a historical view of the novel's relation to the law courts are perhaps best illustrated by another distinctly Scottish work and one of the most important primary texts of the period, James Hogg's *The Private Memoirs and Confessions of a Justified Sin-*

ner, Written by Himself (1824). Understood in conjunction with M. M. Bakhtin's much-neglected treatise *Toward a Philosophy of the Act* (1919–21), this novel can help suggest by way of conclusion why the strange literary category of alibi has haunted me and my understanding of the juridical architecture of the novel as I wrote this book.

Like an alibi, which must tell one story to refigure another, Hogg's story is devilishly divided into two parts that each recount the same set of events but turn out to be completely at odds with each other: first, "The Editor's Narrative," written in the third person, tells the story of the aristocratic George Colwan's torment by his religious half-brother Robert Wringham; then, the "Private Memoirs and Confessions of a Sinner," written in the first person by Robert Wringham, relate that same story from his viewpoint. Part of the achievement of Hogg's novel is to destroy any assurance of what the "truth" might be. The speciously lucid Editor is as untrustworthy and self-interested as the hallucinating Robert Wringham, whose grave the Editor ghoulishly digs up at the end of the story. Readers are better off paying attention to the marginalized local working people. As Gary Kelly sensibly advises, "the only truth apparent to the reader is offered by dialect speakers, not the two principal narrators who use standard written English."[3] These vernacular speeches, which often express the crucial view that "truth" may be self-contradictory and contingent, break through the bifurcation of the story into equally tendentious objective and subjective accounts.

Hogg likewise introduces the law court into the story as a site that momentarily wrests narratorial authority from its ostensible authors, the Editor and Wringham.[4] Just as the standard English–speaking authors are actually triangulated with the dialect speakers, the two written narratives are triangulated with the storytelling forum of the court. In a key trial scene control momentarily shifts from the narrator to a minor character, Bessie Gillies, who speaks commandingly from the witness stand. We see this shift even in the novel's written format; as in a number of other official nineteenth-century novelistic tribunals, we are suddenly provided in this trial scene with identifying tag lines (as in the script of a play): "From the Judge" and "The Judge."[5] The Editor's narrating voice, displaced by the storytelling forum of the court, gives way to Bessie's voice.

Bessie is to prove that some silver spoons, a gown, and other property recovered from Bell Calvert are stolen from her mistress, Miss Logan. The stolen goods are on display in the court. Knowing that Bell will be hanged for taking items Miss Logan can well afford to replace, Bessie commits what would ordinarily be called pious perjury. Yet, rather than simply deny the objects are Miss Logan's, Bessie claims to be unable to *know* that they are the same objects. They may look "like" them, but, as Bessie says, "Bless you, sir, I wadna swear to my ain fore finger, if it had been as lang out o' my sight, an' brought in an' laid on that table" (67). It is a case of apprehending that an object is identical to itself and not simply just like some other object. Mightn't these spoons, in other words, have an alibi? Are they the same spoons? The point at first seems silly, but, as the novel progresses, Bessie's forensic dilemma will recur in a much more disturbing and real form, first for Thomas Drummond, whose inability to prove an *alibi* makes him Wringham's scapegoat (91), and then even more strangely for Wringham himself, the justified sinner, who must ask: is he identical with himself? Is it necessarily the case that he is responsible for acts apparently committed by himself?

"This is unaccountable," Wringham says. "It is impossible that I can have been doing a thing, and not doing it at the same time. But indeed, honest woman, there have several incidents occurred to me in the course of my life which persuade me I have a second self; or that there is some other being who appears in my likeness"(177). In this strange story at some level we understand that Wringham's childhood friend and guide, Gil-Martin, is "actually" the devil and that he is assuming Wringham's likeness to commit all manner of crimes. We readers hardly know what to make of Gil-Martin's presence: he seems a psychological projection of Wringham's, but, if so, are we even sure that simply makes him unreal? We may pass further beyond such impossible factual questions to realize Wringham's turmoil, like the novel's dual structure itself, raises fundamental questions about what it means to be "accountable" at all.

As we near the end of the story, Wringham's incoherence of self only worsens: "I seemed hardly to be an accountable creature; being thus in the habit of executing transactions of the utmost moment, without being sensible that I did them. I was a being incomprehensible to myself. . . . To be in a state of consciousness and unconsciousness, at the same time, in the same body and same spirit, was impossible" (182). Not surprisingly, his story ends with his flight from the law, fearing a trial that would, Kafka-like, require him to account for himself, when this is just what he cannot do. As his servant informs him, "It seems there are some strong presumptuous proofs against you, and I came to warn you this day that a precognition is in progress, and that unless you are perfectly convinced, not only of your innocence, but of your ability to prove it, it will be the safest course for you to abscond, and let the trial go on without you" (191).

A pedant, or perhaps a reader under the spell of the Editor, might point out that Wringham merely needs an insanity defense (he's been in a fugue), and Hogg's novel looks forward to the rise of medical jurisprudence and the changes in the law which arose from the McNaughtan case of 1843. But, as Wringham's metaphysical speculations about his profound lack of self-posses-sion suggest, we are in deeper waters here: by the end of the novel Robert Wringham is somehow living an alibi, a being elsewhere from himself.

Hogg's character-experiment comes remarkably close to what Bakhtin, al-most a century later in an authoritarian Russia, was confusingly trying to ana-lyze in one of his earliest philosophical projects, *Toward a Philosophy of the Act*. In this unfinished work Bakhtin, thinking of alibis primarily in broad, modern terms as excuse stories, suggested that for humans there is "no alibi in being" (*ne-alibi v bytii*): we are (1) stuck with the singularity of our existence and (2) accountable for and to it. At one level the unstoppable and unrepeat-able rush of our existence in the present forms our "once-occurrent event of Being," as Bakhtin calls it. At another level we must fashion a relation to this present, representing it to ourselves and others and thus understanding our lives as "answerable self-activity."[6]

As Wringham realizes to his cost, even if we happen to be unconscious of our acts or find them inexplicable, they are still *ours* as we each uniquely move through time and space. In Bakhtin this bind becomes the ground of a philo-sophical description for human life. In a cosmic sense: I have no alibi, therefore I am. *Ne-alibi v bytii*, no-alibi-in-being, names the lack of an absence that makes for our perpetual presence. Complexly, it purposely names our irre-ducible, moment-by-moment, living presence in the world, our being, from the vantage point of language and of stories with which that beingness is bound up but to which it is not precisely the same. Thus, in Bakhtin's inwoven formula-tion, as beings without alibis for our acts, we necessarily construct stories at-taching an otherwise actually unrepresentable reality to us, constructing our self-consciousness and making our lives accountable—justified. Put in other words, in Bakhtin's theorization it matters that we humans do *not* have an alibi for what has happened to us because, having experienced "life," we produce stories that answer for it, alibi-like, even as those stories shape that experience.

In *Confessions of a Justified Sinner* Hogg toys with a similar gap he sees between representation and actual experience: the Editor's ostensibly objective version of the story turns out to be nothing more than another representation, and Wringham's subjective version is also no more right about reality. (The truest words of the book turn out to be Samuel Scrape's retelling of a fablelike story which provides a miniature version and gloss on Hogg's own story, never trying to adjudge its reality.) By the novel's end Hogg's story has imploded into itself—self-consciously incorporating Wringham's printed confessions, then pulling in the Editor as a character, and finally even portraying Hogg, whose self-depiction as the "Ettrick Shepherd" reflects how others represented him. The result is not a preview of postmodern, reflexive linguistic realities, though it can sometimes feel like that. Rather, Hogg is, I think, playing with a serious and elemental ideological project of the nineteenth-century novel: its attempt to picture—and construct—a social network composed of individual accountable lives being lived, a republic of justifying citizens.

Confessions of a Justified Sinner thus illuminates a basic illusion woven by nineteenth-century novels: to present realistically the account of a life and society as the agglomeration of such intersecting accounts. An unspoken contract with their implied readers is that their representations will construct an "answerable" life, to use Bakhtin's term. This is what I think we mean when we weakly describe the nineteenth-century novel as presenting "linear" or "organic" lives, "integrated egos," or fantasies of coherence, in distinction to the fragmentation or decentering of subjectivity found in modernist works. It is not that nineteenth-century authors or readers naively thought that life actually had a simple coherent and organic shape. The series of traumas and transgressions, liminal states and border crossings, which make up the nineteenth-century novel belie that simplistic notion. Rather, nineteenth-century novels endeavored to work out how that fragmented, actual "once-occurrent" life could be made into answerable self-activity *at the level of representation.*

More than other novels, Hogg's impossibly double story reminds us that this accounting for lives is a construction and is what novels preeminently construct. In a straightforward way we can recognize this as why readers of nine-teenth-century novels typically see different versions of a story, and especially unpublished endings, as a fatal rupturing of the tale: not because the alternate texts are better or worse but because, as readers, we have invested our belief in the singleness of the protagonist's represented experience and given the char-acter what we quite accurately, colloquially, call "life." More complexly, in upending this assumption of accountability in 1824, Hogg's novel helps pin-point the way novels were newly central in imagining ordinary lives as answer-able activity. If we step back and look at the larger, historical epistemological frameworks depicted in this novel, we may see Hogg decimating the earlier claims to truth of both eighteenth-century Enlightenment rationality (the Edi-tor) and religion (Wringham). We can then also perhaps see at work a larger post–French Revolutionary, republican ideology in which the novel is partici-pating: the remaking of society into the agglomeration of its individuals' ac-countable stories. A primary function of the realist novel as an art form is not simply to reflect this state but to express it, to body it forth, producing in its readers the imaginative capacity for accounting for variegated individual lived lives which it exercises, and silently uniting its readers in the project of imagin-ing the world in these always-being-constructed terms.

It is no accident, then, that, as in *Caleb Williams, Frankenstein, Pickwick, Mary Barton, Eugene Aram,* and other novels, Hogg's novel simultaneously exposes and is caught up in a justice system that atomizes society into indi-vidual, self-justifying storytellers—a people tensed toward (narrative) answer-ability, for whom the law courts were newly magnetic. As the title of one of J. H. Riddell's novels would later put it, modernity—increasingly unable to look forward and upward to the retrospection of an ecclesiastical final judg-ment day—was founded on the secularized, here-and-now accountability of *A Life's Assize* (1871). In this modern world a juridical narrative architecture tied the novel to the newly empowered law courts. That tie between the novel and the law courts has been the subject of this book, and, in retracing its rise in the early nineteenth century, I have tried to restore a sense of what the novel was in a time and place when the novel carried an ethical weight that we, having reduced the novel to a marginal form, may mistakenly dismiss as Victorian overearnestness.

Introduction

---

1. Martin Meisel, *Realizations: Narrative, Pictorial, and Theatrical Arts in Nine-teenth-Century England* (Princeton: Princeton University Press, 1983), 296.

2. James Dafforne, "British Artists: Their Style and Character," *Art-Journal,* 3d ser., 1 (1862): 73.

3. "John Trot at the Royal Academy," *Punch* 32 (1857): 200; *Athenaeum,* 19 December 1857, 1592.

4. George Eliot, *Adam Bede,* ed. Stephen Gill (New York: Penguin, 1985), 177.

5. Ian Watt, *The Rise of the Novel: Studies in Defoe, Richardson, and Fielding* (Berkeley: University of California Press, 1957), 31. Kieran Dolin, for instance, quotes Watt in *Fiction and the Law: Legal Discourse in Victorian and Modernist Literature* (Cambridge: Cambridge University Press, 1999), 1.

6. See John Bender, *Imagining the Penitentiary: Fiction and the Architecture of Mind in Eighteenth-Century England* (Chicago: University of Chicago Press, 1987), esp. chap. 6, 165–98.

CHAPTER ONE
From Scaffold to Law Court, from Criminal
Broadsheet and Biography to Newspaper and Novel

---

1. References are, respectively, to Leon Radzinowicz, *A History of English Crimi-nal Law and Its Administration from 1750,* 2 vols. (New York: Macmillan, 1948); Michel Foucault, *Discipline and Punish: The Birth of the Prison,* trans. Alan Sheridan (New York: Vintage, 1979); J. M. Beattie, *Crime and the Courts in England, 1660–1800* (Princeton: Princeton University Press, 1986); V. A. C. Gatrell, *The Hanging Tree: Exe-cution and the English People, 1770–1868* (Oxford: Oxford University Press, 1994); and John Stuart Mill, "Civilization," in *Essays on Politics and Society,* vol. 18 of *Collected Works of John Stuart Mill,* ed. J. M. Robson (Toronto: University of Toronto Press, 1977), 130. Unless otherwise indicated, quotations from Beattie refer to *Crime and the Courts* and from Gatrell to *Hanging Tree,* and they will be cited parenthetically in the text. For a jurisprudential history of the law, see J. H. Baker, *An Introduction to English Legal History,* 3d ed. (London: Butterworths, 1990).

2. See Michael Ignatieff, *A Just Measure of Pain: The Penitentiary in the Industrial Revolution, 1750–1850* (New York: Pantheon, 1978); and "State, Civil Society, and Total Institutions: A Critique of Recent Social Histories of Punishment," in *Crime and Justice: An Annual Review of Research* 3 (1981): 153–92. On transportation, which meant not just to be banished but to be sold as a servant (e.g., into slavelike conditions on a Virginia tobacco farm), see A. Roger Ekirch, *Bound for America: The Transporta-tion of British Convicts to the Colonies, 1718–1775* (Oxford: Clarendon, 1987); and

A. G. L. Shaw, *Convicts and the Colonies: A Study of Penal Transportation from Great Britain and Ireland to Australia and Other Parts of the British Empire* (London: Faber and Faber, 1966). In the words of the epigraph to Marcus Clarke's novel *His Natural Life* (1870–72), quoted from evidence given in the House of Commons in 1837, transportation "may be made more terrible than Death."

3. James Boswell, *Life of Johnson* (London: Oxford University Press, 1953), 1211. Johnson was not being bloodthirsty; see *The Rambler*, no. 114.

4. *Daily News* (London), 15 November 1864.

5. Raymond Williams, *Culture and Society, 1780–1950* (New York: Columbia University Press, 1958), 297–300; and the entry for "Masses" in Williams's *Keywords: A Vocabulary of Culture and Society,* rev. ed. (New York: Oxford University Press, 1983), 192–97.

6. Charles Dickens, letter to the editor, *Times* (London), 14 November 1849. Later Dickens takes the same line with the lingering presence of public whippings, protesting them "not [out of] the least regard or pity for the criminal . . . but in consideration for the general tone and feeling" ("Lying Awake," *Household Words* 6 [1852]: 147). Indeed, immediately after its public prohibition in 1862, whipping in private was reinstated by "the Garroters Act." As Martin J. Wiener reasons of its resurrection: "This turn of events powerfully suggests that what had been most widely upsetting about these penalties (beyond the ranks of committed humanitarians) had not been so much the fact of infliction of bodily pain or death upon malefactors, but its visibility and the psychological consequences that were felt to flow from that act of witness" (*Reconstructing the Criminal: Culture, Law, and Policy in England, 1830–1914* [Cambridge: Cambridge University Press, 1990], 100).

7. See E. P. Thompson, *Whigs and Hunters: The Origin of the Black Act* (New York: Pantheon, 1975); and Douglas Hay, "Property, Authority, and the Criminal Law," in *Albion's Fatal Tree: Crime and Society in Eighteenth-Century England* (New York: Pantheon, 1975), 17–63.

8. Robin Evans, in *The Fabrication of Virtue: English Prison Architecture, 1750–1840* (Cambridge: Cambridge University Press, 1982), places Bentham's panopticon in the larger historical reinvention of prison architecture. References to the law court's architecture are predictably rare in Bentham's work. In *Rationale of Judicial Evidence* (1827) he observes the importance of court architecture in appropriately reinforcing privacy and publicity (bk. 2, chap. 10), and in that work's prefatory, posthumously published "Introductory View of the Rationale of Evidence" he looks forward in a footnote to the enlargement of the courts at Westminster (chap. 8). In *Constitutional Code* (1830) he recommends putting up placards in court (inscribed, for instance, with the greatest happiness principle) and describes in fascinating detail how a night judge's chamber might be divided into separate spaces for the performance of judicial duties and sleeping (see bk. 2, chaps. 12–13).

9. Randall McGowen, "The Image of Justice and Reform of the Criminal Law in Early Nineteenth-Century England," *Buffalo Law Review* 32 (1983): 96–97.

10. See Nikolaus Pevsner, *A History of Building Types: The A. W. Mellon Lectures*

in the Fine Arts, 1970 (Princeton: Princeton University Press, 1976), 53. Pevsner suggests the first stand-alone courthouse in England was John Carr's construction of a court and a prison as look-alike, detached buildings in York.

11. Foucault, *Discipline and Punish,* 9.

12. Ibid., 183.

13. In his next work on power, *The History of Sexuality,* vol. 1: *An Introduction,* trans. Robert Hurley (New York: Vintage, 1980), Foucault seems better to recognize the import of the law courts, arguing that "the judicial institution is increasingly incorporated into a continuum of apparatuses (medical, administrative, and so on) whose functions are for the most part regulatory" (144). Still, the law courts never directly form his subject because he is interested in emphasizing the wider jigsaw of power relations. For a discussion of studying the law courts in the wake of Foucault's work on discipline, see Katherine Fischer Taylor, *In the Theater of Criminal Justice: The Palais de Justice in Second Empire Paris* (Princeton: Princeton University Press, 1993), 106–7.

14. Hay, "Property," 27.

15. Ibid., 30.

16. *Country* here literally means the local county.

17. John H. Langbein, "Shaping the Eighteenth-Century Criminal Trial: A View from the Ryder Sources," *University of Chicago Law Review* 50 (1983): 2; see also "The Criminal Trial before the Lawyers," *University of Chicago Law Review* 45 (1978): 263–316; and "The Prosecutorial Origins of Defence Counsel in the Eighteenth Century: The Appearance of Solicitors," *Cambridge Law Journal* 58 (1999): 314–65. For an elucidation and summary of Langbein's work, see J. M. Beattie, "Scales of Justice: Defense Counsel and the English Criminal Trial in the Eighteenth and Nineteenth Centuries," *Law and History Review* 9 (1991): 221–67.

18. Langbein, "Ryder," 115.

19. F. D. MacKinnon, "The Law and the Lawyers," in *Johnson's England: An Account of the Life and Manners of His Age,* ed. A. S. Turberville, 2 vols. (Oxford: Clarendon, 1933), 2:307.

20. On the history of the jury trial, see Thomas Andrew Green, *Verdict according to Conscience: Perspectives on the English Criminal Trial Jury, 1200–1800* (Chicago: University of Chicago Press, 1985), esp. chap. 7, 267–317, on the jury trial in the eighteenth century; and *Twelve Good Men and True: The Criminal Trial Jury in England, 1200–1800,* ed. J. S. Cockburn and Thomas Andrew Green (Princeton: Princeton University Press, 1988). The jury in the eighteenth century was quite different from its ancient origins as the witnesses called to swear (*jurer*) what they knew of the crime, and it is also quite different from our modern jury. The eighteenth-century jury is perhaps best described as an extension of the bench. It was usually composed of a set of experienced jurors. Once formed, it sat through many trials in a single session and worked expertly under the close direction of the judge. Although the jury had officially established its independence from the judge's direct coercion in 1670, the judge could force the jury to explain its verdict, pressure the jury to change its verdict, recommend a verdict to the jury, and quash guilty verdicts with which he disagreed by organizing a

pardon. Such measures, however, were rarely necessary. Probably only after 1738, when the jury at the Old Bailey adopted the custom of rendering a verdict after each trial, did they even begin to sit together in the courtroom, and this arrangement itself was only necessary because they did not usually retire to deliberate. E. P. Thompson quotes a 1767 report that, "as the custom is now, they sit among the crowd, undistinguished, and it is not easy to know them from the rest of the spectators" ("In Defence of the Jury," in *Making History: Writings on History and Culture* [New York: New Press, 1994], 149).

21. On the impact and history of the Prisoners' Counsel Act, see David J. A. Cairns, *Advocacy and the Making of the Adversarial Criminal Trial, 1800–1865* (Oxford: Clarendon, 1998).

22. Foucault, *Discipline and Punish,* 19.

23. Edward Herbert, "A Pen and Ink Sketch of a Late Trial for Murder," *London Magazine,* February 1824, 166.

24. John Bender, *Imagining the Penitentiary,* 176. It has been commonly noted that the novel presents a "case"; see, for example, J. Paul Hunter, *Before Novels: The Cultural Contexts of Eighteenth-Century English Fiction* (New York: Norton, 1990), 289–90.

25. Bender, *Imagining the Penitentiary,* 177.

26. Charles Cottu, *On the Administration of Criminal Justice in England; and the Spirit of the English Government* (London, 1822), 105–6.

27. "Examine the Prisoner!" cried *All the Year Round* 7 (1862): 306. See E. M. Palmegiano, comp., *Crime in Victorian Britain: An Annotated Bibliography from Nineteenth-Century British Magazines* (Westport, Conn.: Greenwood, 1993); John H. Langbein, "The Historical Origins of the Privilege against Self-Incrimination at Common Law," *Michigan Law Review* 92 (1994): 1047–85.

28. Alexander Welsh, *Strong Representations: Narrative and Circumstantial Evidence in England* (Baltimore: Johns Hopkins University Press, 1992), 8. Jan-Melissa Schramm shows how, on the underside of a historic new emphasis on circumstantial narrative, nineteenth-century novels nonetheless often insisted on depicting its opposite: a model of justice in which the accused speaks. See *Testimony and Advocacy in Victorian Law, Literature, and Theology* (Cambridge: Cambridge University Press, 2000).

29. Adam Smith, *The Theory of Moral Sentiments,* ed. D. D. Raphael and A. L. Macfie (Oxford: Clarendon, 1976), 82–85, 109–13. Note that, as Smith's term *spectator* suggests, Smith's philosophy of justice resonates with the theater, not prose narrative, as David Marshall argues in "Adam Smith and the Theatricality of Moral Sentiments," *Critical Inquiry* 10 (1984): 592–613. In general, on Smith, see Bender, *Imagining the Penitentiary,* 218–28.

30. A new guidebook was introduced in the eighteenth century and became popular in the first half of the nineteenth: *Every Man His Own Lawyer.* And in 1832 "The Society for the Diffusion of Useful Knowledge" thought fit to publish collections of state trials.

31. Margaret Anne Doody, "George Eliot and the Eighteenth-Century Novel," *Nineteenth-Century Fiction* 35 (1980): 287.

32. José Ortega y Gasset, "Notes on the Novel," trans. Helene Weyl, in *The Dehumanization of Art and Other Writings on Art and Culture* (Princeton: Princeton University Press, 1948), 103.

33. See M. T. Clanchy, *From Memory to Written Record: England, 1066–1307*, 2d ed. (Oxford: Blackwell, 1993).

34. *The Eumenides,* the third play of Aeschylus's *Oresteia* trilogy, not only portrays the earliest known Western trial but also models the law court's theatrical form as part of its civics lesson. The complex confluence between the ancient tragic stage and the Athenian law courts has been much discussed; a good example is Kathy Eden's *Poetic and Legal Fiction in the Aristotelian Tradition* (Princeton: Princeton University Press, 1986).

35. Wiener, *Reconstructing the Criminal,* 50.

36. C. J. W. Allen, *The Law of Evidence in Victorian England* (Cambridge: Cambridge University Press, 1997), 149.

37. See Cecilia Lucy Brightwell, ed., *Memorials of the Life of Amelia Opie,* 2d ed. (London: Longman, Brown, 1854).

38. See Lennard J. Davis, *Factual Fictions: The Origins of the English Novel* (New York: Columbia University Press, 1983); and Catherine Gallagher, *Nobody's Story: The Vanishing Acts of Women Writers in the Marketplace, 1670–1820* (Berkeley: University of California Press, 1994), esp. xvi.

39. Henry Mayhew, *London Labour and the London Poor,* 4 vols. (1861–62; rpt., New York: Dover, 1968), 1:223–24, also see 1:229.

40. Ibid., 1:281.

41. Foucault, *Discipline and Punish,* 68.

42. Hannah More, "The History of Mr. Fantom, The New-Fashioned Philosopher and His Man William," in *The Repository Tales,* vol. 1 of *The Works of Hannah More,* 7 vols. (New York: Harper and Brothers, 1836), 1–23.

43. Foucault, *Discipline and Punish,* 68.

44. An example of this complex shift is the Ordinary's *Account,* provided by the prison chaplain, who turned his exclusive access to the prisoner's "Last dying speech and confession" into profit, even if that sometimes meant literally doing some ghostwriting. In the beginning of the eighteenth century the *Account* took the form of broadsheets. By midcentury the *Account* had turned into a longer format, which was more expensive. It was extinct by the 1820s. As Philip Rawlings explains: "It is surely no coincidence that, as the literature of crime, including the biographies, became more sophisticated and more critical in its discussion of crime and the criminal justice system, the *Accounts,* with their simplistic portrayal of the progression to the gallows, began to disappear. But there were also other, longer-term pressures which reduced the importance of the *Accounts.* The improved reporting of trials, both in specialist publications like the OBSP [Old Bailey Session Papers] and in the biographies, showed events as linked together through cause and effect, and the offender as an individual

who is rational and responsible and whose actions can be rationally explained, rather than as directed by a divinely ordained progression from sin to the gallows" (*Drunks, Whores, and Idle Apprentices: Criminal Biographies of the Eighteenth Century* [London: Routledge, 1992], 26). See also P. Linebaugh, "The Ordinary of Newgate and His *Account,*" in *Crime in England, 1550–1800,* ed. J. S. Cockburn (Princeton: Princeton University Press, 1977), 246–69.

45. Richard D. Altick, *Victorian Studies in Scarlet* (New York: Norton, 1970), 113–14.

46. Ibid., 109.

47. [Thomas Denman], "Laws of Evidence—Criminal Procedure—Publicity," *Edinburgh Review* 40 (1824): 171. This is a review article of Et. Dumont, *Traité des Preuves Judiciaires* (Paris, 1823).

48. Scott to Miss Clephane, 23 January 1824, *The Letters of Sir Walter Scott, 1823–1825,* ed. H. J. C. Grierson (1932; rpt., New York: AMS Press, 1971), 160.

49. Altick, *Victorian Studies in Scarlet,* 56.

50. Ibid., 55.

51. James Sutherland, *The Restoration Newspaper and Its Development* (Cambridge: Cambridge University Press, 1986), 49, 49, 47. See also Fredrick Seaton Siebert, *Freedom of the Press in England, 1476–1776: The Rise and Decline of Government Controls* (Urbana: University of Illinois Press, 1952); and James Oldham, "Law Reporting in the London Newspapers, 1756–1786," *American Journal of Legal History* 31 (1987): 177–206. Oldham reports that occasional legal columns began to develop toward 1786 and that "attention to activities in the courts accelerated during the late 1700s, and it is my expectation that this pattern continued to the end of the century and onward" (206).

52. See Langbein, "Before the Lawyers," 270; Beattie, *Crime and the Courts,* 24.

53. Lucy Brown, *Victorian News and Newspapers* (Oxford: Clarendon, 1985), 147. The court did order that the consecutive trials of the Cato Street conspirators could not be published until they were all completed, and an editor was fined for defying this order.

54. Denman, "Laws of Evidence," 199.

55. England enforced strict contempt of court laws that would check "newspaper convictions or acquittals," in marked contrast to the United States. See Arthur L. Goodhart, "Newspapers and Contempt of Court in English Law," *Harvard Law Review* 48 (1935): 885–910.

56. Denman, "Laws of Evidence," 197.

57. "The 'Moral Lesson' of the Gallows," *Punch* 10 (1846): 33.

58. "The Press and the Law of Libel," *Solicitors' Journal* 2 (1858): 657. Not all judicial proceedings of course were, or are, open. Jeremy Bentham anatomizes the tension between publicity and privacy in legal procedure in *Rationale of Judicial Evidence* (1827). He also objects that the courts in Westminster Hall are so small that they physically preclude adequate publicity, and he looks forward to "those architectural im-

provements which have been sometimes talked of" (*The Works of Jeremy Bentham,* ed. John Bowring, 11 vols. [1843; rpt., Bristol: Thoemmes, 1995], 4:26–27).

59. Edward Bulwer Lytton, *A Word to the Public* (London: Saunders and Otley, 1847), 28.

60. Benedict Anderson, *Imagined Communities: Reflections on the Origin and Spread of Nationalism,* rev. ed. (London: Verso, 1983), 35.

61. FitzGerald to John Allen, 3 December 1865, *The Letters of Edward FitzGerald,* vol. 2: *1851–1866,* ed. Alfred McKinley Terhune and Annabelle Burdick Terhune (Princeton: Princeton University Press, 1980), 568. FitzGerald continues his letter with a quotation from John Gay's *Beggar's Opera* (3.1): "The Charge is prepared; the Lawyers are met, / The Judges are rang'd, a terrible show."

62. For example, see Michael McKeon, *The Origins of the English Novel, 1600–1740* (Baltimore: Johns Hopkins University Press, 1987), 96–100, 382–94.

63. As is generally well-known, Newgate was the name of a famous London prison, razed in 1902; less well-known is that the names of imprisoned people taking their trial would be inscribed on an official court document called the "Crown Calendar," or simply the "Calendar." Judgments would also be recorded in the Calendar's margin next to each prisoner's name. Another Newgate Calendar source for novelists was Thomas Salmon's popular *A Compleat Collection of State-Tryals,* first published in 1719, and one of the earliest anthologies was Alexander Smith's *The History of the Lives of the Most Noted Highway-men* (1714). Rayner Heppenstall's *Reflections on the Newgate Calendar* (London: W. H. Allen, 1975) provides a nice tour through the *Newgate Calendar.*

64. Maximillian E. Novak, "'Appearances of Truth': The Literature of Crime as a Narrative System (1660–1841)," *Yearbook of English Studies* 11 (1981): 30.

65. John J. Richetti, *Popular Fiction before Richardson: Narrative Patterns, 1700–1739* (Oxford: Clarendon, 1969); Lincoln B. Faller, *Turned to Account: The Forms and Functions of Criminal Biography in Late Seventeenth-and Early Eighteenth-Century England* (Cambridge: Cambridge University Press, 1987). More recently, displaying a sharp eye for the subversive and novelistic moments that crop up in early gallows writing, trial reports, crime reporting, and criminal biographies, Hal Gladfelder has pinpointed important moments that escape Richetti and Faller's otherwise accurate generalizations; see *Criminality and Narrative in Eighteenth-Century England: Beyond the Law* (Baltimore: Johns Hopkins University Press, 2001).

66. Faller, *Turned to Account,* 195.

67. Richetti, *Popular Fiction before Richardson,* 34.

CHAPTER TWO
Caleb Williams and the Novel's Forensic Form

1. Henry Crabb Robinson, *Henry Crabb Robinson on Books and Their Writers,* ed. Edith J. Morley, 3 vols. (London: Dent, 1938), 1:377.

2. See, for instance, Ian Ousby, *Bloodhounds of Heaven: The Detective in English Fiction from Godwin to Doyle* (Cambridge: Harvard University Press, 1976).

3. In general, Godwin's connection of his novel to the politics of his times and to his work *Political Justice* has kept discussion of this novel grounded in its historical context. The current thread of that historical discussion begins with Gary Kelly, *The English Jacobin Novel, 1780–1805* (Oxford: Clarendon, 1976); and Marilyn Butler, *Jane Austen and the War of Ideas* (Oxford: Clarendon, 1975). Equally important has been the way *Caleb Williams* turns the *telling* of its story into the subject of its story, and this novel was something of a textbook case for deconstructive readings with a political bent. See, for example, chapter 6 of Tilottama Rajan, *The Supplement of Reading: Figures of Understanding in Romantic Theory and Practice* (Ithaca: Cornell University Press, 1990), 167–94; or Karl N. Simms, "Caleb Williams' Godwin: Things as they Are Written," *Studies in Romanticism* 26 (1987): 343–63.

4. An important exception is John P. Zomchick's study of the eighteenth-century formation of a juridical subject—a term by which he refers to characters broadly constituted through internalizing their society's public legal discourse. Zomchick traces eighteenth-century literature up to Caleb Williams; see *Family and the Law in Eighteenth-Century Fiction: The Public Conscience in the Private Sphere* (Cambridge: Cambridge University Press, 1993). Here I take Godwin as the beginning, rather than the end, of a literary school, my thinking in this respect shaped by Pamela Clemit, *The Godwinian Novel: The Rational Fictions of Godwin, Brockden Brown, Mary Shelley* (Oxford: Clarendon, 1993).

5. At the most basic level connections are reconstructed, as in Nancy Jane Tyson's *Eugene Aram: Literary History and Typology of the Scholar-Criminal* (Hamden, Conn.: Archon, 1983), while in the most sophisticated treatment, as in Eric Rothstein's work, the allusions to criminal biography are explained as a complex part of the way Godwin has Caleb telling his story (see *Systems of Order and Inquiry in Later Eighteenth-Century Fiction* [Berkeley: University California Press, 1975], esp. 212, 219–21, 231). Specific attention has been paid to Godwin's self-conscious construction of a world of print within his novel in Garrett A. Sullivan Jr., "'A Story To Be Hastily Gobbled Up': *Caleb Williams* and Print Culture," *Studies in Romanticism* 32 (1993): 323–37.

6. William Godwin, *Caleb Williams,* ed. David McCracken (London: Oxford University Press, 1970), 222. Further references to the novel are from this edition and are included in the text.

7. Marilyn Butler and Mark Philp, introduction to *The Collected Novels and Memoirs of William Godwin, Volume 1,* ed. Mark Philp (London: Pickering, 1992), 26, 43.

8. For a different but related view of the characters' use of narrative conventions, see Donald R. Wehrs, "Rhetoric, History, Rebellion: *Caleb Williams* and the Subversion of Eighteenth-Century Fiction," *Studies in English Literature, 1500–1900* 28 (1988): 497–511.

9. Kenneth W. Graham, *The Politics of Narrative: Ideology and Social Change in William Godwin's* Caleb Williams (New York: AMS, 1990), 70.

10. Gary Handwerk, "Of Caleb's Guilt and Godwin's Truth: Ideology and Ethics in *Caleb Williams,*" *ELH* 60 (1993): 953. Handwerk's essay provides an example of the continuing, increasingly acute critical attempts to reconstruct the relationships

between the contents of the novel and the contents of *Political Justice*. For further considerations of the ending's "tendency"—that is, "the actual effect it is calculated to produce upon the reader," which Godwin discusses in "Of Choice in Reading" in *The Enquirer: Reflections on Education, Manners, and Literature* (Dublin: J. Moore, 1797), 136—see, for instance, Rajan, *Supplement of Reading*, 183–90; Kristen Leaver, "Pursuing Conversations: *Caleb Williams* and the Romantic Construction of the Reader," *Studies in Romanticism* 33 (1994): 589–610; and Robert W. Uphaus, "*Caleb Williams*: Godwin's Epoch of Mind," *Studies in the Novel* 9 (1977): 279–96.

11. *Morning Chronicle*, 8 February 1793.

12. Novak, "Literature of Crime," 45.

13. Ibid., 45.

14. William Godwin, *Enquiry Concerning Political Justice, with Selections from Godwin's Other Writings*, ed. K. Codell Carter (Oxford: Clarendon, 1971), 5.

15. Shortly after *Caleb Williams*'s publication, Godwin was in court supporting his colleagues being prosecuted in the famous treason trials of the 1790s. Aided by Godwin's "Cursory Strictures on the Charge delivered by Lord Chief Justice Eyre to the Grand Jury" (*Morning Chronicle*, 21 October 1794), the defense did challenge, in part, the contemporary institution of the law in these trials; see John Barrell, *The Birth of Pandora and the Division of Knowledge* (Philadelphia: University of Pennsylvania Press, 1992), 119–43.

16. *Morning Chronicle*, 8 February 1793.

17. Mary Shelley, quoted in C. Kegan Paul, *William Godwin: His Friends and Contemporaries*, 2 vols. (London, 1876), 1:80. *Political Justice*'s actual price (at thirty-six shillings) was less than two guineas; *Caleb Williams* first sold for nine shillings or so (*British Critic* 1 [1793]: 307; *British Critic* 4 [1794]: 70; *Critical Review* 11 [1794]: 290).

18. *Morning Chronicle*, 30 March 1793.

19. Paul, *William Godwin*, 1:126.

20. Thompson, *Whigs and Hunters*, 267.

21. See "Of The Right of Private Judgement," bk. 2, chap. 6, in Godwin, *Political Justice*, 90–96; the trials violate that fundamental right in Godwin's philosophy: that of private judgment. Godwin's quarrel is not with any specific trial procedures or specific laws; as he makes clear in an exchange of public letters with an agitated lawyer, he is concerned with the larger social field and structuring of individuals which is constructed by the current justice system (see *British Critic* 5 [1795]: 444–47; and *British Critic* 6 [1795]: 94–95).

22. William Hawkins, *A Treatise of the Pleas of the Crown . . .* , 2 vols. (London: 1716–21), 2:400.

23. William Godwin, Manuscript of *Caleb Williams,* 3 vols., National Art Library, Victoria and Albert Museum, 2:25, quoted in Graham, *Politics of Narrative,* 62. Godwin quotes from *Hamlet,* 2.2.598.

24. John Bender, "Impersonal Violence: The Penetrating Gaze and the Field of Narration in *Caleb Williams,*" in *Vision and Textuality,* ed. Stephen Melville and Bill Readings (Durham: Duke University Press, 1995), 256–81.

25. Roy Pascal, *The Dual Voice: Free Indirect Speech and Its Functioning in the Nineteenth-Century European Novel* (Manchester: Manchester University Press, 1977).

26. See Dorrit Cohn, *Transparent Minds: Narrative Modes for Presenting Consciousness in Fiction* (Princeton: Princeton University Press, 1978), esp. 107–16. Ann Banfield would argue that the narratorial sentences presenting characters' speech or thought are better described as narratorless, and another approach here might be to see Caleb as aspiring, lawyerlike, for his story to speak itself; see *Unspeakable Sentences: Narration and Representation in the Language of Fiction* (Boston: Routledge, 1982).

27. Godwin creatively and productively participated in the reconstruction of the novelistic narrator which was in full swing at the turn of the century. Writing in the wake of such formally innovative novels as his friend Elizabeth Inchbald's *A Simple Story* (1791), he helped stretch the relation of quotation to narration—rearranging the grammar of relations between self and other. On this link between authority and literary form, particularly free indirect discourse, see V. N. Voloshinov [and M. M. Bakhtin], *Marxism and the Philosophy of Language,* trans. Ladislav Matejka and I. R. Titunik (New York: Seminar Press, 1973).

28. Harald Kittel, "Discovering, Naming and Translating the Impossible: (Self-) Narrated Discourse in *Caleb Williams* (English and French)," in *Histories, Systems, Literary Translations,* ed. Harald Kittel (Berlin: Erich Schmidt, 1992), 346.

29. Robinson, *On Books and Their Writers,* 1:216

CHAPTER THREE
Mary Shelley's Legal *Frankenstein*

---

1. Mary Wollstonecraft Shelley, *Frankenstein, or The Modern Prometheus: The 1818 Text,* ed. James Rieger (Chicago: University of Chicago Press, 1982), 27. Further references to the novel are from this edition and are included in the text.

2. Ann Marie Frank, "Factitious States: Mary Shelley and the Politics of Early Nineteenth-Century Women's Identity and Fiction" (Ph.D. diss., University of Michigan, 1989), 56, 49, 54.

3. Beth Newman, "Narratives of Seduction and the Seductions of Narrative: The Frame Structure of *Frankenstein,*" *ELH* 53 (1986): 148.

4. For a chronology of *Frankenstein*'s composition, see Charles E. Robinson, *The Frankenstein Notebooks: A Facsimile Edition of Mary Shelley's Manuscript Novel, 1816–17 (with Alterations in the Hand of Percy Bysshe Shelley)* . . . , 2 vols. (New York: Garland, 1996), lxxvi–cx.

5. "Chancery Papers Relating to Shelley's Children by Harriett [*sic*]. The Children's Petition Dated 8 January 1817," reprinted in Thomas Medwin, *The Life of Percy Bysshe Shelley,* rev. ed. (London: Oxford University Press, 1913), 464.

6. Percy Bysshe Shelley, "Declaration in Chancery," in *Percy Bysshe Shelley, Mary Wollstonecraft Shelley, Volume 22, Part Two, A Facsimile and Full Transcript of Bodleian MS. Shelley adds. c. 5* . . . , ed. Alan M. Weinberg (New York: Garland, 1997), 259. Mary probably transcribed the declaration on 2 February 1817. E. B. Murray assesses

that "Mary somewhat freely copied a rather rough draft, implementing some creative additions of her own as she copied" (*The Prose Works of Percy Bysshe Shelley, Volume 1*, ed. E. B. Murray [Oxford: Clarendon, 1993], 410). For a summary of the Chancery proceedings, see Edward Dowden, *The Life of Percy Bysshe Shelley*, 2 vols. (London: Kegan Paul, 1886), 2:76–95.

7. Medwin, *Life of Percy Bysshe Shelley*, 467. The newspapers more logically referred to the case as "Shelley *v.* Westbrooke [*sic*]."

8. Anne K. Mellor, *Mary Shelley: Her Life, Her Fiction, Her Monsters* (New York: Methuen, 1988), 41.

9. Percy Shelley to Eliza Westbrooke, 18 December 1816, in Leslie Hotson, "Shelley's Lost Letters to Harriet," *Atlantic Monthly* 145 (1930): 175.

10. Medwin, *Life of Percy Bysshe Shelley*, 471, 466.

11. Ellen Moers forever coupled our understanding of *Frankenstein* to Mary Shelley's traumatic experiences of birth and parenting in *Literary Women* (Garden City, N.Y.: Doubleday, 1976), and scholars—including Sandra Gilbert and Susan Gubar, Mary Jacobus, Barbara Johnson, and Mary Poovey—have since extensively explored the ways in which the novel portrays a monstrous birth. Discussion has ranged from specific focuses on the creation, as in Alan Bewell, "An Issue of Monstrous Desire: *Frankenstein* and Obstetrics," *Yale Journal of Criticism* 2 (1988): 105–28, to more wide-ranging discussions, as in Anne K. Mellor, *Mary Shelley: Her Life, Her Fiction, Her Monsters*. Also helpful to the discussion in this chapter has been Mellor's essay on Mary Wollstonecraft's *Maria*, "Righting the Wrongs of Woman: Mary Wollstonecraft's *Maria*," *Nineteenth-Century Contexts* 19 (1996): 413–24.

12. See Tilottama Rajan, introduction to *Valperga*, by Mary Shelley (Peterborough, Ont.: Broadview, 1998), 14. Especially since Robert Kiely's study *The Romantic Novel in England* (Cambridge: Harvard University Press, 1972) it has been better recognized that *Frankenstein* presents not veiled portraits but complex and often ambivalent responses to the philosophies and personalities of Mary Shelley's intellectual circle.

13. Percy Bysshe Shelley, "Declaration in Chancery," 253.

14. William Blackstone, *Commentaries on the Laws of England, A Facsimile of the First Edition of 1765–1769*, vol. 1: *Of the Rights of Persons (1765)* (Chicago: University of Chicago Press, 1979), 447. According to Blackstone, a father must provide his bastard children with maintenance, protection, and education (responsibilities later eliminated under the New Poor Law of 1834). The children may also "gain a surname by reputation" (447), as the human creature we now commonly call "Frankenstein" has.

15. Percy Shelley to Mary Shelley, 11 January 1817, *The Letters of Percy Bysshe Shelley*, vol. 1: *Shelley in England*, ed. Frederick L. Jones (Oxford: Clarendon, 1964), 528; *The Journals of Mary Shelley, 1814–1844*, ed. Paula R. Feldman and Diana Scott-Kilvert, 2 vols. (Oxford: Clarendon, 1987), 1:178.

16. *Morning Chronicle*, 27 August 1817.

17. *Examiner*, 31 August 1817.

18. *Journals of Mary Shelley*, 1:152; Godwin had told her that in eloping she was

"committ[ing] a crime," provoking Mary to write a vindication, now lost; see Emily W. Sunstein, *Mary Shelley: Romance and Reality* (Boston: Little, Brown, 1989), 89.

19. Percy Shelley to Mary Godwin, 16 December 1816, *Letters,* 1:521; to Byron, 23 April 1817, 1:540.

20. Percy Shelley to Claire Clairmont, 30 December 1816, *Letters,* 1:525.

21. Percy Bysshe Shelley, *Queen Mab* (1813; rpt., Oxford: Woodstock Books, 1990), 145.

22. Ibid., 147, 151.

23. *Journals of Mary Shelley,* 2:560.

24. Percy Shelley to Eliza Westbrook, 18 December 1816, in Hotson, "Shelley's Lost Letters," 175.

25. Percy Shelley, "Declaration in Chancery," 255.

26. Medwin, *Life of Percy Bysshe Shelley,* 468.

27. Joyce Zonana, "'They Will Prove the Truth of My Tale': Safie's Letters as the Feminist Core of Mary Shelley's *Frankenstein," Journal of Narrative Technique* 21 (1991): 170–84.

28. It seems likely that the trial letters would have come to Mary Shelley's attention before or as she rewrote the section of her draft (now lost) which contained the De Lacey chapters; Robinson calculates that the major rewriting of the original draft which produced these chapters certainly occurred after 5 December 1816 and most likely after April 1817 (*Frankenstein Notebooks,* 317).

29. Ibid., 173.

30. [John Wilson Croker], *Quarterly Review* 18 (1818): 381.

31. A gendered double standard of caretaking may originally have been indicated in this moment. The text in Mary Shelley's hand reads, "I turned with loathing from the woman who could utter so unfeeling a speech to a *man* just saved, on the very edge of death" (Robinson, *Frankenstein Notebooks,* 513; emph. added). Percy later changed *man* to *person.*

32. Here we may hear echoes of Percy Shelley's protests that his trial suggests that people must "live in daily terror that a court of justice may be converted into an instrument of private vengeance" (167); as well as that "it is . . . sheer revenge" (Percy Shelley to Mary Shelley, 11 January 1817, *Letters,* 1:527); and "legal persecution" (Percy Shelley to Lord Byron, 23 April 1817, *Letters,* 1:539). Percy himself rages directly against the lord chancellor in his poem "To the Lord Chancellor" (1818).

33. See Olaudah Equiano, *The Interesting Narrative of the Life of Olaudah Equiano, or Gustavus Vassa, the African,* in *The Classic Slave Narratives,* ed. Henry Louis Gates Jr. (New York: Penguin, 1987), 3.

34. Mary Wollstonecraft, *A Vindication of the Rights of Woman, An Authoritative Text, Backgrounds, the Wollstonecraft Debate, Criticism,* ed. Carol H. Poston, 2d ed. (New York: Norton, 1988), 8.

35. Heinrich von Kleist, *Michael Kohlhaas,* in *The Marquise of O——, and Other Stories,* trans. David Luke and Nigel Reeves (New York: Penguin, 1978), 210. *Michael Kohlhaas* was first published in 1810.

36. Inasmuch as *Frankenstein* can read like a series of violent acts, it underscores Robert Cover's association of the law's monopolization of violence with its constructions of narratives; see *Narrative, Violence, and the Law: The Essays of Robert Cover,* ed. Martha Minow, Michael Ryan, and Austin Sarat (Ann Arbor: University of Michigan Press, 1992).

37. *Frankenstein,* for instance, appropriately forms part of discussions of the ethics of cloning, for example, George J. Annas, "Why We Should Ban Human Cloning," *New England Journal of Medicine* 339 (1998): 122–25.

38. Percy Bysshe Shelley, "Continuation of the Shelley Papers, On 'Frankenstein,'" *Athenaeum,* 10 November 1832. Percy's review was published posthumously.

CHAPTER FOUR

Victorian Courthouse Structures, *The Pickwick Papers*

---

1. *The Life of Mary Russell Mitford, Told by Herself in Letters to Her Friends,* ed. A. G. K. L'Estrange, 2 vols. (New York: Harper and Brothers, 1870), 2:198.

2. John Sutherland, *Victorian Novelists and Publishers* (Chicago: University of Chicago Press, 1976), 22. See also N. N. Feltes, *Modes of Production of Victorian Novels* (Chicago: University of Chicago Press, 1986); Robert L. Patten, *Charles Dickens and His Publishers* (Oxford: Clarendon, 1978); and Bill Bell, "Fiction in the Marketplace: Towards a Study of the Victorian Serial," in *Serials and Their Readers, 1620–1914,* ed. Robin Myers and Michael Harris (New Castle, Del.: Oak Knoll, 1993), 125–44.

3. Charles Dickens, *The Posthumous Papers of the Pickwick Club,* ed. Robert L. Patten (New York: Penguin, 1972), app. A, 899. Further references to the novel are from this edition and are included in the text.

4. See David M. Bevington, "Seasonal Relevance in *The Pickwick Papers,*" *Nineteenth-Century Fiction* 16 (1961): 219–30.

5. James Kinsley, introduction to *The Pickwick Papers,* by Charles Dickens, ed. James Kinsley (Oxford: Clarendon, 1986), xlvii.

6. See Richard A. Posner, *Law and Literature: Revised and Enlarged Edition* (Cambridge: Harvard University Press, 1998); Ian Ward, *Law and Literature: Possibilities and Perspectives* (Cambridge: Cambridge University Press, 1995); and the anthology *Law's Stories: Narrative and Rhetoric in the Law,* ed. Peter Brooks and Paul Gewirtz (New Haven: Yale University Press, 1996). For a critical discussion of the history of the field, see Brook Thomas, "Reflections on the Law and Literature Revival," *Critical Inquiry* 17 (1991): 510–39.

7. Philip Collins, *Dickens and Crime,* 3d ed. (London: Macmillan, 1994), 182–83.

8. John Forster, *The Life of Charles Dickens,* ed. A. J. Hoppé, 2 vols. (London: Dent, 1966), 1:73.

9. Dickens to Chapman and Hall, 1 November 1836, *The Letters of Charles Dickens,* vol. 1: *1820–1839,* ed. Madeline House and Graham Storey (Oxford: Clarendon Press, 1965), 189.

10. Aptly enough, the brief letter by Mary Mitford quoted at the beginning of this

chapter goes on, after celebrating *Pickwick,* to disparage "another book, which is much the fashion . . . Mr. Sergeant Talfourd's 'Life of Charles Lamb'" (*Life of Mary Russell Mitford,* 2:199). Talfourd was also a barrister in the *Norton v. Melbourne* case that Dickens reported as court reporter (*Morning Advertiser,* 23 June 1836) and then later drew upon in his depiction of the *Bardell v. Pickwick* case.

11. Steven Marcus, "Language into Structure: Pickwick Revisited," *Daedalus* 101 (1972): 187. The date as a beginning is underscored again in the next chapter of *Pickwick:* "That punctual servant . . . the sun, had just risen, and begun to strike a light on the morning of the thirteenth of May, one thousand eight hundred and twenty-seven, when Mr. Samuel Pickwick burst like another sun from his slumbers" (72).

12. Charles Dickens, *David Copperfield,* ed. Nina Burgis (Oxford: Clarendon Press, 1981), 290.

13. Anny Sadrin, "Fragmentation in *The Pickwick Papers,*" *Dickens Studies Annual* 22 (1993): 23.

14. Dickens to Chapman and Hall, 1 November 1836, *Letters,* 1:189. This comment and *Pickwick* itself should be read against the letters concerning *Pickwick's* workaday progress. In the letters, which often conflate *Pickwick* the book and Pickwick the character, both *Pickwick* and Pickwick take on a different complexion in lines such as: "Whether they, having all the *Pickwick* machinery in full operation, could not obtain for them a much larger sale" (Dickens to John Forster, 17 June 1837, *Letters,* 1:273); and "When you have quite done counting the sovereigns, received for Pickwick, I should be much obliged to you, to send me up a few" (Dickens to Chapman and Hall, 6 August 1836, *Letters,* 1:161).

15. John Glavin, "Pickwick on the Wrong Side of the Door," *Dickens Studies Annual* 22 (1993): 14.

16. Dickens to Madame De la Rue, 17 April 1846, *The Letters of Charles Dickens,* vol. 4: *1844–1846,* ed. Kathleen Tillotson (Oxford: Clarendon, 1977), 534.

17. See Daniel Duman on the barristers, "Pathway to Professionalism: The English Bar in the Eighteenth and Nineteenth Centuries," *Journal of Social History* 13 (1980): 615–28. For a brief discussion of the professionalization of solicitors in the 1820s, see Gatrell, *Hanging Tree,* 429–39. See chapter 10, "The Legal Profession," in J. H. Baker, *Introduction to English Legal History,* 177–99, for a longer historical view as well as a cogent historical explanation of the sergeants at law, whose fading order ended in the Victorian period, when its remaining privileges were made available to all barristers.

18. Fred Kaplan, *Dickens: A Biography* (New York: William Morrow, 1988), 47.

19. Robert Smith Surtees, "Jorrocks in Trouble," *New Sporting Magazine* 2 (1832): 248–56; later reprinted after *Pickwick's* publication with revisions and additions as a chapter in *Jorrocks's Jaunts and Jollities* (1838). Surtees's piece laid the foundation for Dickens's own comic misconstruction of his protagonist by lawyers. It lacked, however, the element of extended plot which makes the trial scene in Dickens's story into something like the center of a loose web.

20. Especially for Dickens, who later became famous for his public readings, the genre of the novel was not only a silent art, produced by one scribbling like a solicitor,

but also a performance like the barrister Buzfuz's. As Kathleen Tillotson points out, ongoing serial novels such as *Pickwick* "gave back to story-telling its original context of performance" (*Novels of the Eighteen-Forties* [Oxford: Clarendon, 1956], 36).

21. J. Hillis Miller, *Charles Dickens: The World of His Novels* (Cambridge: Harvard University Press, 1958), 16.

22. M. M. Bakhtin, *The Dialogic Imagination: Four Essays,* ed. Michael Holquist, trans. Caryl Emerson and Michael Holquist (Austin: University of Texas Press, 1981), 27.

23. Just a few years after finishing *Pickwick,* Dickens put the lawyers on trial in a court of print once again. In letters to the *Morning Chronicle* he protests "that license which is extended to counsel" of the sort Buzfuz takes (21 June 1840, reprinted in *The Letters of Charles Dickens,* vol. 2: *1840–41,* ed. Madeline House and Graham Storey [Oxford: Clarendon, 1969], 88). Outraged over a barrister's "right to defeat the ends of truth and justice by wantonly scattering aspersions upon innocent people," Dickens calls for a restraint of "their too free flights" (26 June 1840, *Letters,* 2:91). Fiction making is, in short, dangerous in court; it should be left to the professionals. Predictably equivocal, Dickens announces at the outset of the 21 June letter that the "profession . . . is accounted (and justly so, when its duties are becomingly exercised) a highly honourable one" (*Letters,* 2:86–87).

24. Samuel Warren, *Ten Thousand a-Year,* 3 vols. (Boston: Little, Brown, 1894), 1:344, 2:130–33, 2:298.

25. Baker, *Introduction to English Legal History,* 44.

26. Pevsner, *History of Building Types,* 53.

27. David B. Brownlee, *The Law Courts: The Architecture of George Edmund Street* (Cambridge: MIT Press, 1984), 55. See also M. H. Port, *Imperial London: Civil Government Building in London, 1850–1915* (New Haven: Yale University Press, 1995), 103–13. If architecture is expression in space, the Royal Courts themselves seem shaped in form and function like a Victorian novel. The member of parliament who said of the Royal Courts that "we have set ourselves to build a sort of Tower of Babel" (qtd. in Brownlee, *Law Courts,* 191) might also have added that this particular Tower of Babel would be remarkable for the fact that, despite its monstrous size, it carefully organized the separation and intersections of its denizens with what the *Times* declared were "plans ten times more intricate and incomprehensible than the Labyrinth of Crete" ([London], 19 November 1867, qtd. in Brownlee, *Law Courts,* 102).

28. Brownlee, *Law Courts,* 55.

29. Ibid., 40.

30. Ibid., 52.

31. Glavin, "Pickwick," 14.

CHAPTER FIVE
Mary Barton's Telltale Evidence

1. See Hilary M. Schor, *Scheherezade in the Marketplace: Elizabeth Gaskell and the Victorian Novel* (New York: Oxford University Press, 1992). Unlike Dickens in *Pickwick,* Gaskell does not imaginatively figure her first novel or her debut as novelist in terms of the all-male Victorian legal profession. As her depiction of the lawyers indicates (see, for example, chap. 26), Gaskell knows only too well her contemporary legal system's invidious gender divisions. For a wide-ranging discussion of the nineteenth-century novel's depictions of women as witnesses in court, see Anthea Trodd, *Domestic Crime in the Victorian Novel* (New York: St. Martin's, 1989).

2. Elizabeth Gaskell, *Mary Barton: A Tale of Manchester Life,* ed. Edgar Wright (Oxford: Oxford University Press, 1987), 378. Further references to the novel are from this edition and are included in the text.

3. Robyn R. Warhol, *Gendered Interventions: Narrative Discourse in the Victorian Novel* (New Brunswick: Rutgers University Press, 1989), 48. Gerald Prince labels a narrator who does not appear as a character (that is, is heterodiegetic) and whose narrating occurs apart from the fictional story (that is, is extradiegetic) but who nevertheless is self-referential, "self-conscious," and "immanent"; see *A Dictionary of Narratology* (Lincoln: University of Nebraska Press, 1987), 65–66, 84. I prefer here the label *self-referential* because it emphasizes how this narrator's "I" creates a literal, not just psychological, presence.

4. Gillian Beer, "Carlyle and 'Mary Barton': Problems of Utterance," *1848: The Sociology of Literature, Proceedings of the Essex Conference on the Sociology of Literature, July 1977,* ed. Francis Barker et al. (Colchester: University of Essex, 1978), 243.

5. Roland Barthes, "L'Effet de réel," *Communications* 11 (1968): 84–89.

6. Schor, *Scheherezade,* 30.

7. Roland Barthes, "From Work to Text," in *Image, Music, Text,* trans. Stephen Heath (New York: Hill and Wang, 1977), 156–57. Gaskell even more directly manipulates novelistic form to accord with the material conditions she depicts in *Cranford;* see Tim Dolin, "*Cranford* and the Victorian Collection," *Victorian Studies* 36 (1993): 179–206. Linda K. Hughes and Michael Lund detail the way in which documents are meaningfully ubiquitous in *Mary Barton* in *Victorian Publishing and Mrs. Gaskell's Work* (Charlottesville: University Press of Virginia, 1999), 35–48.

8. See J. L. Austin, *How to Do Things with Words,* ed. J. O. Urmson and Marina Sbisà, 2d ed. (Cambridge: Harvard University Press, 1962). At issue here, as elsewhere in this section, are the distinctions, if not the terminology, that Austin makes in his theory of speech acts (for example, Mrs. Wilson's persuasive testimony might be called a "perlocutionary act").

9. Raymond Williams, *Culture and Society,* 91.

10. Gaskell's attempt to sway her readers' judgment forms the subject of her novel's second epigraph, which extends the first epigraph's concerns with her novel's effect on its readers and her own act of authorship. This second epigraph—written in German

and unfortunately mistranslated in every modern edition and everywhere misapprehended as a cryptic reference to the death of her baby—invokes the novel's goal of providing a spiritual ferrying for the masters and the workmen:

> Take only ferryman, take the fare,
> That I gladly three times offer.
> The two that came over with me,
> Were spiritual natures.
>   (My trans.)

11. McKeon, *Origins of the English Novel,* 16.

12. Gaskell to John Potter, 16 August 1852, *The Letters of Mrs. Gaskell,* ed. J. A. V. Chapple and Arthur Pollard (Manchester: Manchester University Press, 1966), 196.

13. Dorothy Thompson, *The Chartists* (London: Temple Smith, 1984), 78.

14. Ibid., 295.

15. Asa Briggs, *Chartism* (Phoenix Mill, Eng.: Sutton, 1998), 75.

16. Ibid., 75.

17. Williams, *Culture and Society,* 91.

18. Gareth Stedman Jones, "The Language of Chartism," in *The Chartist Experience: Studies in Working-Class Radicalism and Culture, 1830–60,* ed. James Epstein and Dorothy Thompson (London: Macmillan, 1982), 3–58.

19. The narrative structures patterning mid-Victorian social problem novels such as *Mary Barton* and *Sybil,* and the interrelations of these novels, are explained by Rosemarie Bodenheimer in *The Politics of Story in Victorian Social Fiction* (Ithaca: Cornell University Press, 1988).

20. Catherine Gallagher, *The Industrial Reformation of English Fiction: Social Discourse and Narrative Form, 1832–1867* (Chicago: University of Chicago Press, 1985), 68. Gallagher shifted discussion of the industrial novels from concerns with their ideological effectiveness and the reality of their depictions to historically oriented analyses of their structure and form.

21. *Bronterre's National Reformer, in Government, Law, Property, Religion, and Morals,* 4 February 1837. For readers in the United States it is important to keep in mind that the separation between judicial and legislative branches is historically much less clear in England, where the House of Lords is England's highest court.

22. Gaskell to Mary Ewart (late 1848), *Letters of Mrs. Gaskell,* 67.

23. See Hughes and Lund, *Victorian Publishing,* 40–44, for instance, for the suggestion that Mary Barton should be read as a detective figure.

24. *Times* (London), 11 February 1867.

25. See Brownlee, *Law Courts,* 91. Katherine Fischer Taylor provides the much-needed beginnings of an expert analysis of the architecture of the Old Bailey's courtrooms; see Taylor, *In the Theater of Criminal Justice,* 10–14.

26. Alfred Waterhouse, "A Short Description of the Manchester Assize Courts," *Papers Read at the Royal Institute of British Architects, Session 1864–65* (London,

1865), 167. Compare the *Morning Chronicle*'s 4 June 1824 report on the new Court of Common Pleas: "The New Court is considerably larger than the old one, and instead of there being but one door through which Judges, Counsel, Students, Jurors, Attorneys, and Witnesses, were obliged to pass, there are now six, each of which communicates only with a particular portion of the Court."

27. See Gaskell, *Mary Barton,* 96–98; one key to dating the story lies in whether John Barton attends the first or second Chartist petitioning of parliament (1839 or 1842); arguments can be made for either.

CHAPTER SIX

The Newgate Novel and the Advent of Detective Fiction

---

1. William Makepeace Thackeray, *Catherine: A Story,* ed. Sheldon F. Goldfarb (Ann Arbor: University of Michigan Press, 1999), 116, 19.

2. See Keith Hollingsworth, *The Newgate Novel, 1830–1847: Bulwer, Ainsworth, Dickens, and Thackeray* (Detroit: Wayne State University Press, 1963). Besides Hollingsworth's authoritative study, there are, inexplicably, few illuminating discussions of the Newgate novel. I pick up where Hollingsworth ends; as he provocatively theorizes at the conclusion of his study: "At a time when Bulwer and Dickens . . . would have extended the author's prerogative of omniscience as a technique for psychological exploration, Thackeray's [successful denigration of Newgate novels] constituted in some degree a hindrance" (228).

3. This advertisement appeared in an 1869 edition of *Catherine* and in a number of subsequent editions; it is reprinted in Thackeray, *Catherine: A Story,* 190. Modern advertising of "Newgate fiction" reflects the fact that the label has shed its pejorative connotations.

4. Edward Bulwer Lytton, *Paul Clifford,* Knebworth Edition (London: Routledge, [1875–78]), 415. Further references to the novel are from this edition and are included in the text. Bulwer became Bulwer Lytton in 1843; I refer to him as Bulwer throughout this chapter because it largely focuses on his work in the 1830s.

5. See Patrick Brantlinger, *The Spirit of Reform: British Literature and Politics, 1832–1867* (Cambridge: Harvard University Press, 1977), 35–38, 44–45.

6. *Examiner,* 17 January 1841. This critique is from an unsigned review of Bulwer's *Night and Morning* (1841).

7. Edward Bulwer Lytton, *Eugene Aram: A Tale,* Knebworth Edition (London: Routledge, [1875–78]), 116. Further references to the novel are from this edition and are included in the text.

8. Andrew Knapp and William Baldwin, *The Newgate Calendar; Comprising Interesting Memoirs of the Most Notorious Characters . . . ,* 4 vols. (London: J. Robins, 1824–28), 2:246–57.

9. Bulwer Lytton, *Word to the Public,* 39 (full bibliographic details at chap. 1 n. 59). In the year *A Word to the Public* was first published (fifteen years after the appearance of *Eugene Aram*) Thackeray was still eagerly attacking Bulwer's Newgate novels; see the

parody of Bulwer in the brief tale "George de Barnwell," which ran under the heading "Punch's Prize Novelists," *Punch* 12 (1847): 136–37, 146–47, 155.

10. The contrasting narratorial perspectives at issue in the Newgate controversy were neatly captured when a contemporary *Newgate Calendar,* Charles Whitehead's *Lives and Exploits of English Highwaymen, Pirates, and Robbers, Drawn from the Earliest and Most Authentic Sources, and Brought Down to the Present Time,* 2 vols. (London: Bull and Churton, 1834), struck back at Bulwer's *Eugene Aram* after its own summary of Aram's life, protesting that "Aram has been deemed a fit hero for a popular novel; and the execration with which he should have been consigned to posterity has been attempted to be converted into a sentimental commiseration" (2:313).

11. Thackeray, *Catherine,* 133.

12. Edward Bulwer Lytton, *Lucretia, or the Children of the Night,* Knebworth Edition (London: Routledge, [1875–78]), 178. Further references to the novel are from this edition and are included in the text.

13. Edward Bulwer, "On Art in Fiction," *Monthly Chronicle* 1 (1838): 144.

14. George Eliot, *Adam Bede,* 425 (full bibliographic details at intro. n. 4). Further references to the novel are to the aforementioned edition and are included in the text.

15. Bulwer, *Paul Clifford,* xi.

16. George Eliot, "History of 'Adam Bede,'" in *The George Eliot Letters,* ed. Gordon S. Haight, 9 vols. (New Haven: Yale University Press, 1954–78), 2:503–4; the "History" is originally from Eliot's journal entry for 30 November 1858.

17. Bulwer Lytton, *Word to the Public,* 30.

18. Bulwer to John Blackwood, 14 April 1860, in *George Eliot: The Critical Heritage,* ed. David Carroll (London: Routledge, 1971), 122.

19. Fergus Hume, *The Mystery of a Hansom Cab* (Melbourne: Sun Books, 1971), 193.

20. Bulwer Lytton, *Word to the Public,* 54.

21. Frederick R. Karl, *George Eliot, Voice of a Century: A Biography* (New York: Norton, 1995), 27. Contrast Karl's comment with the opening of Edith Simcox's 1873 review of *Middlemarch,* in which she follows her suggestion that theoretical ideas about the English novel are largely based on "one or other of the masterpieces" with this list: "*Tom Jones, Clarissa Harlowe, Waverley, Pride and Prejudice, Vanity Fair, Adam Bede*—to which some might wish to add *Eugene Aram, Pickwick,* and *Jane Eyre*" (*Academy* 4 [1873]: 1). Bulwer is rightly enough remembered today largely for his unintentionally comic melodramatic writing (the famous line "It was a dark and stormy night" begins *Paul Clifford*), but his subjects and approaches were in their time often significantly innovative.

22. Sightlines, like acoustics, within the courtroom are obviously carefully constructed, not least so that the jury may view the witnesses and the prisoner. In England overhanging, separate galleries were often provided for the public, unlike in France, where the public typically had a place on the court floor (see Taylor, *In the Theater of Criminal Justice,* 10–14).

23. Charles Dickens, *Oliver Twist,* ed. Kathleen Tillotson (Oxford: Clarendon,

1966), 129–30. Further references to the novel are from this edition and are included in the text.

24. Hilary M. Schor, *Dickens and the Daughter of the House* (Cambridge: Cambridge University Press, 1999), 19–32.

25. Thackeray, *Catherine,* 30. With less sophistication than Bulwer, Dickens also defends *Oliver Twist*'s Newgate form, and Nancy in particular, three years after its publication in one of the lengthiest prefaces he wrote to any of his novels.

26. William Makepeace Thackeray, "Going to See a Man Hanged," *Fraser's Magazine* 22 (1840): 155.

27. "Charles Dickens and His Works," *Fraser's Magazine* 21 (1840): 394.

28. See D. A. Miller, *The Novel and the Police* (Berkeley: University of California Press, 1988), 4–10.

29. R. H. Horne, ed., *A New Spirit of the Age,* 2 vols. (London: Smith, Elder, 1844), 1:38.

30. Elizabeth Barrett Browning to Mary Russell Mitford, 27 November 1842, *The Letters of Elizabeth Barrett Browning to Mary Russell Mitford, 1836–1854,* ed. Meredith B. Raymond and Mary Rose Sullivan, 3 vols. ([Waco, Tex.]: Armstrong Browning Library of Baylor University, Browning Institute, Wedgestone Press, and Wellesley College, 1983), 2:93.

31. Thackeray, *Catherine,* 132.

32. "Charles Dickens and His Works," 394.

33. Ousby, *Bloodhounds of Heaven,* 82 (full bibliographic details at chap. 2 n. 2).

34. Robert Tracy, "'The Old Story' and Inside Stories: Modish Fiction and Fictional Modes in *Oliver Twist,*" *Dickens Studies Annual* 17 (1988): 1–33.

35. Edgar Allan Poe, "The Murders in the Rue Morgue," in *Edgar Allan Poe: Poetry and Tales,* ed. Patrick F. Quinn (New York: Library of America, 1984), 423. When Poe wrote this new sort of mystery (described by himself as "something in a new key"), the word *detective* did not yet even exist; see Julian Symons, *Bloody Murder, from the Detective Story to the Crime Novel: A History* (New York: Viking, 1985), 39, 35.

36. Wilkie Collins, *The Moonstone,* ed. John Sutherland (Oxford: Oxford University Press, 1999), liii, 163. Further references to the novel are from this edition and are included in the text.

37. See Miller, *Novel and the Police,* 33–57.

38. See Edmund Wilson, "Why Do People Read Detective Stories?" in *Classics and Commercials: A Literary Chronicle of the Forties* (New York: Farrar, Straus, 1950), 231–37; Miller, *Novel and the Police,* 33–37; and Franco Moretti, "Clues," in *Signs Taken for Wonder: Essays in the Sociology of Literary Forms,* trans. Susan Fischer, David Forgacs, and David Miller (London: Verso, 1983), 130–56.

39. Thackeray to Mrs. Carmichael-Smyth, March 1840, *The Letters and Private Papers of William Makepeace Thackeray,* vol. 1: *1817–1840,* ed. Gordon N. Ray (Cambridge: Harvard University Press, 1945), 433.

40. Sheldon F. Goldfarb, "Historical Commentary," in Thackeray, *Catherine,* 139–41.

41. Charles Dickens, "Hunted Down," in *Victorian Tales of Mystery and Detection: An Oxford Anthology*, ed. Michael Cox (Oxford: Oxford University Press, 1992), 65.

42. It is a premise of my argument that, just as there had been wide cultural and legal transformations stemming from the professionalization and expanded trial presence of the lawyers, there were later different transformations associated with the arrival of the modern police departments. Clive Emsley stresses the historic difference the new police made in *The English Police: A Political and Social History* (New York: St. Martin's, 1991): "The traditional historians of police have tended to see a logical progression from the Fieldings and the developments in Bow Street, through the Middlesex Justices' Act and the work of Colquhoun, to the appearance of the Metropolitan Police in 1829. Yet the force which was created in 1829 bore little resemblance to what had gone before in London" (23). A much repeated but nonetheless amazing fact is that only by 1860 had the word *police* narrowed its meaning from governing in a general sense and attached itself to the new branch of the state organized to prevent and track crime. There was simply no police state in the modern sense at the beginning of the nineteenth century. Before the "police," such an organized, living force would have been understood as a standing or occupying army, and the first blue-clad police uniforms were partly designed to differentiate the new domestic soldiers.

43. See Symons, *Bloody Murder*, 13. At the furthest pole from those who would take a narrow inventory of the mystery genre is David I. Grossvogel, for whom *mystery* names a profound repeating figure in which literature has variously confronted humankind's encounters with the limits of our understanding (see *Mystery and Its Fictions: From Oedipus to Agatha Christie* [Baltimore: Johns Hopkins University Press, 1979]).

44. See Symons, *Bloody Murder,* in which he argues that after 1940 the detective genre begins (again) to emphasize the detective's life as enmeshed in and part of the criminal's underworld and thereby transmutes from mystery into crime novel, abandoning clues in favor of characters.

45. Anne Humpherys, "Who's Doing It? Fifteen Years of Work on Victorian Detective Fiction," *Dickens Studies Annual* 24 (1996): 272. Humpherys has also suggested that the "mysteries" serials, such as G. W. M. Reynold's *The Mysteries of London* (1844–48), stood formally and historically between the Newgate and detective mystery genres, in "Generic Strands and Urban Twists: The Victorian Mysteries Novel," *Victorian Studies* 34:455–72.

Conclusion

1. One must remember that Scotland's legal system was separate and different from England's, though ultimately, as Scott's novel shows, united under appeals to the king or queen.

2. Walter Scott, *The Heart of Midlothian,* ed. Claire Lamont (Oxford: Oxford University Press, 1982), 14. Further references to the novel are from this edition and are included in the text.

3. Gary Kelly, "Romantic Fiction," in *The Cambridge Companion to British Romanticism,* ed. Stuart Curran (Cambridge: Cambridge University Press, 1993), 214.

4. Modern readers might pause to compare the role of standard English, dialect, and the trial in Zora Neale Hurston's *Their Eyes Were Watching God* (1937).

5. James Hogg, *The Private Memoirs and Confessions of a Justified Sinner,* ed. John Carey (Oxford: Oxford University Press, 1969), 68. Further references to the novel are from this edition and are included in the text.

6. M. M. Bakhtin, *Toward a Philosophy of the Act,* ed. Michael Holquist and Vadim Liapunov, trans. Vadim Liapunov (Austin: University of Texas Press, 1993). For the repercussions of this idea in Bakhtin's work, see his comments on how the novel is symbiotic with the courts in *Speech Genres and Other Late Essays,* ed. Caryl Emerson and Michael Holquist, trans. Vern W. McGee (Austin: University of Texas Press, 1986), 12; and *Dialogic Imagination,* 33. Relevant here is Terry Eagleton's argument that after Kant (who is also Bakhtin's starting point) a new aesthetic ideology helped construct ethics as immanent in the world, simply a part of what it meant to be a subject; see *The Ideology of the Aesthetic* (Cambridge: Blackwell, 1990).